Lucifer Unveiled

Lucifer Unveiled

EXPOSING THE KINGDOM OF DARKNESS

V. Lynn

Revelations Publishing House LLC

Contents

Copyright — vii
Dedication — viii
Thy Queendom Come — ix
Disclaimer — x

Introduction

Star Wars — 7
1. Cosmic Combat — 8
2. Lord of the Rings — 16
3. Black Cube of Saturn — 30
4. The Santa Clause — 39
5. Star Gate — 46

Serpent's Seed — 52
6. The Serpent — 53
7. The Little Mermaid — 78

Unholy Grail — 82
8. Illuminati Bloodlines — 83
9. Our Lady of Secrets — 93
10. Order of the Dragon — 100
11. Symbology — 106

Babylon Rising — 114
12. The Lost Tribe — 115
13. X-Man — 123
14. Cain's Mark — 134

Lucifer's Legions — 138
15. Fallen Angels and Nephilim — 139
16. Anunnaki — 158

United Nations Of Lucifer — 167

17 United Nations of Lucifer — 168

Lucifer Unveiled! — 200

18 Lucifer Unveiled! — 201

19 Conclusion — 236

About The Author — 241
Extra Extra — 243
Bibliography — 247
Bible Index — 255
Index — 257

Copyright © 2022 by V. Lynn

LUCIFER UNVEILED
Exposing the Kingdom of Darkness
Mystery Babylon Series Volume Two
Copyright © 2022 by Revelations Publishing House Mailing:
43000 West 9 Mile Rd. Ste. 109, #209
Novi, Michigan 48375
www.revelationsbooks.com info@revelationsbooks.com
All rights reserved. No part of this book may be reproduced in any manner whatsoever except in the case of brief quotations embodied in critical articles and reviews, properly cited. Otherwise, no part of this publication may be reproduced, stored in a retrieval system, or transmitted in any form or by any means: copying- distributing-scanning- recording-broadcasting-electronic mail-facsimile-scanning, or any other medium without written permission from the publisher.
First Printing, 2023
Unless otherwise noted, all Scripture quotations are from the King James Holy Bible KJV
E-Book -979-8-218-07912-3
Print - 979-8-9866976-6-6
LCN- 2022915995

DEDICATION

To everyone who has been;
Called Crazy
Labeled a Conspiracy Theorist
Told your views are Radical
Accused of being Rebellious
Laughed at, Mocked and Scorned

You are the TRUE Defenders of the Faith and
Warriors for CHRIST!

This book is dedicated to YOU
They called Noah crazy as well… until it started RAINING!

My Lord and Savior
Y'SHUA HAMASHIACH
JESUS CHRIST THE MESSIAH
THE ONLY WISE GOD AND SAVIOR
BE GLORY AND MAJESTY
DOMINION AND POWER
BOTH NOW AND EVER
AMEN

Mystery Babylon Series Vol. One

THY QUEENDOM COME

The Devil's Secret Agenda

BELIEVERS-YOU DON'T KNOW YOUR ENEMY!

500 Pages
220 References
100+ Documents and Pictures
Historical Records
Secret Society
Occult
New Age
Secrets of America
Mystery Religion
Mystery Schools
Demonology
ANTI-CHRIST

DEFEND THE FAITH! WE ARE AT WAR!

V. LYNN

"And upon her forehead was a name written, MYSTERY, BABYLON THE GREAT, THE MOTHER OF HARLOTS AND ABOMINATIONS OF THE EARTH"
Revelation 17:5

Disclaimer

The Mystery Babylon Series of books is a journalistic review of the teachings, beliefs, and plans of the enemies of CHRIST.

Quotes, research, and information from the highest sources of instructional manuals, religious texts, theologians, historians, and commentators are compiled in our materials.

Revelations Publishing House does not support nor agree with these teachings, and our position is to EXPOSE the works of darkness as the Word of God instructs us (Ephesians 5:11).

The Mystery Babylon Series does not attack individual groups or religions. Our goal is to expose the systems which contradict Biblical beliefs and the methods and organizations in which the deceptions are funneled.

"And ye shall know the truth, and the truth shall make you free."
John 8:32

Revelations Publishing House
www.revelationsbooks.com

Introduction

Shocked, amazed, in disbelief, bewildered, and even, a bit angered (if I can be honest)! These were just a few of the feelings that surrounded me as I researched the first installment of the *Mystery Babylon Series*; "Thy Queendom Come, The Devil's Secret Agenda." If you have not read the first installment, you must do so to thoroughly understand the enemy's very masterful plan.

I have been a professional writer for nearly two decades. I have also done work in independent journalism and investigations dating back to the Flint Water Crisis of 2014. Before we go forward, I want to reflect and share, in brief, how this journey all began so that the reader will better understand my research method.

My career as a writer and journalist completely changed in March 2020. The year that the world experienced a pandemic that changed our society forever. I began doing daily news reports covering the rapidly increasing Covid death numbers and cases. The focus of the investigations was the discretions on the mainstream news networks versus the actual data from the CDC and other health organizations.

This national crisis was in full swing in May of 2020 when all of a sudden, constant Covid coverage halted due to the murder of *George Floyd* on Monday, May 25, 2020, in Minneapolis, Minnesota. The horrific video of George Floyd pinned down on the concrete by *Officer Derek Chauvin* sparked outrage worldwide. It was not this heinous act that prompted my interest to travel to Minneapolis, it was the protests that had begun immediately after his death.

Something about the many videos I'd watched of protestors being attacked by local police didn't add up in my journalistic mind. I watched almost non-stop "live" social media videos of protestors attacked by local law enforcement. By Thursday, May 28, 2020, three days after the death of Floyd, I had landed in Minneapolis with only a cell phone to record the events that captivated the nation.

The entire time I was in Minneapolis, I filmed "live" so viewers had a front-row seat to all the action, or as you will see, in-action, that was happening. Without going into painstaking detail, everything you saw on television about the protests and riots (not the murder) was one of the biggest hoaxes in modern American media history! There were no riots, there was no violence, and there were no unruly mobs. What you witnessed was a mass media theatrical production; many of my viewers could see that live and in color. Covid was still wrecking the world, and now George Floyd protests were shaking the world. I didn't think this was a coincidence, that both events were global agendas.

From the moment I landed on the ground on May 28, 2020, my life has never been the same.

Although I have never trusted corporate media because of my personal experiences, this was different. I'll give you an example of media deception. On May 28 or early May 29, news stations nationally replayed a bunch of rowdy young people overrunning a police precinct in Minneapolis. Logically speaking, had these events occurred in real time, agents of the Minneapolis Police Department, County Sheriffs, State Police, area municipalities, and federal forces would have immediately descended on Minneapolis.

Here is what really happened on that day. I arrived at the central area of the protests (near the Target store on Lake Street) on Thursday, May 28, 2020, in the early afternoon. I was floored by what I observed. I was anticipating mass protests and heavy police presence. Instead, there was a party-like atmosphere with zero police in the vicinity, which contradicted what was on mass media. I recorded inquiries to the locals about the police presence or the absence thereof. I uncovered that earlier in the day, the police vacated the entire precinct, "they just packed up and left." Not under distress or threat, but in an orderly fashion, moved out. All of this was odd because this designated protest area was a few miles removed from Cup Foods, the actual location of the murder.

I then left the protest area and proceeded reluctantly to the location of the murder, the Cup Foods convenience store. Cup Foods' intersection was solemn and peaceful, with people visiting and paying their respects with artwork, stuffed animals, cards, and prayers. It was very surreal and serene. People in the protest areas and at the vigil were welcoming, friendly, and not hostile in the least.

You can imagine my shock when the following day, Friday, May 29, 2020, news outlets nationwide broadcast the overtaking and burning down of an entire police precinct! That news story and broadcast were not the truth! The news showed the precinct ravaged and burned by an angry mob that frightened trained officers of the law out of their building. The angry crowd was unarmed college-aged young people vandalizing an already vacant building! Certainly not a criminal, unruly, violent mob. I was there! Many locals also testified on camera that the fires in Minneapolis were professional arson jobs, and many residents named law enforcement professionals as the culprits. Deception is the word for what occurred on that monumental weekend.

That was it; my eyes were open to the fear-driven, narrative-pushing media, and the rabbit holes were deep!

Next, it was time to "follow the money." On the surface level—George Floyd protests and the Covid pandemic (exercises and vaccines) appeared as two different unconnected events. To my shock, the same companies, businesses, and organizations had financial ties in the protests and the pandemic. It was all one big operation headed by a few mighty organizations.

By this time, I was full-fledged into independent journalism when I discovered the "Communist Manifesto" written in 1840 by *Karl Marx* and *Friedrich Engels*. The manifesto, in no uncertain terms, called for the abolishment of:
all religion
all morals
all family
all national borders
all property rights

As I read document after document, this agenda became apparent in every area of our lives, including agriculture, medicine, education, politics, business, and most importantly, the systematic breakdown of the family and religious life as we know it.

The picture was becoming very clear; underneath all of these political aims was a clear spiritual agenda, although many of these organizations claim they are religiously tolerant (except for followers of Christ) and are more atheistic.

Underneath another layer still was the most prominent organization in the world, the United Nations, and its many arms and schemes. One such *scheme* is the United Nations Agenda 21/2030. On the surface, the environmental program of the United Nations Agenda 21/2030 is a humanitarian effort for the betterment of the world. Under a microscope, this program slowly implements total control of the world and its resources. I have done quite a bit of investigation into this plan. Agenda 21/2030 is the blueprint for the world's nations to implement the New World Order. Even in its name, United Nations is a reversing of the Tower of Babel; GOD divided the countries (Genesis 10), and the U.N. wants to bring the nations back together. Agenda 21/2030 is the repackaged Communist Manifesto which would eliminate borders, truly creating ONE UNITED WORLD.

The U.N. also played a crucial role in the pandemic through its World Health Organization and the George Floyd protests through its "peace-keeping" efforts.

With some appropriate digging, you will find the *Lucis Trust*, a spiritual partner of the U.N. The original name of this company was *Lucifer Publishing*! The Lucis Trust is on the grounds of the United Nations (866 United Nations Plaza). Directly on the Lucis Trust website, the organization gives homage to the "solar angel" *Lucifer* and his sacrifice! I wish I could tell you this was a fiction novel, but it is not. The U.N. is the largest organization in the world, connected to every country in the world, and gives public honor (through the Lucis Trust) and reverence to the enemy of the MOST HIGH; Lucifer!

Everything was clear. Behind the attacks on the financial system, technology, gender, and race wars, the family and faith in Christ (in particular) were not merely an economic, social, or industrial agenda. The agenda is to prepare the world for Lucifer's *Satanic Kingdom on earth* and it's being done right before our eyes.

At this time, I started veering into older writings on anything I could find about secret societies, the New World Order, and the planned global agenda. Pandora's box, the rabbit hole, and the matrix are all appropriate words to describe the schemes I read about that have been planned for millennia.

Fast forward to the release of *Thy Queendom Come* (September 2022). I was listening to a broadcast entitled "The Hour of the Time" by host *Bill Cooper* ("Behold a Pale Horse"), perhaps one of the best-known *conspiracy exposers* of modern times. Bill Cooper died in 2001 at the hands of Arizona law enforcement, but he left for the world thousands of radio shows, documents, and evidence of this new Luciferian Kingdom or the One World, New World Order, as you would.

Have you ever wondered the purpose of the all-seeing eye, Egyptian pyramid and the phrase, *Novus Ordo Seclorum* (New Order of the Age) printed on the dollar bill?

I was listening to an old broadcast of Bill Cooper's (early 1990s) where he discussed an official gathering of a secret society. Bill Cooper had uncovered private proceedings from 1916 regarding the design of the back of the dollar bill. This classified file not only revealed the cryptic code of the design, but the true purpose for the colonization of the United States of America. The facts according to this secret society contained major bombshells! I was left with the question, "where do I live?" What is the purpose of this country called the United States of America?

> "And upon her forehead was a name written, MYSTERY, BABYLON THE GREAT, the mother of harlots and abominations of the earth." [Revelation 17:5]

Mystery Babylon has been attributed to the United States of America by many esteemed theologians and eschatologist. However, investigating the "city" or the location of "Mystery Babylon" was not my assignment. My focus was on the "Mother of Harlots" and the identity of the woman who possibly inspired the passage. The search for this mysterious woman led;

all around the world,

into every secret society,

every religious and pagan belief,

the occult, and every demonic anti-Christ agenda that is on the horizon.

The conclusion of the investigation led to a shocking, unexpected source that all the organizations and religions had in common. This mysterious "source" was identified in the 1916 document about the dollar bill. I was also puzzled that every book of; witchcraft, magic, occultism, and secret societies I reviewed, had one "religious" belief in common. This false religious system is a return to the Babylon Mystery System, where Lucifer (under many names) is the supreme deity. At its basis, this mystery religion is the lie given to Eve in the garden by the serpent;

- Question God's authority.
- Immortality-You "surely won't die."
- You can become "as gods."

The first installment of the *Mystery Babylon* series ended with 500+ pages, 300+ resources, and 100+ documents and pictures! The inaugural research revealed fascinating connections that I could not fit into *Thy Queendom Come*. Specifically the subjects of the solar system, the spirit world, fallen angels, the Nephilim, the Serpent, the Holy Grail, and royal bloodlines. These areas will be the focus of Volume II in the Mystery Babylon series, *Lucifer Unveiled*.

In this book, the reader will obtain a deep understanding of the following;
- Fallen Angels and the Nephilim
- Gods of Mythology
- Black Cube (Saturn) Cult
- The Real Star Wars
- Fairy "tails" and Mermaids

- Santa Claus unmasked
- Illuminati Bloodlines
- Order of the Dragon
- Unholy Grail
- Black Madonna
- Synagogue of Satan
- The Lost Tribe
- Mark of Cain
- United Nations of Lucifer
- Anunnaki and Human Hybrids
- Star Gates
- The biggest lie in history
- 666-The Serpent Exposed

The purpose of this book is of several natures;
1. Likened to the original, we can't fight an enemy we don't know, and I can tell you, believers still don't see the enemy.
2. Supply research and documentation to the body of Believers in their search to understand the *end times*.
3. To expose the works of darkness so that all may come to repentance and the truth of our Lord and Savior, JESUS CHRIST (Y'SHUA HAMASHIACH).

I consider this series of books an investigation. As with any research, it's always about connecting the dots, finding common denominators, and discovering the thread that holds everything together.

Lucifer knows he has but a short time but still believes he can EXALT himself above the THRONE OF GOD, and this false angel of light is deceiving the masses.

As a snake sheds its scales, this book will shed the Luciferian agenda and the silent, divisive weapons used to conquer the faithful followers of CHRIST. Fear not! THE LORD reminds us to;

> Be of good cheer; I have overcome the world." [John 16:33]

Note: Throughout this book, we examine all records and measure everything against the Word of God, which is the ultimate authority. Other works are used solely for research, information, and historical purposes.

SECTION I

Star Wars

STAR WARS

1

Cosmic Combat

After a deep dive into the beliefs of the occult regarding the solar system, one thing became apparent; planetary movements govern the decisions of the world's elite. This belief system goes far past the habit of reading weekly horoscopes (which, as a believer in CHRIST, you should cease immediately). Many books of esoteric teaching gave human attributes, emotions, and alliances to individual planets and stars. Their movements dictated everything from land geography, building plans, agriculture, names of buildings and organizations, and important dates like Presidential Inaugurations. Planetary movements also served as a "guide" for the powers-that-be, not only in centuries past but the present day. Many believe this is the sole reason for NASA and the many space programs. This battle is principally a spiritual war; Lucifer and the fallen are indeed, *spiritual wickedness in high places.*

> "For we wrestle not against flesh and blood, but against principalities, against powers, against the rulers of the darkness of this world, against spiritual wickedness in high *places.*"[Ephesians 6:12]

Celestial War in the Heavens

"Survival of the Fittest" reigned supreme from the moment that *Kosmos* manifested into being... the battles fought between stars and constellations, between Moon and planets later on incarnated as Kings and mortals, hence also the *War in Heaven of Michael and his Host* against the Dragon (Jupiter and Lucifer- Venus), when a third of the stars of the rebellious host were hurled down into space, and "its place was found no more in Heaven." (Blavatsky No Shadow No Light. Page 202)

It is important to note, as was exposed in *Thy Queendom Come*, the Hermetic principle which governs the entire occult world, *As Above, So Below* (Lynn Chapter 8 Occult Philosophy. Page 63). In the simplest terms, if it happens in the heavens, there is duplicating action in the earth and vice versa. Planets were also given governorship over particular countries, regions, vegetation, animals, emotions, and colors according to their Luciferian belief system.

In the above quote from *Madame Blavatsky* (Queen of the occult and the New Age), she explains the actual cosmic combat or star wars for the "Survival of the Fittest" in the heavenly realm. In this planetary war, the same concept applies as on earth; if a person ascends to a place of prominence (by whatever method), they deserve to be in that position. In the same respect, if a person finds themselves at the low end of the socio-economic totem pole, it's because of accumulated karma, heritage, bloodline, or lack of personal ambition. These factors dictate that they belong at the bottom. Only the fit will survive. This scenario perfectly applies to the hermetic philosophy, *As Above, So Below*, as claimed by Blavatsky.

Note: Madame Blavatsky's theories are responsible for much of the sci-fi material you watch in movies and read in books today.

"The great gods...appear explicitly as planets. In the *Titanic Wars* vividly depicted by ancient chroniclers, the planets moved on erratic courses, appearing to wage battles in the sky, exchanging electrical discharges, and more than once menacing the earth. " (Talbott Myth and Catastrophe)

Egypt

Egypt stands as a worldwide wonder and a center for hidden knowledge and ancient activity, this passage may hold a key to Egypt's secret;

"Do you not know that *Egypt* is an image of heaven? Or, so to speak more exactly, in **Egypt all the operations of the powers which rule and work in heaven have been transferred down to earth below?** The purpose to which these powers were harnessed, in the Hermetic view, was to facilitate the initiate's quest for immortality." (The Book of Secrets – Reflections and Notes on the Royal Families of the Grail Page 76)

Rulers Celestial and Terrestrial

"On the fourth day I commanded that there should be great lights on the heavenly circles. On the first uppermost circle I placed the stars, *Kruno*, and on the second *Aphrodit*, on the third *Aris*, on the fifth *Zoue*s, on the sixth *Ermis*, on the seventh, the lesser moon, and the adorned it with the lesser stars." (Schnieders, Paul C. Chapter 30. Page 133)

Although the language is ancient, this creation account shows that the Greek gods in mythology were actually planets, which eventually had a mythological counterpart on earth; *Aphrodite, Aries, Zeus, Hermes.*

"Among classical writers (*Herodotus, Diodorus, Plutarch*) the idea prevailed that *Osiris* lived on our earth as a man or man-god. Egyptian sources, too, often portray him in human form. Yet the early religious texts say again and again that Osiris was the supreme light of heaven, ruling from the cosmic centre. He was, in fact, "the lord of the gods." His body formed the celestial residence of the gods. And the secondary gods themselves constituted the limbs of Osiris." (Talbott The Age of Kronos)

Cosmic Trinity

"The Trinity was, in truth, only an astronomical triad unless they accepted the more abstract and metaphysical meanings given to it by the Gentiles composed of;

- the Sun (the father)
- and the two planets Mercury (the son)
- and Venus (the holy ghost), *Sophia*, the spirit of wisdom, love and truth
- and Lucifer, (as Christ), the bright and morning star

Because, if the father is the Sun (the elder brother in the Eastern philosophy), the nearest planet to it is Mercury (*Hermes, Buddha, Thoth*), the name of whose mother on earth was *Maia*, the planet which receives seven times more light than any other which fact led the Gnostics to call their Christos, and the Kabbalists their Hermes (in the astronomical meaning), the seven-fold light." (Talbott The Age of Kronos)

The doctrine of the *Holy Trinity* is one of the most controversial aspects of Christendom. However, we will leave that argument to the scholars and theologians. There is no place in the Word of God, the Holy Scriptures, or The Bible that waters our Great Creator down to the Sun or the planets; in fact, HE CREATED THEM!

> "In the beginning GOD created the HEAVEN and the earth." [Genesis 1:1].

It's critical, however, to understand this is one of the end-times deceptions. This doctrine is straight out of the playbook of anti-Christ, anti-Creator, and anti-Biblical ideology that claims the Bible is but a zodiacal explanation for the heavens. The 12 Tribes of Israel, and the 12 Apostles of Jesus, are equated to the 12 houses of the Zodiac. According to this doctrine, all Biblical accounts only retell the stories of the heavens. This blasphemy even puts YAHUAH Himself (as is shown) as but a planetary creation, meaning there is one higher than Himself. Our GOD, Our FATHER, The CREATOR, is... THE "MOST HIGH! Lucifer lost his place in Heaven and created deceptions about the ONE who removed him!

Moon

"When God punished the envious moon by diminishing her light and splendor, so that she ceased to be the equal of the Sun as she had been originally, she fell, and tiny threads were loosed from her body. These are the stars." (Ginzberg, Legends of the Jews The Fourth Day. Page 109-110)

" [4] And the moon shall alter her order, and not appear at her time. [5] And in those days the Sun shall be seen and he shall journey in the evening on the extremity of the great chariot in the west." [Enoch 80: 4-5]

These passages about the "moon" appearing to be an "independent woman" are an exacting parallel to many goddess myths and the "divine feminine" aspect. Principally, *Lilith*, who, in Jewish Talmudic tradition, was Adam's first wife (before Eve). Lilith did not want to be submissive to Adam but wanted to be his equal. The Gnostic's Sophia is also a prototype for this account. Sophia (a high spiritual emanation) moved out of her heavenly abode to "create" things without her consort. Lastly, *Shekhinah* also had a mind of her own and became separated from her "spouse." The moon is mostly always regarded as "feminine." So it's a principal reason many women in witchcraft worship the moon. It's not a far reach at all to see the struggle in the cosmos of the *independent moon*, is parallel to the feminist movement on earth. (Lynn Chapter 15 Gnosticism, Chapter 28 Babylonian Demonology, Chapter 36 Come out of Her!)

"Moon demons inhabit the "Dark Side of the Moon," where they play a legitimate role in the spiritual economy of the cosmos, helping to tear corruption from human spirits after death. However, if they break through into the earthly realm, they appear as *malevolent dwarves*. The height of a six or seven-year-old child with large, hypnotic eyes, they sometimes emit an ear-splitting yell that can freeze a human with fear. More powerful when the moon is waning, these demons may account for some modern encounters with aliens, which in a physical form at any rate play no part in esoteric cosmology." (Booth Chapter 7 The Age of Demi-Gods and Heroes The Ancient Ones • The Amazons • Enoch • Hercules, Theseus and Jason)

Sirius

The Sirius star (Greater Dog star) is one of the most sacred cosmic bodies in the ancient mysteries and still today. Sirius is seen as the brightest star in the sky, giving off different light colors. The Sirius star, in many traditions, is kept hidden. We covered the Sirius star briefly in Chapter 11 of *Thy Queendom Come*. A former victim of the CIA's MK Ultra (mind control) program exposes a technique used to brainwash victims in connection to the Sirius star that is both eye-opening and equally disturbing;

"Blue beams of light are used as a hypnotic induction for slaves who are given the cover story of being abducted by aliens. The *All-Seeing Eye* is used to represent the planet Sirius. Sirius is important to the Hermetic magicians, and some of the programmers are deeply into hermetic magic. **Satan is said to come from Draco or Sirius**, esp. The dog star Canis major. *Masonic* programming may well have the "blazing star" portrayed in the programming as a pentagram, with the name Sirius. Sirius may represent the *Master*, the creator of the system, in some systems where the programmer is steeped in Masonic philosophy. A *s*ickle may be involved with the *Garden of Eden* story for some victims of this type of programming, because supposedly the *Golden Age* ended with a sickle splitting heaven from earth. The moon is waning, these demons may account for some modern encounters with aliens, which in a physical form at any rate play no part in esoteric cosmology." (Booth Chapter 7 The Age of Demi-Gods and Heroes The Ancient Ones • The Amazons • Enoch • Hercules, Theseus and Jason)

Sirius – Connections

We all know the familiar, perhaps, most popular children's nursery rhyme TWINKLE TWINKLE LITTLE STAR. This famous song, no doubt, is about SIRIUS. This great bluish-white luminary is not only the brightest star in the cosmic atmosphere but it "twinkles." The Twinkle of Sirius is brilliant in the clear night sky. The Twinkle, along with the color of serious, is said to be a breathtaking wonder. As you can ascertain by the etymology, Sirius connects with the Egyptian goddess, Isis.

"Robert Temple's book, *The Sirius Mystery*, maintains that the Dog Star, Sirius, was the location of **intelligent beings who visited earth in ages past and taught mankind the body of sacred alchemical traditions** that have been preserved in the Egyptian mysteries." (The Book of Secrets – Reflections and Notes on the Royal Families of the Grail Page 36)

Robert Temple also asserts about the Dogon Tribe in Mali, Africa, "For the Dogon differentiates very clearly between the fiery, roaring landing craft which they describe as bringing the Nommos to Earth and the new star which appeared in the sky while they were here, which would seem to be a reference to their larger base parked in orbit. This is called the "Star of the Tenth Moon." The Dogon do three drawings of it showing it in separate stages, which seem to imply that it could be expanded and contracted as a sphere at will." The Dogon tribe claims to have received Sirius visitors. The Dogon also describes two stars (A and B) that rotate around Sirius. These legends are thousands of years old and predate any telescopic technology. The Dogon tribe is quite a mystery, and we will discuss them further in the coming chapter.

"The serpent is *Ophis*, so too is *Sophia* (Wisdom), as in S-ophis, another name for *Isis* and the **Sirius star**. " (Gardiner and Osborn Chapter Seven The Serpent in Classical Myth. Page 136)

Taurus

Mechanical Bull
Commonwealth Games 2022

Out of all the Zodiac signs, the symbolism of the Bull, Taurus, continues to be displayed prominently worldwide, above the other eleven signs. The *Commonwealth Games* is a massive sporting event similar to the Olympics, which brings all 72 countries of the British Commonwealth together in various athletic competitions. The games recently took place in Birmingham, England (summer of 2022). The undisputed highlight of the opening ceremony was a giant mechanical bull that was both worshiped, feared, and illuminated. The sign of the Bull and its "horns" are everywhere. As in all esoteric symbolism, let's examine the true meaning of Taurus, the sign of the Bull.

"*The Festival of Unification*, which begins the process of understanding or enlightenment of the mind, is referred to as a *Taurean festival*. The sign of Taurus is taken as representing the initiating impulse that starts the process of illumination. **Taurus the Bull is the great Bestower of Light**, who fertilizes the minds of mankind with seeds of light. In the East the festival of the Buddha, called the *Wesak festival*, is celebrated at the same full moon as the *Beltane festival* in the West - for they are one and the same. The festival is described as being the time when "**light is gathered**," concentrated and poured out to stimulate the mental state of humanity with wisdom, and incline men towards love and brotherhood. The festival is associated with the birth of the Buddha, for Buddha means 'the Enlightened One', which is a description of the enlightened mind or soul of man."

"It should be noticed...that the so-called 'Unification of the Two Lands' in Ancient Egypt, which marked the start of the first cycle of Pharaonic dynasties, began with the commencement of the astronomical **Age of Taurus, c**. 3,240 BC. The symbol of the bull was of particular importance for Egypt throughout its history."

"At the time that the Pharaonic civilization of Ancient Egypt was supposed to have begun, c. 3.240 BC, the Spring Equinoctial Sun arose in the middle of the **zodiacal sign of Taurus**, and the *May Day* festival Sun was on the cusp of the signs of Cancer and Gemini."

"New Agers think that commencing the Great Work **under the sign of Taurus**, as prophesied by *Aleister Crowley*, will ensure 'the rebirth of the New Age of Enlightenment' under the leadership of this angelic bloodline."

"*Orion, the Hunter*, is a prominent constellation, perhaps the best-known in the sky. At the time of the *Grand Planetary Alignment* on May 5, the five planets (Mercury, Venus, Mars, Jupiter and Saturn) were in the process of leaving the constellation Aries and entering Taurus. It is indeed auspicious that the constellation of Orion appears in the sign of Taurus, which opens or '**births' the Golden Age of Saturn**. According to "The Saturn Myth" by David Talbot, Orion was known as *Tammuz* in Babylon and *Saturn* in Rome: "The story of Orion preceded astrology. (In fact, Orion is widely acknowledged to be the Greek version of the Babylonian Tammuz-Ninurta, the planet Saturn.)" (The Book of Secrets – Reflections and Notes on the Royal Families of the Grail Page 55-56)

After a review of this information, the logical question is; when Lucifer and his angels were kicked out of the 3rd or highest heaven, was their abode the 2nd heaven or the solar system? Did these "beings" take up residence on the planets? Is this the spiritual wickedness in high places?

Connecting the Dots

Dragon = Jupiter and Venus (Lucifer)
Gods of the earth = planets
Osiris = light of heaven, cosmic center, limbs of the secondary gods
Mercury = Hermes, Buddha, Thoth
Serpent = Venus (Lucifer), Sophia, Isis, Sirius
Moon = created the stars
Satan = comes from Draco or Sirius
Sirius = location of the fallen angels (intelligent beings), Isis, Sophia
Taurus (bull) = bestow-er of light, Buddha, birthed Golden Age of Saturn
Golden Age ended = when the heavens separated from earth (firmament)
72 = Countries in the British Commonwealth

2

Lord of the Rings

The mystery and splendor of Saturn constitutes particular attention. Were you aware that Saturn is a common word for *Satan*? What does this mean, and how does it connect here in *the below*? Uncovering Saturn's secrets will quickly reveal there is much more to this ominous planet than its infamous appearance. Saturn is the undisputed "Lord of the Rings."

"Saturn is thought to be the first planet in the solar system to be formed by God. "Let there be lights on the firmament of the heaven to divide the day from the night; and let them be for signs and seasons and days and years," God said in Genesis 1:11. As a result, it was Saturn, a god of agriculture, who is responsible for the growth of plants. Saturn is also said to have ruled over the signs of the zodiac, as well as being the god of time." (Sela)

Saturn as god

"In fact, Saturn was the one "great god" invoked by all mankind. The first religious symbols were symbols of Saturn, and so pervasive was the planet god's influence that the ancients knew him as the creator, the King of the world, and Adam, the first man." (Talbott Introduction)

"A cloud harvests souls with a sickle, and we discover one like the *Son of Man* in Revelation 14:4. **Saturn, the God of Harvest, was particularly associated with the sickle.**"

Note: the sickle is an interesting item as it frequently appears in creation myths, including those of Greek and Egyptian antiquity. The ruling god usually is castrated with a sickle, and the "seed" from the castration creates other gods or beings.

In creation accounts, Saturn emerged from the cosmic sea and the watery chaos and produced a *New Order*. The people worshiped him as the supreme *lord of the heavens*.

A glance back into the annals of history reveals that Saturn, to the ancients, was much more than this great ring in the sky. Ancient images of Saturn show;

- Saturn on a celestial ship
- Saturn having several goddesses as consorts
- Saturn revolving around islands, cities, and temples
- Saturn connected with the paradise of Eden
- Saturn and the lost city of Atlantis.

Other familiar images of Saturn include; a one wheeled chariot of god, the fountain of youth, the all-seeing eye, and the serpent dragon of the watery deep.
(Talbott II The Great Father) (Talbott Myth and Catastrophe)

"Above the arch of the heavens **Saturn is the dwelling of the different powers controlling the universe.** The Supreme Council of gods is composed of 12 deities, six female and six male which correspond with the positive and negative signs of the Zodiac. The six gods are Jupiter, Vulcan, Mars, Apollo, Neptune, and Mercury. The six goddesses are Juno, Ceres, Vesta, Minerva, Venus, and Diana." (Hall, The Secret Teachings of All Ages The Scheme of the Universe according to the Greeks and Romans. Page 33)

"Saturn, the father of the gods and the true illuminator of all humanity." (Hall, The Secret Teachings of All Ages Seven Wonders of the World. Page 64)

Saturn as Earthly King

Saturn was considered the ruler of the heavens as the great father and an actual earthly ruler. There is an unresolved debate among history scholars whether Saturn was an earthly ruler venerated in the sky, another name for an ancient ruler, or simply a myth. Saturn is said to have sired both gods and mortal men on earth.

As an earthly King and god, Saturn was the founder of a Kingdom of extraordinary splendor where he ruled peacefully and balanced all things. During the reign of Saturn, the land produced wonderful vegetation, there were no regional borders (similar to the Communist Manifesto), and all people lived in harmony.

Legends also claim that, as an earth-man, Saturn was a vast primordial giant whose body reached the heavens.

"The same cosmic figure whom the oldest races knew as the creator and supreme god appears in the myths as a terrestrial King, reigning over the *Golden Age*. His rule was distinguished for its peace and abundance, and he governed not one land alone but the entire world, becoming the model of the good King. Every terrestrial ruler, according to the Kingship rites, received his charisma and authority from this divine predecessor." (Talbott II The Great Father)

These epics of a *Golden Age* give way to images of ancient *Atlantis*, which we covered in great detail in *Thy Queendom Come*. As with Saturn, there is debate whether Atlantis truly existed, was simply a myth, or was a metaphor for something else. Many scholars say that Atlantis was the original Egyptian dynasty, and many compare it to the time of Eden before *the fall*. This Golden Age represents a time when there was peace on earth and goodwill for all men, but something happened. At the end of Saturn's reign, he then became the prototype for all proceeding Kings who became types of Saturn themselves;

"No mythical figure remains more enigmatic than the great King to whom so many ancient peoples traced their ancestry. Who was *Osiris*, the legendary ruler who led the Egyptians out of barbarianism and reigned as King of the entire world? Who was *Enki*, whom the ancient Sumerians revered as the "universal lord" and founder of civilization? The same figure appears repeatedly as one passes to India, Greece, China, and the Americas. For the Hindus it was *Yama*; for the Greeks, *Cronos*; for the Chinese, *Huang-ti*. The Mexicans insisted that *Quetzalcoatl* once ruled not only Mexico but all mankind. In North America the same idea is attached to the primordial figure *Manabozo*." (Talbott The Universal Monarch)

"In the original age of cosmic harmony and human **innocence the gods dwelt on earth**. Presiding over the epoch of peace and plenty was the *Universal Monarch*, who founded temples and cities and taught humanity **the principles of agriculture, law, writing, music, and other civilized arts**. This Golden Age, however, ended in the god-King's catastrophic death." (Talbott The Universal Monarch)

In Greek mythology, Cronos is the father of the most famous Greek god *Zeus*. Cronos is also known as Saturn, the god of time. Many places in Italy bore the name of Saturn as Cronos. There are even stories that his reign as an earthly King was explicitly in the Italian region. However, that may be a different geographic area in today's terms. As for the demise of Saturn, he vanished suddenly. Still, his memory lived on throughout the ages in shrines, temples, hills, and high holy places.

"Cronos is preeminently the good King, his darker side concealed. First of all the deathless gods who dwell on Olympus made a **golden race of mortal men who lived in the time of Cronos** when he reigned in heaven. And they lived like gods without sorrow of heart, remote and free from toil and grief: miserable age rested not on them." (Talbott The Age of Cronos)

"Through identification, the sacred history of the race or nation merges with the history of the gods, for **each organized community viewed itself as a duplication of the celestial "race."** Each line of historical Kings leads back to a first King who is not a man, but Saturn, the supreme power of heaven; in the same way, **the race as a whole traces its ancestry to a generation of gods or semi-divine beings who inhabited the "earth" raised in the creation.** By this universal tendency, Saturn's paradise becomes the ancestral land, the place where history began. Does not every nation claim that its ancestors descended from a race of gods, who occupied a happy garden at the centre and summit?"

"The ancients laid out their first political settlements, taking the cosmic habitation as the prescribed plan. The purpose was to establish **Saturn's Kingdom on earth,** repeating the creator's defeat of *Chaos* and founding a central authority whose power extended to a protective "border" separating the Kingdom of light from the powers of darkness and disorganization (the "barbarians")." (Talbott The Enclosure as Prototype)

Note: this is classic, As Above, So Below theory. This "protective border" sounds like the firmament when GOD separated light from darkness.

"In classical tradition, Cronos and Saturn are treated as the same personages, but the character of the Roman Saturn is quite different from that of the Greek Cronos. In the mythical legends of Rome, Saturn was celebrated as a very ancient King of Italy, who introduced agriculture industry, social order and the habits of civilized life. He was suddenly removed from the divine abodes and became a god. These legends were in ancient Italy long before Rome was built. The Greek, Egyptian, and Ethiopian legends made *Dionysus* contemporary with Saturn, or Cronus, and his sons. And Cronus, undoubtedly the same personages, and by the Greeks and Romans admitted to be so, are definitely portrayed in their mythical narratives." (Baldwin Dionysus, Cronus, Zeus. Page 285-286)

"*An*, the oldest and highest of the Sumero-Babylonian gods, whose primordial age was "the year of abundance," **signified Saturn**, according to Jensen. The same verdict is tacitly maintained by Jeremias and Langdon, who identify the great **god Ninurta as both the planet Saturn and a form of Anu. The shepherd Tammuz was likewise Saturn**, according to Jeremias. And one can add the well-known fact that the **Sumerian Enki (Babylonian Ea, the Oannes of Berossus) came to be translated Cronos (Saturn)** by the Greeks." (Talbott The Great Father Saturn)

In the above context, Saturn could be the cosmic title for the earthly King. Signifying that as Saturn ruled the heavens according to the ancients, the paralleled earthly King would himself rule the world as *Saturn*.

"Paul A Philips tells us that: "Since ancient times in occult symbolism Saturn has been known to represent negativity such as that found in limitations in space and time, conflict and death." (Love)

"The Greeks and the Romans worshiped Saturn as a cruel deity: Since ancient times, sages gazed at the stars, admiring their heavenly glow and attributing them godly powers, based on their effect on humans. Before the Great Flood, Saturn was regarded by all mankind as the supreme god and ruler of the kings. Occult researchers affirm that Saturn ruled the kingdom of Atlantis and became the divine ancestor of all earthly patriarchs and kings." (Love)

Here the veil is taken off of the beneficent deity Saturn and a cruel side, more like the Satan we are accustomed to, is revealed. This research also claims to trace Saturn back to the kingdom of Atlantis which brings clarity to earlier suspicions.

Fragmentary records preserved by the early Greeks and Phoenicians tell of a King by the name of Saturn who ruled over the ancient continents of Hyperborean, Polaris, and Atlantis. Because these continents and their secrets lie beneath the oceans, their symbols have frequently been rocks or stones on which supports the emerging of *new lands, new races, and new empires.* (Hall, The Secret Teachings of All Ages Stones, Metals and Gems. Page 97)

Saturn's Divine Feminine

Every pagan belief centers on the androgynous or dual nature of their gods, consisting of equal male and female personalities, hermaphrodites in nature. This belief envelops everything in our current world system. It is a significant part of the mystery religion covered in *Thy Queendom Come*. With Saturn, we revisit some familiar divine feminine themes with familiar names.

"The Hebrews regarded the Shekhinah (the creator's encircling "aura," "anima," or "glory") as "the Mother" leads to the same conclusion: **the great god's halo was his own spouse**. Accordingly, the *Tibetan* ritual invokes the great god as "the centre of the Circle, enhaloed in radiance, embraced by the (divine) Mother." (Talbott The Great Mother)

"To the ancients, the "universe" (Cosmos) meant Saturn's home, not a boundless expanse. That Saturn's Cosmos **acquired a dual character as the god's "body" and as his "spouse"** is sufficient to explain the primordial **Father-Mother**."

"The hermaphrodite or androgyne, *Eliade* tells us, is "the distinguishing sign of the original totality [i.e., the All]." Its customary form is "spherical," he notes. We thus arrive at the following equation; "Band of the enclosed Sun=Cosmos (island, egg, cord, girdle, shield, circle of the gods)=body of the great father=womb of the great mother." (Talbott The Hermaphrodite)

"In the New Testament (Book of Revelation) one finds a fascinating equation of primeval goddess and primeval city. In his vision, John beholds "the great whore that sitteth upon many waters: With whom the Kings of the earth have committed fornication . . . and upon her forehead was a name written, 'MYSTERY, BABYLON THE GREAT, THE MOTHER OF HARLOTS AND ABOMINATIONS OF THE EARTH." Who was this "mother of harlots"? The angel explains: "And the woman which thou sawest is that great city, which reigneth over the Kings of the earth. "The language points to the ancient rites of Kingship, in which every local ruler took as his consort the city *(womb) on the cosmic waters*. In ranging over the myths and symbols of the created earth, paradise, wheel, throne, and city, one thus remains in the shadow of a single mother goddess, **who contains within her womb the first organized domain in heaven, the island of Saturn's Cosmos**." (Talbott The City of Heaven)

Saturn's Divine Offspring

"Two of the tombs of *Osiris* and *Isis*. On one was this inscription: "I am Isis, Queen of this country. I was instructed by *Mercury*. No one can destroy the laws which I have established. **I am the eldest daughter of Saturn,** most ancient of the gods. I am the wife and sister of Osiris the King. I first made known to mortals the use of wheat. I am the mother of *Horus the King*. In my honor was the city of Bubaste built. Rejoice, O Egypt, rejoice, land that gave me birth!"

"And on the other was this, "I am Osiris the King, who led my armies into all parts of the world, to the most thickly inhabited countries of India, the North, the Danube, and the Ocean. **I am the eldest son of Saturn.** I was born of the brilliant and magnificent egg, and my substance is of the same nature as that which composes light. There is no place in the Universe where I have not appeared, to bestow my benefits and make known my discoveries." (Pike Page 253)

"Osiris, Isis, *Nephtys* and *Set* were siblings, their parents were *Geb*, the earth god and *Nut*, the sky goddess. They were the descendants of *Ra*, the Sun god." (Lynn Chapter 13 Egyptian. Page 165)

This text makes a fascinating connection. As discussed earlier, Saturn could be the title of all earthly Kings (similar to the Pharaohs), and Saturn could also be the name of an actual ruler. In Egyptian mythology, Osiris and Isis were siblings that married. But here, *Albert Pike*, the foremost authority of Freemason doctrine, connects Isis and Osiris as children of Saturn.

"Cronos, the Greek Saturn, had six sons, and by *Astar*te seven daughters, the Titanides." (Pike Page 466)

Note: Cronos having children by the famous goddess Astarte (the goddess with many names) is fascinating. Cronos is a part of Greek mythology and Astarte Canaanite and Phoenician mythology. Titans are considered the giant offspring of the "sons of God" (angels) and the daughters of men spoken of in Genesis 6. We will explore this in detail in the coming chapters.

"Without the presence of the greater gods to keep them down, the crab-like progeny of Saturn that had been imprisoned in underground caves began to creep up into the daylight again, infesting the surface of the earth and preying on humankind. Sea monsters also leapt on to the shore to drag off members of the tribe who had strayed too close. Giants carried off cattle and sometimes preyed on human flesh, too." (Booth Chapter 7 The Age of Deni-Gods and Heroes The Ancient Ones • The Amazons • Enoch • Hercules, Theseus and Jason)

Saturn as the Sun

It's difficult to imagine that at one time in history, Saturn, not the Sun that we know today, was considered to be the "greater light" of the day. The image of Saturn in our minds does not emit light; it's nearly the opposite of light.

However, the symbolism may give us a clue into this ancient myth. Think of a halo, the round orb that adorns celebrities, religious statues and pictures, and other fanciful artwork. Could the halo secretly represent the rings of Saturn, which many consider the original "Sun?"

"The "Great god" or "Universal Monarch" of the ancients **was not the Sun, but Saturn,** which once hung ominously close to the earth and visually dominated the heavens. Saturn dominated the earth as a Sun, presiding over the universal Golden Age." (Talbott Introduction)

"The most common symbols of antiquity, which our age universally regards as solar emblems…were originally unrelated to our Sun. They were literal pictures of Saturn, whom the entire ancient world invoked as "the Sun." In the original age to which the myths refer, Saturn was no remote speck faintly discerned by terrestrial observers; the planet loomed as an awesome and terrifying light. And if we are to believe the wide-spread accounts of Saturn's age, the planet-god's home was the un-moving celestial pole, the apparent pivot of the heavens, far removed from the visible path of Saturn today."

Ancient symbols for Saturn

Let's consider two important themes of the Saturn of times past;

1. Saturn, not the solar orb, was the authentic "Sun-god" of ancient ritual.
2. Throughout Saturn's reign, this Sun-planet remained fixed at the **north celestial pole**.

"These two themes, affirmed by the straightforward testimony of ancient sources, compose a global memory: in the beginning Saturn did not move on its present remote orbit, but ruled as the central Sun around which the other heavenly bodies visually revolved." (Talbott III. The Polar Sun)

Helios and Saturn were one and the same god.

"The equation of sun and Saturn is very old, with roots in Sumerian-Babylonian astronomy. Of the Babylonian star-worshippers the chronicler *Diodorus* writes: "To the one we call Saturn they give a special name, "Sun- Star." Among the Babylonians the "sun"-god par excellence was *Shamash*, the "light of the gods."

Fall of Saturn

If, in times past, Saturn was, indeed, the great light of the heavens, what happened? Did a cosmic war cause this planet to lose its place? Could a cosmic dual of Saturn and the Sun be a metaphor for the *Fall of Satan or Lucifer*? Considering the defeat of the Greek god Cronos (Saturn), it's not strange to go along with this line of thinking. Remember, the occult hides its agenda in signs, symbols, metaphors, and stories; look at any Hollywood Sci-fi, and you will see.

"Old Saturn fell to *Death's dark country.*" There is not a race on earth that forgot this cataclysmic event—the death of Saturn, the *Universal Monarch*; or the *fall of Adam*, the *Heaven Man*. And peoples the world over, for thousands of years, awaited the full turn of *Time's wheel,* when **Saturn's Kingdom would appear again** to rescue the world from a decadent age of Iron (the present age, marking the lowest of the descending ages after the Golden Age). The powerful memory of Saturn's age gave rise to a prophesied return, as announced in the famous lines of *Virgil*: That Saturn governed the Golden Age is a supreme tenet of the ancient mysteries." (Talbott The Great Father Saturn)

If we ponder on the fall of Saturn, we must go back to the beginning.

Scholars and theologians are re-examining the Genesis creation account. The re-examination is not about the validity of Scripture but rather about the traditional interpretation of Scripture. Have we followed the "traditions" of men when it comes to Scripture interpretation? Or are we looking at the Scripture for how the MOST HIGH intended them to be understood? For example, traditional teaching regarding the *first day*, accounts for the creation of the Sun, but let's examine what the text says;

> [1] In the beginning God created the heaven and the earth. [2] And the earth was without form, and void; and darkness was upon the face of the deep. And the Spirit of God moved upon the face of the waters. [3] And God said, Let there be light: and there was light. [4] And God saw the light, that it was good: and God divided the light from the darkness. [5] And God called the light Day, and the darkness he called Night. And the evening and the morning were the first day. [Genesis 1:1-5]

Firstly, the text doesn't say Sun at all; the text reads *light*. Further down on day four, we see the creation of what we would call "the Sun," but the Scriptures refer to it as the "greater light." There is not a Bible believer that wouldn't instinctively interpret the "light" of creation to be the Sun.

> [16] And God made two great lights; the greater light to rule the day, and the lesser light to rule the night: he made the stars also. [17] And God set them in the firmament of the heaven to give light upon the earth, [18] And to rule over the day and over the night, and to divide the light from the darkness: and God saw that it was good. [19] And the evening and the morning were the fourth day. [Genesis 1:16-19]

The greater light, which most consider our Sun, was not created until day four. What happened to the original light, or what was the original light on day one? Did the original light lose its place? Did it fall? Without going into the various gap theories, (which are all valid in my humble estimation), many put the angelic fall of Lucifer, right between Genesis 1:1 and 1:2.

> "[1] In the beginning, God created the heaven and the earth."[Genesis 1:1]

GAP THEORY HERE (fall of Lucifer)

> "² And the earth was without form, and void; and darkness was upon the face of the deep." [Genesis 1:2]

Why do scholars put the fall of Lucifer after verse one? Because GOD would never create anything and its original state was *without form and void*. According to gap theorists, something catastrophic happened between verses one and two.

"The gap theory attempts to resolve the apparent conflict between Scripture and modern geology by inserting a gap of unknown time between the first two verses of Genesis 1. The gap theory doesn't just insert a gap of time in order to give room for geological eras; it also theorizes that because of Satan's fall, the original creation became ruined and devastated, which supposedly explains the evidence of mass animal death before the fall as seen in the fossil record. Genesis 1:2 is describing not merely that the earth was formless and void but also that it was in a state of ruin and destruction, an accursed state under God's judgment. The gap theory suggests that verse 1 describes God's original work of creation, verse 2 describes the result of the original creation's destruction, and verse 3 and following describe its restoration or re-creation. For this reason, the theory has also been called the ruin-restoration theory." (Irons)

The "GAP" of time in creation to the enemies of Christ is the foundation of their entire false belief system. The occult acknowledges the fall of both man and Lucifer; this is a universal belief. The conflict is; they believe Lucifer and the fallen angels were fighting for mankind to be free from an angry and unjust GOD. This belief is Occultism 101 with few exclusions. We will delve into this further in another chapter.

Saturn in Creation

To completely understand the mindset of the Luciferians, you must know how they believe the world came into existence. Everything in their belief system is rooted in their account of creation.

In the beginning, there was nothing. There was only a void. A *cosmic mist* emerged that was more subtle than light. This gas or mist was called the *Mother goddess*, the *Mother of all living* which within herself had everything needed to create life. They interpret this from the Bible as "the earth was without form and void" [Genesis 1:2]. There is a sharp contrast here between that theology and Biblical theology, especially regarding the gap theory.

To their account, the darkness in Genesis was *an attack in the form of a dry wind*. This wind nearly destroyed the mother goddess' potential to bring forth life. In their account, the mother goddess was the first emanation of God, and then this *hot wind* or this *storm* was the second emanation of God. The enemy of the mother goddess was called the *Dark lord*. In appearance, the Dark lord was long and bony, with red piercing eyes and white scaly skin. This dark lord will be known as the *god of Saturn*.

While the mother goddess was unlimited, Saturn was limited. Saturn appearing in creation meant there was potential for other objects to exist. Saturn, was the first manifested object. Saturn was not omnipresent or everywhere at the same time. Saturn can only be in one place at one time. Saturn then became the *Rex Mundi*, king of the world, or *prince of this world*, because he controls the material world or the material life. Because Saturn could exist, it also meant he could cease to exist. Thereby Saturn is the *god of destruction*. Saturn eats his children and is "old father time" and "death" himself. Saturn influences everything in our lives and contains the seed within himself.

- Consequently, what Saturn feeds us also destroys us
- Because of Saturn, our lives are complex
- Because of Saturn, every sword is double-edged
- Every crown is a crown of thorns
- If we sometimes feel our lives are almost too hard to bear,
- if we bruise and do cry out to the stars in despair,
- it is because Saturn pushes us to our limits

Throughout history, Saturn returns at different times and in various forms to mummify humanity and squeeze the life out of it. At the end of earthly history, one of Saturn's most divisive interventions will take place, something long predicted by secret societies. Saturn, in their account, holds tyranny over mother earth and wants to squeeze all potential life out of the cosmos. Saturn has done this over time. Saturn's reign of terror eventually ended; Saturn was not destroyed but kept "in check." Their account for this is when God said in Genesis, *let there be light, and there was light.* The light pushed back against the darkness brooding over the waters. So, according to this account, the first two creations were an earth goddess or mother earth and Saturn. The earth goddess was a mist, not a form. Saturn was a solid form.

Next, in their creation account, the *seven-fold Sun god* comes to rescue mother earth from Saturn. This seven-fold Sun god has *seven emanating rays* that make up his nature. Statues and celebrities adorn themselves with these seven rays; the most famous seven-ray statue is the *Statue of Liberty*. The Sun god is called; *Apollo, Krishna, Mithra,* and many others. The Sun god pictured is a beautiful and radiant young man. He rides a chariot and is a musician.

Note: this sounds very close to Lucifer, who was bright, beautiful, and had pipes within himself.

Rising from the storm, the Sun god fights the darkness, Saturn, until Saturn becomes like a

dragon or serpent and encircles the cosmos (ouroboros). The Sun then warms mother earth to new life. The Sun god then lets out a roar that vibrates the entire universe of creation and causes the cosmic womb to dance and form patterns. In esoteric traditions, this process is sometimes called *the dance of the substances*. Over time this matter formed into strange shapes. The material world was coming into existence through the sound of the singing from the Sun god.

The mystery schools teach that this transition began to bring forth the mineral cosmos and plant life. Eventually, these germs formed vast floating structures like webs that filled the universe. In the Indian Vedas sacred books, this process is called the *Net of Indra,* where luminous living threads interweave like light waves. These waves appear and then dissolve again and again. The waves continued this pattern until treelike forms came into existence.

This vast vegetable with soft and luminous limbs stretched to all four corners and was called *Adam* (paradise). Adam lived in an endless springtime, and nature gave an infinite supply of a milky sap which nurtured Adam. This symbology can be seen in the multi-breasted mother goddess from many cultures but most popularly, *Diana*. In this sense, life developed from minerals, vegetables, and animals to humans. Humans evolved over a stage of evolution. This vegetable element in man is said to be a part of us today and is associated with flowers on a tree and the Chakras which operate the solar plexus. Chinese medicine follows this flow and life force which they call *chi*.

Adam's body, they teach, was soft and amorphous and delicate, but it began to harden. Adams's green limbs, warmed by the Sun, started tingling with pink. As Adam physically solidified, he also became divided into two. Adam was a hermaphrodite who reproduced asexually. It was by this plant-like method of reproduction that Eve was born out of Adam's body molded from the waxy cartilage which served Adam as bone. Adam and Eve reproduced children asexually and procreated by "sound." Freemasons consider this sound, *the word that was lost*. Adam and Eve's progeny were immortal, but they sometimes went to sleep to refresh. This stage of the *Garden of Eden* could not go on forever if man wanted to evolve from being a vegetable.

This "creation account" was acted out in dramas during mystery school initiation rituals.

At this stage, a giant serpent wrapped itself around Adams's vegetable trunk in a coil. The coiling represented moving from vegetable to animal life, a painful but necessary process. **Lucifer was the serpent that coiled Adam**. *Lucifer and his legions infested the earth with a plague of glistening serpents.* The planet began populating with primitive animal life.

This evolution from vegetable to animal man bought torment, "I will greatly multiply thy sorrow and conception, and to Adam curses the ground." So no longer would Adam and Eve reproduce asexually by sound, they were now having intercourse to bring forth children. The serpent, in this sense, is considered Lucifer. Lucifer and Satan are not considered the same beings.

Lucifer and Saturn are both names for planets. *Lucifer is Venus*, the bright morning star; *Satan is Saturn*, the dark Lord, one light and one dark.

Lucifer and Venus's symbology is present in the horned figure and feathered snake god *Quetzalcoatl*. The apple is the fruit of Venus. Lucifer is evil, but Lucifer is a necessary evil. Without Lucifer, according to the mystery school tradition, man would have never evolved from the vegetative form of life. However, this evolution contained animal desires, and now the planet is reaped with animal lust and desires. *Frederick Nietzsche* said, "Without chaos inside you, you could not give birth to a dancing star; Humans would never have been able to become freely creative, brave, or loving if they had not made mistakes, seeing things as other than they are, and believed something to be different." In other words, this was necessary chaos, just as the motto of the 33rd Degree of Freemasonry says, *Ordo Ab Chaos* "order out of chaos."

(Booth Chapter 4 Lucifer, The Light of the Light of the World, The Apple of Desire, War in Heave, The Secrets of the Days of the Week)

This apparent fall of Saturn, the so-called original Sun, brings us to another heavy doctrinal belief even inside many fringe denominations such as Mormonism and Jehovah's Witness. These groups claim Lucifer and Jesus are brothers, both sons, and creations of God. Many believe Satan, or Lucifer in this sense, was the first created or older "son of God." These doctrines don't account for the SON of GOD, Y'SHUA, as a part of the GODHEAD but as a created being separate from the FATHER, THE MOST HIGH.

This belief is one of the main end-times deceptions. The enemy is perfectly fine with a person believing in JESUS, as a prophet, a Holy Man, as an example of love and sacrifice, as long as the person denies the deity and supremacy of CHRIST. What separates the believer of CHRIST is the belief in the deity and GODHOOD of CHRIST JESUS, our LORD. Understand, if you believe that the SON of GOD is but a creation of GOD, and not GOD manifest in the flesh (while on earth), your beliefs are aligned with the occult and are heretical. HE is the ONLY way to the FATHER. You cannot believe in this universal religion (the idea that there is one God but many paths to that God) that the Vatican is now pushing.

"[1] **In the beginning was the Word, and the Word was with God, and the Word was God**. [2] The same was in the beginning with God. [3] **All things were made by him; and without him was not anything made that was made.** [4] In him was life; and the life was the light of men. [5] And the light shineth in darkness; and the darkness comprehended it not. [6] There was a man sent from God, whose name was John. [7] The same came for a witness, to bear witness of the Light, that all men through him might believe. [8] He was not that Light but was sent to bear witness of that Light. [9] That was the true Light, which lighteth every man that cometh into the world. [10] **He was in the world, and the world was made by him, and the world knew him not.** [11] He came unto his own, and his own received him not. [12] But as many as received

> him, to them gave he power to become the sons of God, even to them that believe on his name: ¹³ Which were born, not of blood, nor of the will of the flesh, nor of the will of man, but of God. ¹⁴ **And the Word was made flesh, and dwelt among us, (and we beheld his glory, the glory as of the only begotten of the Father,) full of grace and truth.**" [John 1:1-14]

> "⁶ Jesus said to him, "I am the way, the truth, and the life. No one comes to the Father except through Me." [John 14:6]

Lucifer's central end-time deception is to convince you that mankind, the earth, the heavens, the animals, and all life, were not created by YAH. The goal is to put doubt in your heart about the Genesis "account of creation." This "doubt" is how the serpent, under the influence of Lucifer, deceived Eve. Suppose he and his agents can make you believe the fanciful stories of evolution. In that case, it unravels the entire belief system. Lucifer's goal is to get you to doubt GOD and believe him.

> ## *Connecting the Dots*
>
> **Saturn (names)** Osiris (Egypt), Enki (Sumeria), Yama (Hindu), Cronos (Greeks), Huang-ti (Chinese), Quetzalcoatl (Mexico), Manabozo (North America), Dionysus, Shamash, Helios, An
>
> **Saturn**=first planet, first light, father of time, ruler of heavens, creator, first man (Adam), father of harvest, connected with Eden, Atlantis, All Seeing-Eye, ruled golden age, rules zodiac, father of mortals and gods, light of the gods, universal monarch, founded temples, cities, taught humanity agriculture, law, writing, music, and other civilized arts, establish a Kingdom on earth, created a golden race of mortal men, reigned in Italy (Roman Saturn), power extended to a protective "border" separating the Kingdom of light from the powers of darkness (the "barbarians"), original sun, death (disappeared), memory venerated, fall of Adam, people await the return to the golden age, destruction, matter, first created "being", tyranny, dragon, serpent, ouroboros, halo (Saturn's spouse)
>
> **Mother goddess**=cosmic gas or mist, the mother of all living, "earth was without form and void"
>
> **The Sun god** = Apollo, Krishna, Mithra
>
> **Lucifer**=Venus, serpent, legions infested the earth with glistening serpents
>
> **Lucifer/Venus** = horned figure, *Quetzalcoatl*
>
> **Apple**=Venus
>
> **Isis**=instructed by Mercury, oldest daughter of Saturn
>
> **Osiris**=eldest son of Saturn

3

Black Cube of Saturn

Black cubes

The Black Cube, or as many call it, *The Cube of Saturn*, to the eye, looks like a three-dimensional cube, not serving much of a purpose. This obscure object, however, can be found everywhere. This cube appears in movies, business logos, commercials, music videos, games, art structures, and, more importantly, a significant focus for religious worship and reverence. Let's uncover the hidden meaning of the black cube and its connection to the planet Saturn.

"Saturn occult symbolism is [represented] by a black cube. Without many people ever knowing its sinister origin, it can be seen all over the world and is used in the entertainment industry, [various] religions and for corporate logos. As the saying goes, If you haven't seen it, then your eyes haven't been opened. It has been said that, the world's ruling elite pay homage to the worship of the Saturn cube." (Phillips)

Black

"The path belongs to Saturn, and the color of Saturn is black." (The Black Arts pg. 47, The Occult, Colin Wilson Pg. 268)

"Saturn's colour, black, and his emblem, the sarcophagus, accompany the soul as it emulates the planetary god's involvement in the feminine principle." (Theosophy Trust, Saturn Pg. 2)

"Each Planet and god was associated with its own color, and the color of Saturn was black, Hence, the planet Saturn was known as the black Sun, the dark Sun, the black square."
(Saturn: Lord of Time, Worship of Saturn, Touching the Astrology of Saturn.)

History

The fall or defeat of Saturn caused this once bright Sun to transform into a symbol of death, thus becoming the "black" or "dark" planet.

Legend says Adam bought a foundation stone from the Garden of Eden. Originally a purely white stone, but through the continual sins of mankind, the stone's color has become black and dark, distorted by the world's evils.

"The solar system was organized by forces operating inward from the great ring of the Saturnian sphere; and since the beginning of all things were under the control of Saturn, the most reasonable inference is that the first forms of worship, were dedicated to him in his peculiar symbol—**the stone**. Thus the intrinsic nature of **Saturn is synonymous with that spiritual rock which is the enduring foundation of the Solar temple**." (Hall, The Secret Teachings of All Ages Stones, Metals and Gems. Page 97)

In the tradition of the mysteries, men's spirits are Saturn's powdered bones. To the initiate of the mystery schools, the famous "grim reaper" skeleton figure, holding a sickle (which he used to mutilate his sire), denotes Saturn or Cronos, the father of the gods. The stone was always worshiped as Saturn because Saturn represented the base or footing stone, the element which held creation together.

Kaaba Stone in Mecca

Circumambulation around the Kaaba

"The stone, which Islamic tradition holds fell at the time of Adam and Eve, is framed in pure silver at the southeast corner of the Kaaba, itself said to have been constructed by *Abraham* and his son *Ishmael*. During the Hajj, which Muslims are instructed to complete at least once in their lifetime, pilgrims perform *Tawaf*, or circumambulation, seven times counterclockwise, around the Kaaba. Worshipers usually touch, kiss, or wave at the al-Hajar al-Aswad stone when walking past it. Observant Muslims around the world pray toward the Kaaba five times a day." (TOI Staff)

"According to Muslim tradition, the stone was originally white, but turned black from being in a world where it absorbed humanity's sins. According to Islamic tradition, the stone was set intact into the Kaaba's wall by the Islamic prophet *Muhammad* in the year 605 AD." (Hill)

"In Muslim legends about Adam some of these features are retained, Adam, the *Khalifa*, brought the later, "black stone," then a white hyacinth, from paradise to the spot of the Ka'ba, and it served Adam as a throne to sit upon." (Wensinck The Navel and the Universe. Page 55)

In the Enochian magick tradition, the *Cube of Saturn* centers around paths called *aethers* which circle the cube. Each corner faces the four cardinal directions. The Kaaba in Mecca also meets all four cardinal directions.

There are no direct connections in Islamic teachings about the Kaaba and Saturn. Many authorities, even some Islamic scholars, indicate that the stone was a meteorite or from outer space. The frequent references to the Kaaba and Saturn include;

- The apparent color and shape of the monument
- The counterclockwise circle that pilgrims rotate around the Kaaba
- This motion appears to emulate the rings of Saturn.

Cult of Saturn

Members of The Fraternitas Saturni

"The "great god Pan," the horned deity, represented Saturn in ancient paganism. This half-man half-goat creature is considered the ancestor of our modern depictions of Satan. "Pan was a composite creature, the upper part–with the exception of his horns–being human, and the lower part in the form of a goat. The *pipes of Pan* signify the natural harmony of the spheres, and the god himself is a symbol of Saturn because this planet is enthroned in Capricorn, whose emblem is a goat." (Hall, The Secret Teachings of All Ages The Myth of the Dying God. Page 35)

"So Pan was depicted with **horns due to the fact it represented Saturn**, the ruler of the house of Capricorn which symbol is a goat. Pan was the controlling spirit of the lower worlds. He was portrayed roaming through the forests, penis erect, drunk and lascivious, frolicking with nymphs and piping his way through the wild. We might say he ruled the lower nature of man, its animal side, not unlike Satan."

"It has been said that, the world's ruling elite pay homage to the worship of the Saturn cube." (Phillips)

"Despite acknowledging its association with *Evil*, secret societies find the veneration of Saturn necessary to obtain illumination. It is the necessary counterpart of the principle of *Good*. Masonic authors clearly associate Saturn with Satan;

"Saturn is the opposite to Jupiter; his symbol is the cross above the sign of Luna. He is the Satan, the Tempter, or rather the Tester. His function is to chastise and tame the unruly passions in the primitive man." - J.S. Ward, *Freemasonry and the Ancient Gods*

"Probably the most extreme example of a secret society worshiping Saturn's Evil principle is the "Fraternitas Saturni." This occult organization is based in Germany and openly embodies the hidden side of Saturn worship. The Fraternitas Saturni (FS), the Brotherhood of Saturn, has become known to English readers through fragmentary descriptions which emphasize the sensational, sex-magical aspects of this lodge's work or else its darker, more Satanic, side. This is understandable in light of the fact that the FS is (or was) the most **unabashedly Luciferian organization in the modern Western occult revival**, and its practice of sexual occultism perhaps the most elaborately detailed of any such lodge. The FS represents a unique blend of astrological cosmology, neo-Gnostic daemonology, sexual occultism, and Freemasonic organizational principles. This grand synthesis was originally the vision of one man, the long-time Grand Master of the FS, *Gregor A. Gregorius*."

- Stephen E. Flowers, *Fire & Ice: The History, Structure, and Rituals of Germany's Most Influential Modern Magical Order: The Brotherhood of Saturn*

Note: The Fraternitas Saturni is one of the darkest, Luciferian, occultic, sexually perverted Satanic cults.

Star of David (Hexagram of Saturn)

Hexagram (Seal of Solomon, Six pointed star)

The Star of David symbol does not appear in the Holy Bible in any interpretation or version; there is no such thing as a Biblical Star of David. Instead, this hexagram goes back into antiquity. Black magic, witchcraft, sorcery, alchemy, occultism, and astrology are all dark arts that use this unholy symbol. In my journalistic research, I can attest that there is no book of magic, secret societies, or spells that do not contain this most wicked of symbols.

"A Hexagon is a 2D projection of 2 interlocking 3D tetrahedrons one inside each other. Think of it as a kind of a 3d version of the Israeli flag or the Jewish Star." (Richard C. Hoagland, Hyper-dimensional Hexagon, Coast to Coast)

The word hex means to put a hex on someone. According to former satanist *Bill Schnoebelen*, "A hexagram must be present to call forth a demon, and it is a potent tool to invoke Satan." The hexagram also appears on the *Great Seal* of the United States. This hexagram, also called *The Seal of Solomon*, was bought to popularization in 1648 by Viennese Jesuits. Then in 1897 it became a symbol for the Zionist movement funded by the Rothschilds and connected with Freemasonry.

You will find this hexagram everywhere in major religions, including; Catholicism, Islam, Hinduism, the Kabbala, and, as earlier mentioned, various occult practices. But this symbol never has, and never will be, the sign of *King David, King of Israel*, which is an indisputable Biblical fact.

On top of the north pole of Saturn, a hexagram shape appears. The book of Amos also talks about this symbol;

> "²⁶But ye have borne the tabernacle of your Moloch and Chiun your images, the star of your god, which ye made to yourselves." [Amos 5:26]

From the Jewish Encyclopedia:

"A word occurring in connection with "Siccuth" in Amos v. 26. Scholars have long been puzzled to know whether in this passage they are common nouns or proper names. "Siccuth" is probably the Assyrian "Sakkut" (Schrader, "K. A. T." pp. 442 et seq.), an epithet of *Ninib* and *Anu*. **Ninib was identified with Saturn** (Jensen, "Kosmologie," p. 136), the Assyrian name of which was "Kaiman" ("Kaiwan")." (Jastrow and Barton)

"Saturn, under the name of Remphan, was worshiped among the Copts." (Pike Page 308)

"Prominent Roman historians such as *Tacitus* (56–120 CE) and *Cassius Dio* (ca. 155–after 229), as well as Church fathers like *Augustine* (354–430), acknowledged a special link between Saturn and Saturday, the holiest day of the week for the Jews. That Jewish society of the Talmudic period recognized the same association is shown by the fact that the Babylonian Talmud (Shabbat 156a) refers to Saturn as i.e., the star of Shabbat (Saturday)."

"*Abraham Ibn Ezra* (ca.1089–ca.1161) removes the sting of this embarrassing linkage by stressing that Saturn is actually conducive to a Jew's religious faith. In his long commentary on Exodus 20:13, Ibn Ezra associates Saturn with the fourth commandment, ordaining one to "remember the Sabbath day and keep it holy" (Ex. 20:8), and explains that this correspondence allows the Jews, by not occupying themselves with everyday matters but devoting themselves solely to the fear of God on this day, to protect themselves from Saturn's baneful influence and also to improve the quality of their religious belief."

"In the Jewish faith, Saturn is considered to be a very important planet. It is said to be the planet of divine order and justice and is associated with the *Archangel Gabriel*. Saturn is also said to be the planet of the Messiah and is believed to be the ruling planet of the Jewish people."

"Saturn expelled the Idaei, or Judaei, from the solar system, establishing the Jewish race as its founder. Jupiter, the sky god, represents the Aryan force overthrowing the Jewish or proto-Jewish power in order to establish a eugenic future through *Apollo*, Jupiter's son, according to some interpretations of the story. The Greeks referred to Cronos as a Phoenician god of Time, *El Olam* (Oulomos in Greek), which translated as the Phoenician god of Time El Olam."

Note: Aryan is not the white supremacist group as it is familiarly known. Aryan is an evolved race in Madame Blavatsky's Seven Root Races of mankind. See Thy Queendom Come Chapter 19 Root Races.

"According to this study, castrating deities like Cronos/Saturn and *Kumarbi* could have influenced Jewish circumcision practices. The seven-day week is Levantine and astrological in origin, most likely from Semitic and Assyrian calendars that followed lunar cycles."

"Saturn (Shabbetai in Hebrew) is the planet in charge of Jews and is linked to Saturday (Shabbat in Hebrew)."

"Both Hellenistic and Arab astrology believed that peoples had their own presiding planet and indicated Saturn as the planet of the Jews. And the Jews indeed observed as their holy day Saturday, i.e. Saturn's day. A whole school of Jewish sages and philosophers, well versed in astrology and combining astrophysical themes with the Kabbalah, also took for granted that Saturn was indeed the planet presiding over Israel. Hence the further idea that the coming Messiah will have a special relationship with Saturn." (Ruark)

Tefillin

Men wearing Tefillin "prayer" boxes

"In Judaism, the six-pointed *Star of David* represents Satan and originates from Saturn. Orthodox Jews wear *The Black Cube of Saturn* on their forehead (like the third Eye) and call it *The Tefillin*." (Satan and the Black Cube of Saturn)

There is no Biblical scripture instructing the use of Tefillin prayer boxes. The Tefillin prayer box is from rabbinical tradition, as the Bible calls it, "the tradition of men."

For clarity, the connection between Saturn and the Jewish people is not Biblically-based. The enemy takes everything YAH created and perverts it, including the days of the week.

"³ But he answered and said unto them, Why do ye also transgress the commandment of God by your tradition?" [Matthew 15:3]

Connecting the Dots

Saturn's symbols = color (black), stone, hexagram, cube

Saturn = ruler of Hyperborean, Polaris, and Atlantis, Saturday, planet of Archangel Gabriel, planet of Jews, Pan, Capricorn, goat, ruler of lower nature of man, tempter, tester, opposite of Jupiter, black sun, dark sun, Siccuth, Sakkut, Ninib, Kaiman

Apollo = Jupiter's son

Stone = new lands, new races, new empires

4

The Santa Clause

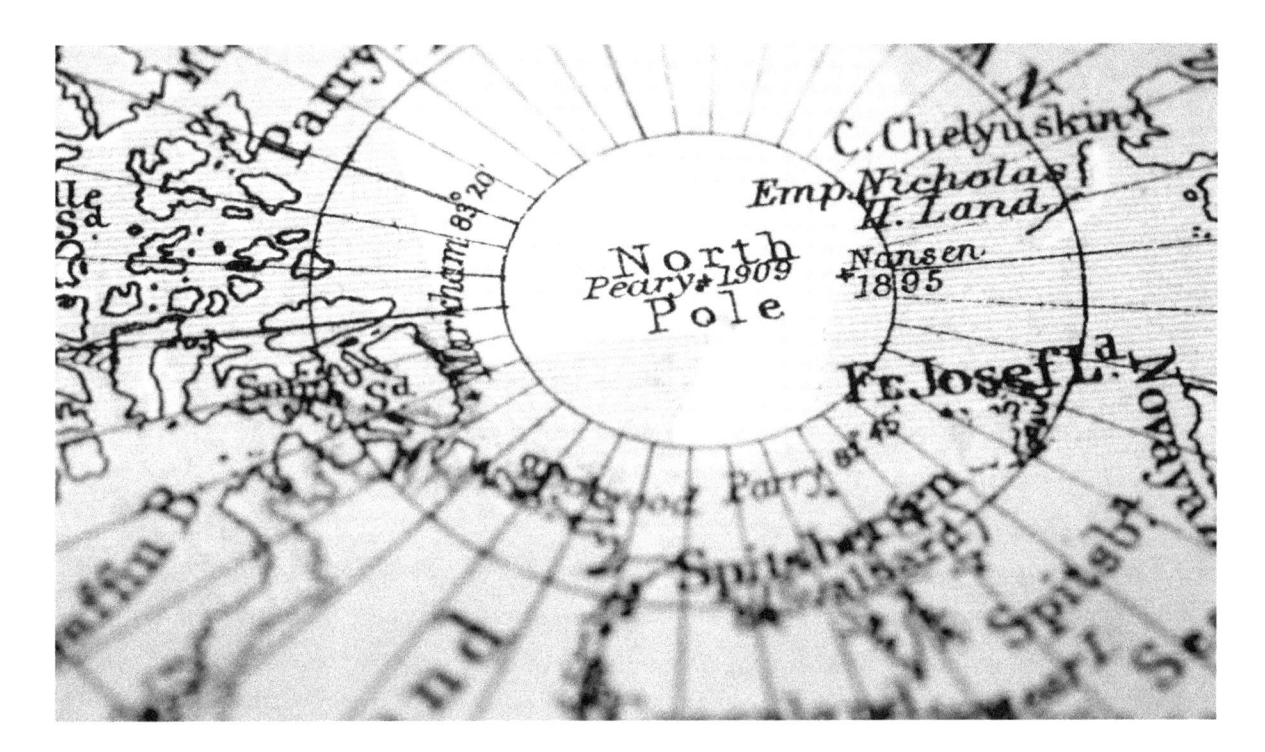

At this juncture, we take a shocking turn towards the NORTH, the NORTH POLE, to be exact. Mention the North Pole, Jolly Old St. Nick's symbolism comes to mind; this appears to be yet another secret veil. A veil that has been told to countless generations of innocent children and unsuspecting parents to venerate the worship of their god, Saturn, secretly. This connection to Saturn-the North Pole-the celestial god – all weave together like an intricately woven spider web.

North Pole

"The Saturn cube is derived from the planet's **North Pole called the '6-pointed star.'** The cube is a 3-dimensional representation of the 2-dimensional hexagonal North Pole 6-pointed star." (Love)

"As God in his heavenly sanctuary sits upon his throne, so the king sits in the earthly sanctuary upon his throne. **The center of the earth and the pole of heaven**, both are intimately connected with the throne. We find this thought already in the legends about Adam. In the center of the earth Adam is inaugurated by God as a king and a priest and set upon a throne. All this is meant typically of course; here the analogy is proclaimed between heaven and earth, godhead and kingship, navel and throne." (Wensinck The Navel of the Universe. Page 54-55)

"Egyptians knew the pole as the "midst" or "heart" of heaven—"the single, immovable point around which the movement of the stars occurred."

Primitive sled
Egyptian Hieroglyphic

"The Egyptian hieroglyph for Atum is a primitive sledge, Clark tells us that "**the celestial pole is 'that place' or 'the great city.'**" (Talbott Egypt)

"The common identification of *Mithra* with the Zoroastrian Zurvan/Saturn cannot be ignored. Iranian cosmology, as reported by *de Saussure,* esteemed the celestial pole as the centre and summit of heaven, where resided "the Great One in the middle of the sky." Who is equated with Kevan, the planet Saturn." (Talbott The Americas)

"The whole machinery of the world is drawn by the infernal fire at the North Pole," notes *Jung*. An alchemical text proclaims, "At the Pole is the heart of *Mercurius*, which is the resting place of his lord." Most important of all for an interpretation of Mercurius," Jung writes, "is his relation to Saturn. Mercurius senex [the aged Mercurius] is identical with Saturn."

"Records of numerous nations around the world stand as a collective witness to a strange, yet consistent idea— an idea which finds no explanation in the heavens we know. Global myths insist that when the first civilizations rose from barbarism a brilliant light occupied the celestial pole. This steadfast light was the ancient Sun-god, repeatedly identified as the planet Saturn, the Universal Monarch." (Talbott The Americas)

But originally, Saturn was the polar Sun, the central source of the directional streams, and it was only to be expected that the other four planets, like the four seasons, four colours, or four elements, came to symbolize the powers of the four quarters, their symbolic location possibly being decided by the element with which each planet was identified. **As to the "center," Saturn could be the only choice. The order was:**

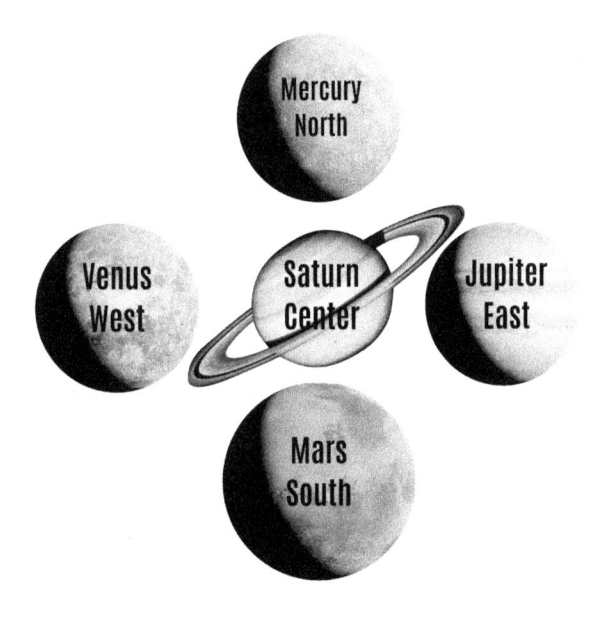

Planetary alignment
Revelations Publishing House

(Talbott Symmetrical Elaborations Of The Sun-Cross)

"The Egyptian *Set* is the primordial serpent or dragon but set also means "mountain." The mythical *Mountain of Set*, in fact, is the acknowledged Egyptian counterpart of the Hebrew *Zaphon* in "the farthest reaches of the north. And like the Mexicans, the Egyptians knew the "Serpent Mountain," a figure of the pole, according to Massey." (Talbott The Serpent/Dragon)

"Associated in esoteric knowledge with this role of high Kingship is **the symbol of the North Pole Star - the crown of the world** - and the circumpolar constellations. Of these, the Lesser and the Greater Bear are the most important: the former providing the present North Pole Star. The *Bear* is a veil to the real name, which means Dove, or Sheepfold, or Chariot." (The Book of Secrets – Reflections and Notes on the Royal Families of the Grail Page 14)

"Saturn is the "pillar." The connection bears on an enigmatic reference to Saturn in the Old Testament. The prophet *Amos* charges Israel with having "borne the tabernacle of your Moloch and Chiun, your images, the star of your god." The term Chiun refers to the "pillar" or "pedestal" of the star-god worshipped by the Israelites in the desert. It is the name of the planet Saturn and traces back to the Babylonian *Kaiun*, also Saturn—the "steady star upon a foundation." Plutarch gives the title *Kiun* to the Egyptian *Anup*, the "god who is on his pole." Kiun, states Massey, "denotes the highest point, at the centre, and is applied to the founding of the world. The name was assigned to Saturn as the god in the highest." (Talbott The Cosmic Mountain Personified)

As Above, So below

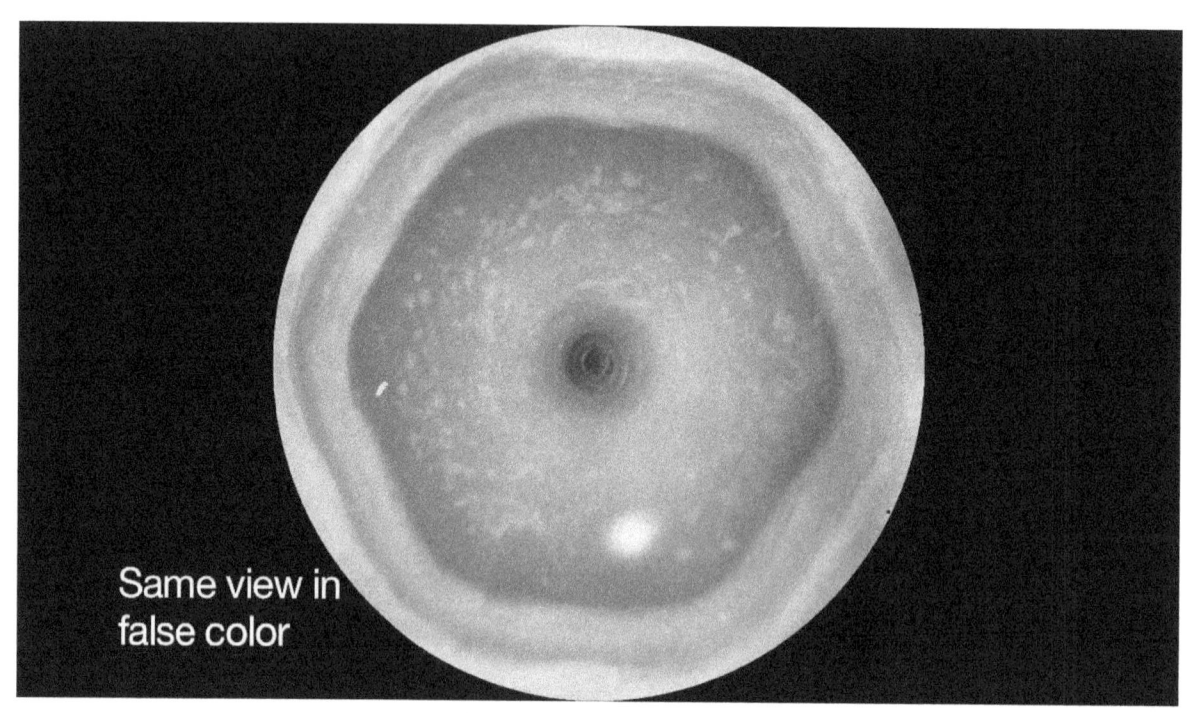

North pole of Saturn hexagram
NASA Cassini spacecraft

Directly from NASA, you can see the hexagram located at the North Pole of Saturn, parallel to the North Pole of earth.

"A bizarre six-sided feature encircling the north pole of Saturn near 78 degrees north latitude has been spied by the visual and infrared mapping spectrometer on NASA's Cassini spacecraft. This image is one of the first clear images ever taken of the north polar region as seen from a unique polar perspective."

"Originally discovered and last observed by a spacecraft during NASA's Voyager flybys of the early 1980's, the new views of this polar hexagon taken in late 2006 prove that this is an unusually long-lived feature on Saturn." (NASA)

The Santa Clause

Shocking as this may be, there is yet more symbolism to unfold about this great North Pole and its celestial occupant.

"When Saturn ruled the world, his home was the summit of the world axis: with this point all major traditions of the great father agree. Even today, in our **celebration of Christmas, we live under the influence of the polar Saturn.** For as *Manly P. Hall* observes;

"Saturn, the old man who lives at the north pole, and brings with him to the children often a sprig of evergreen (the Christmas tree), is familiar to the little folks under the name Santa Claus."

"Santa Claus, descending yearly from his polar home to distribute gifts around the world, is a muffled echo of the Universal Monarch, the primordial **Osiris, Yama,** or **Kronos spreading miraculous good fortune.** His polar abode, which might appear as an esoteric aspect of the story, is in fact an ancient and central ingredient. Saturn, the "best Sun" and king of the world, **ruled from the polar zenith.** But while popular tradition located Santa Claus at the geographical pole, the earlier traditions place his prototype, **the Universal Monarch, at the celestial pole, the pivot of the revolving heavens.**

"The religions of all ancient nations, associate **the abode of the supreme god with the North Pole,** the centre of heaven; or with the celestial space immediately surrounding it. [Yet] no writer on comparative theology has ever brought out the facts which establish this assertion." (Talbott Saturn and the Pole)

Ho x3!

Interesting note, Santa Claus says, *Ho Ho Ho*. You can also hear rappers chant, Say *Ho Ho Ho*, well I was surprised to see this CHANT in a New Age book of mantras and invocations. Here are a few excerpts from the chant;

- Ho! Ho! Ho! I AM the alchemist and I AM clearing my place! I am clearing my force-field.
- Ho! Ho! Ho! then, the structure of atoms and electrons that would interfere with the word made manifest…

In essence, *Ho Ho Ho* is a New Age proclamation that is used in summoning and releasing various entities and energies in the dark realm.
(Prophet and Prophet 10.2 Here and Now, I AM the Victorious One. Page 210)

Mistletoe

"In the Mystery schools it was taught…the higher gods would find it difficult to descend further than the moon. Their visits to the surface of the earth became infrequent and fleeting. It was believed that on these visits they accidentally **left behind the strange and unearthly mistletoe**, a plant which cannot grow in the soil of the earth, but which grew naturally on the moon." (Booth Chapter 7 The Age of Demi-Gods and Heroes The Ancient Ones • The Amazons • Enoch • Hercules, Theseus and Jason)

Christmas is not a Biblically-based holiday. There is much information about the pagan traditions of this holiday. This much more profound revelation shines a light on the very dark meaning of this holiday that has absolutely nothing to do with our Lord and Savior.

Connecting the Dots

North Pole = hexagram, six pointed star, great city, midst of heaven, heart of heaven, home of the great god, great light (Saturn), unmovable, Saturn's (old man) abode, pivot of heavens

Mithra = Zurvan/Saturn, Mercurius

Saturn = Set (Egyptian serpent/dragon, mountain), pillar (Chiun), brings children sprigs of evergreen, Santa Claus

North=Mercury, **South**=Mars, **West**=Venus, **East**=Jupiter, **Center**=Saturn

North Pole Star= the crown of the world – the Lesser and the Greater Bear

The Bear =Dove, or Sheepfold, or Chariot

5

Star Gate

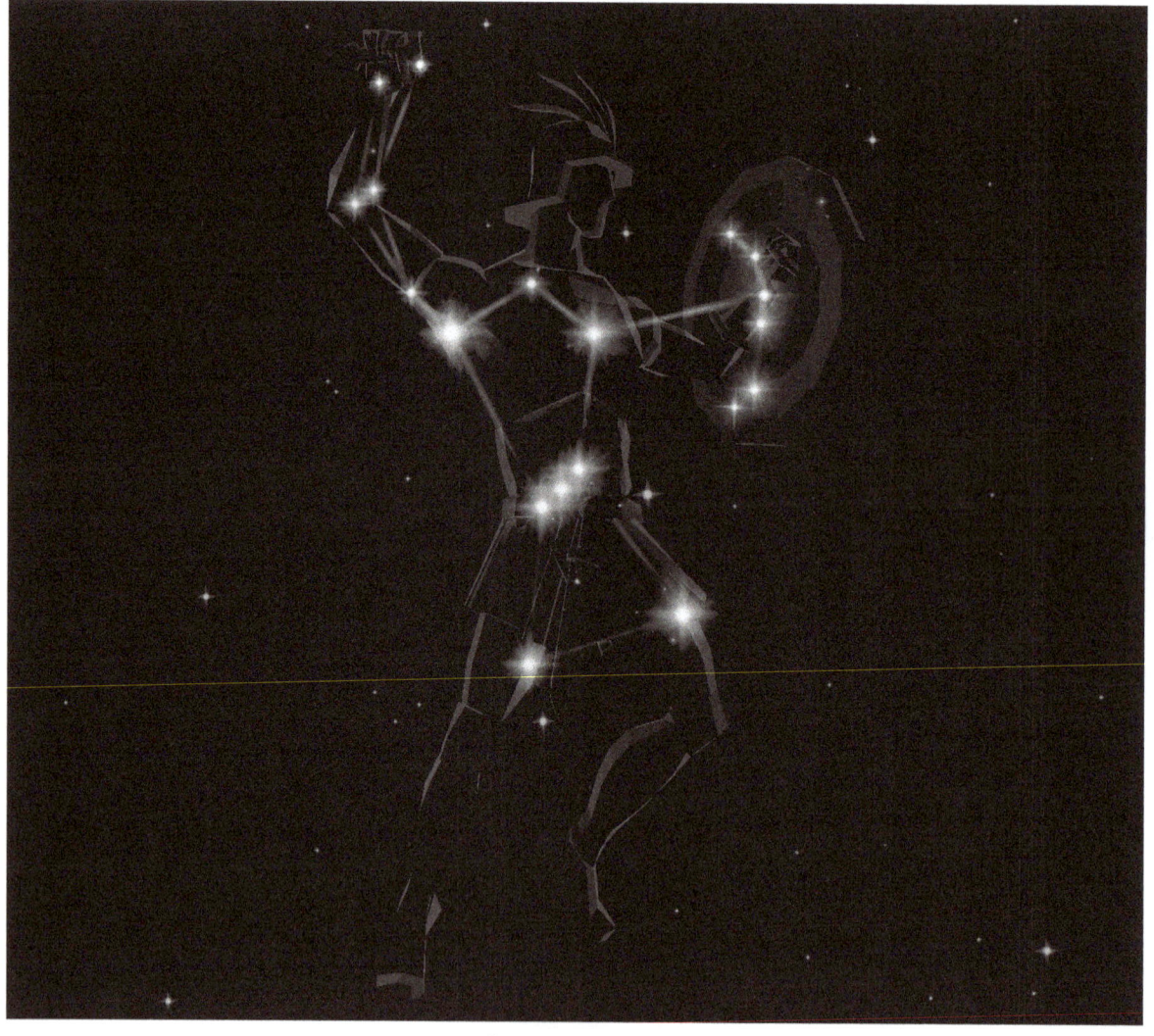

Orion Constellation

The constellation Orion is the most known and famous in the cosmos. It's what we learned about in science class as early as elementary school. This warrior, who looks like he is holding a shield or a bow and arrow with a missing head and limbs, serves as a symbol for nearly all earthly god-men. Orion serves as not only a "prototype" for the "hero" but for alignment and portals for these fallen angels to gain access to the earth once the "stars align." As mentioned, "As above, So below" is a never changing theme in the mystery religion of Lucifer.

"Orion is the warrior-prince with a sword on his side and his foot on the hare or serpent. Eridanus, the torturous River, is the River of Judgment belonging to Orion." (Prophecy Central)

"Orion…has always been my favorite constellation and one of the first ones that, as a child, I was able to identify." - D. James Kennedy

"**As Nimrod became the constellation Orion after his demise**, the Egyptian Sun god, Osiris, whose untimely death was mourned by Isis and all of Egypt, is also universally identified as the *soul of Orion*." (The Book of Secrets – Reflections and Notes on the Royal Families of the Grail Page 69)

"The name of a scorpion in Chaldee is Akrab; but Ak-rab, thus divided, signifies 'THE GREAT OPPRESSOR,' and this is the hidden meaning of the Scorpion as represented in the Zodiac. **That sign typifies him who cut off the Babylonian god and suppressed the system he set up**. It was while the Sun was in Scorpio that Osiris in Egypt 'disappeared' (Wilkinson, vol. iv., p.331), and great lamentations were made for his disappearance. Another subject was mixed up with the death of the Egyptian god; but it is specially to be noticed that, as it was in consequence of a conflict with a scorpion that Orion was 'added to the stars,' so it was when the scorpion was in the ascendant that Osiris disappeared." (The Book of Secrets – Reflections and Notes on the Royal Families of the Grail Page 72)

"It seems that, after the flood and their expulsion from the earth, **the Nephilim left the Sphinx, pyramids and Nile River as markers** indicating their whereabouts in the heavens. As the three pyramids of Giza correspond to the belt stars of Orion, there are also three pyramids in Mexico which correspond to the Giza pyramids. This design would give credence to speculation that **Osiris and Quetzalcoatl** were the same god, whose soul is claimed to now reside in Orion."

"Archaeo-astronomers making use of the latest star-mapping computer programmes had recently demonstrated that the three world-famous pyramids on Egypt's Giza plateau formed an **exact terrestrial diagram of the three belt stars in the constellation of Orion**. Nor was this the limit of the celestial map the Ancient Egyptian priests had created in the sands on the west bank of the Nile. Included in their overall vision…there was a natural feature—the river Nile—which was exactly where it should be had it been designed to represent the Milky Way." (The Book of Secrets – Reflections and Notes on the Royal Families of the Grail Page 72-73)

"Osiris means 'place of the eye'; his place is in Orion. When the Sun is directly over Orion at high noon, **the Stargate opens**, through which *Osiris and the Pharaohs ascended to the heavens*. This is the meaning of the **all-seeing eye in the capstone of the pyramid on the dollar bill.**

According to *David Calvert-Orange*, author of *Isis, Osiris, Divine Kingship and Resurrection*, "The Great Pyramid of Khufu or Cheops…was nothing more than an elaborate Stargate to effect the transmutation of the soul of the dead Pharaoh into the essence of light to enable its assimilation to Osiris in his heavenly abode of Orion." (The Book of Secrets – Reflections and Notes on the Royal Families of the Grail Page 81)

"Orion is the celestial pyramid." (Hurtak Page 47)

"Because of pre-cession the Sun is no longer in Leo at the solstice but on the cusp of Gemini and Taurus. In fact it now stands on a position in the zodiac exactly over the outstretched 'hand' of Orion. Curiously enough this position (which I call the 'shake-hands position') is where according to the ancients there **exists one of the gates of heaven.** There were in fact two of these imaginary gateways at the points where the ecliptic, or pathway of the Sun, crosses over the Milky Way. One of these gates was in Gemini over the hand of Orion and the other in Sagittarius over the sting of Scorpio."

Benben Stone

"This gateway seems to be what is symbolized by the Sahu (Orion) figure as inscribed on the

Benben stone of *Amenemhet III* at the Cairo Museum. He is depicted as a small walking figure holding a scepter in one hand and cupping a star in the other. This star or 'S'ba' to give it its Egyptian name has a dual meaning as a hieroglyphic. On the one hand it means "star" but on the other it means "gateway." Thus Orion is correctly shown holding in his hand what we might call a *star-gate*.

"Now the positioning of the Sun at the solstice at a star-gate is a very extraordinary phenomenon and unique to our present age. It has not happened since around 10,880 BC at around the time when many believe the destruction of Atlantis occurred. The fact that this is now occurring and is somehow linked with the Khafre pyramid seems to me to be an important portent and to symbolize the *opening of a gate in heaven*. This I don't take in some sci-fi way as symbolizing the arrival of aliens or some such but it is, I believe, **symbolic of the birth of a new age of mankind.** I take it to symbolize the beginning of a new era and a new cycle of possibilities." (The Book of Secrets – Reflections and Notes on the Royal Families of the Grail Page 80-81)

"If we consider the star fields as giving some mapping of where the Earth's biosphere as a water prism stands in relationship to given star fields, we will understand why the ancient Egyptian texts refer to lhm-'sk and why the Great Pyramid was aligned with Mintaka (delta), Alnilam (epsilon), and Alnitak (zeta) in Tak-Orion (Orionis). These are the central threshold controls or the region of "positive programming" used by the *Elohim lord of lights* to connect the many galaxies to our father universe...these threshold controls are necessary in coordinating celestial navigation between universes. Through the energies of Orion, the Central Threshold Control, the higher *beings of light* move across the waters of the deep." (Hurtak Page 43)

"According to Masonic sources, the missing head and legs of Orion are symbolized by the **"Skull & Crossbones,"** which strongly indicates that the Freemason's veneration of John the Baptist (who was beheaded) is really the worship of Orion (Nimrod/Tammuz)."

"It would seem that Orion has had his legs and his head chopped off! A similar practice was observed by the Knights Templar when they were buried. By adopting this practice the deceased **Knights Templar became as one with Orion and, by implication, Osiris.** The 'skull and crossbones'...Orion's missing head and legs...were also adopted by the Knights Templar as their emblem, their symbol of recognition. As we shall soon discover, **the severed head of Orion is in fact the Sun**. Moreover it is the headless Orion which is the source of legends about severed heads." (The Book of Secrets – Reflections and Notes on the Royal Families of the Grail Page 63)

"Orion lies partly in the Milky Way, the alleged 'Galactic Stellar Womb' from which the rest of the galaxy was conceived and born: *Orion, the giant, Hunter, and Warrior*, admired in all historic ages as the most strikingly brilliant of the stellar groups, lies partly within the Milky Way, extending on both sides of the celestial equator entirely south of the ecliptic, and so is visible from every part of the globe." (927:303-4) The pre-flood giants, the Anunnaki, were said to travel through the Milky Way by way of a *planet ship named Nibiru*, also called *the Mothership*. **The Anunnaki, which the Bible calls Nephilim**, came to Earth to 'pro-create' the human race (Gen. 6) and conveniently relocated to Orion after the Deluge (Gen. 7). The Bible states that no flesh survived the Great Flood, leaving open the possibility **that the fallen angels, the Nephilim/Anunnaki, may have escaped:**

"Genesis 7:21-23 stress the theme of universal death: "And all flesh died that moved upon the earth... So He destroyed all living things which were on the face of the ground... They were destroyed from the earth. Only Noah and those who were with him in the ark remained alive."(The Book of Secrets – Reflections and Notes on the Royal Families of the Grail Page 65)

"According to "Star Myths of the Greeks and Romans" by *Theony Condos*, "*Hesiod* says that Orion was the son of *Euryale*, the daughter of *Minos* and of *Poseidon* and that to him was granted the ability to walk on the sea as he did on the land." (570:147) Recall that, **being a giant, Orion** could wade through the sea with only his head protruding from the water. Neptune is the **Bistea Neptunis — the Beast out of the Sea and Orion was his son.** As the son of the Beast out of the **sea, it is interesting that Orion has 17 stars, equaling 7 heads and 10 horns:**

"The total [of stars in Orion] is seventeen. Hesiod says this is Neptune's son by Euryale... To him was granted the ability to run on the water as he did on the land."

"And I stood upon the sand of the sea, and saw a beast rise up out of the sea, having seven heads and ten horns, and upon his horns ten crowns, and upon his heads the name of blasphemy. Rev. 13:1. Scripture says that sitting upon this 7-headed, 10-headed Beast, which is full of names of blasphemy— **Orion/Saturn/Tammuz/Nimrod/Horus/Osiris—is a woman, the Great Harlot; and that the 7-heads are the 7 mountains or hills of Rome, which were named after the Sun and moon and five planets.**" (The Book of Secrets – Reflections and Notes on the Royal Families of the Grail Page 67)

"Fellow travelers headed by the one known as Zeus, or more familiarly as Metatron."

Note: Fellow travelers is a Freemason code word, Metatron is a cabbalistic fallen angel whom they parade as an Angel of Light.

Connecting the Dots

Orion=warrior-prince, sword, foot on the hare or serpent, Nimrod, Osiris, oppressed by

Scorpio, pyramids of Giza, Quetzalcoatl, star gate opens (sun), ascend to heaven, celestial pyramid, central threshold, waters of the deep, skull and bones (missing limbs), John Baptist (missing head), worship of Nimrod/Tammuz, sun (severed head), giant, son of Poseidon, 17 stars, equaling 7 heads and 10 horns

Isis=mourned death

Scorpio=great oppressor, but off Babylonian system, Osiris disappeared, Orion added to stars

Markers=Nephilim=Sphinx, pyramids, Nile river, Giza Pyramids

Osiris= place of eye, Orion, all seeing eye

Milky Way=Galactic stellar womb, galaxy was conceived and born, Anunnaki travel through the Milky Way by way of a planet ship named Nibiru

Nibiru=Mothership.

Anunnaki=relocated to Orion after the Deluge

Zeus=Metatron

SECTION II

SERPENT'S SEED

6

The Serpent

Quetzalcoatl (plumed serpent)

The serpent's identity is a major theological stumbling block for many believers. To deny the importance of the serpent would be unwise; this "being" appears from the book of Genesis to the very end of Revelation. In this chapter, we shed the skin on this mysterious figure and prayerfully shed light on this dark enemy of God and man.

Nachash

> "Now the **serpent** [H5175 nachash] was more subtil than any beast of the field which the LORD God had made. And he said unto the woman, Yea, hath God said, Ye shall not eat of every tree of the garden?" [Genesis 3:1]
>
> "And the woman said unto the **serpent** [H5175 nachash], We may eat of the fruit of the trees of the garden." [Genesis 3:2]
>
> "But of the fruit of the tree, which is in the midst of the garden, God hath said, Ye shall not eat of it, neither shall ye touch it, lest ye die. [Genesis 3:3]
>
> "And the **serpent** [H5175 nachash] said unto the woman, Ye shall not surely die:" [Genesis 3:4]
>
> "For God doth know that in the day ye eat thereof, then your eyes shall be opened, and ye shall be as gods, knowing good and evil."[Genesis 3:5]
>
> "And the LORD God said unto the woman, What is this that thou hast done? And the woman said, The **serpent** [H5175 nachash] beguiled me, and I did eat." [Genesis 3:13]
>
> "And the LORD God said unto the **serpent**[H5175 nachash], Because thou hast done this, thou art cursed above all cattle, and above every beast of the field; upon thy belly shalt thou go, and dust shalt thou eat all the days of thy life:" [Genesis 3:14]
>
> "And I will put enmity between thee and the woman, and between **thy seed** and her seed; it shall bruise thy head, and thou shalt bruise it's heel." [Genesis 3:15]

The word serpent is *nachash* in Hebrew as it appears in Genesis. The following is the Strong's Hebrew Concordance definition;

- H5175-serpent, snake, serpent, image (of serpent), fleeing serpent (mythological)
- Root H5172-to practice divination, divine, observe signs, learn by experience, diligently observe, practice fortunetelling, take as an omen
- Nachash, naw-khash'; a primitive root; properly, to hiss, i.e. whisper a (magic) spell; generally, to prognosticate: — X certainly, divine, enchanter, (use) X enchantment, learn by experience, X indeed, diligently observe. (Strong's Concordance)

Dr. Michael Heiser, who is considered one of the foremost experts in the supernatural worldview

of the Bible, says this about the nachash under the concept of the *Serpent/Shining One Imagery*:
Nachash English meaning;

- Noun- serpent
- Verb-to use divination, give omens
- Adjective- bronze, brazen

Regarding the concept of the nachash;

- Word play; triple entendre
- Image of the serpent (divine throne guardian)
- Information from the divine realm (divination)
- Shining appearance associated with divinity (brazen)

Regarding the curse of the serpent "dust thou shalt eat all the days of thy life."

"The nachash was cursed to crawl on its belly, imagery that conveyed being cast down (Ezekiel 28:817; Isaiah 14:11-12,15) to the ground. In Ezekiel 28 and Isaiah 14, we saw the villain cast down to the *erets*, a term that refers literally to the dirt and metaphorically to the underworld. The nachash who wanted to be the "most high," will be "most low" instead cast away from God and the council to earth, and even under the earth. He is hidden from view from life in God's world. His domain is death." (Heiser Chapter 11: Like the Most High? Page 90-91)

Upon closer examination, the nachash appear to be divine celestial beings, not a garden snake or cobra. Although we have only our imagination to ponder how these angelic hosts physically appeared, historical and non-Biblical records mention them.

"The serpent, too, is other than it was at first. Before the fall of man it was the cleverest of all animals created, and **in form it resembled man closely**. It stood upright and was of extraordinary size. Afterward, it lost the mental advantages it had possessed as compared with other animals, and it degenerated physically, too; it was deprived of its feet, so that it could not pursue other animals and kill them. The mole and the frog had to be made harmless in similar ways; the former has no eyes, else it were irresistible, and the frog has no teeth, else no animal in the water were sure of its life." (Ginzberg, Legends of the Jews The Sixth Day. Page 185-186)

Serpent's Seed

In the first installment, we exposed that the occult world believes Eve and the Serpent had relations that resulted in the birth of *Cain*. To stay away from this taboo subject would deny the reader the proper information to come to a Biblical conclusion. Let's first examine the many accounts of Cain's birth according to the position of the Serpent and Eve having relations;

"But after the fall of Eve, Satan, in the guise of the serpent, approached her, and the fruit of their union was Cain, the ancestor of all the impious generations that were rebellious toward God, and rose up against Him. Cain's descent from Satan, who is the angel *Samael*, was revealed in **his seraphic appearance**. At his birth, the exclamation was wrung from Eve, "I have gotten a man through an angel of the Lord." (Ginzberg, Legends of the Jews The Birth of Cain. Page 3)

"And it was said by the rabbis that menstruation was the result of **Eve's relations with the serpent** in the Garden of Eden. In Abyssinia it was thought that girls were in danger of being raped by snakes until they were married."

"**Q'ayin's father was Enki**. In Sumerian history he is referred to as *Ar-wi-um, King of Kish*, the son of *Masda* and successor to *King Atabba* (the Adama). Under his alternative names of Masda and *Mazdao*, Enki was the ancestral forebear of the Magian spiritual master *Zarathustra* (Zoroaster). The name Mas da (from Mas-en-da) means one who prostrates himself (as a serpent). Ar-wi-um is related to the Hebrew word *awwim* which denotes **serpents**. In the Persian tradition Enki was called *Ohrmazd* (or Ormuzd) meaning *Serpent of the Night*, while in this context Mazda is also equivalent to Lord." (Gardner, Genesis of the Grail Kings Chapter Ten The Tree of Knowledge. Page 132-134)

Those that defend the serpent seed doctrine have Genesis 3:15, *the seed of the woman, crushing the serpent's seed* as the Scriptural foundation. The philosophy; If the Messiah came through an actual bloodline, the serpent's seed must have also come through a lineage.

> "15 And I will put enmity between thee and the woman, and between thy seed and her seed; it shall bruise thy head, and thou shalt bruise it's heel." [Genesis 3:15]

Here are the varying beliefs regarding the "dual seed" or "serpent seed" doctrine;

- The forbidden fruit was a sexual act
- Eve had sexual relations with the serpent being
- Eve had sexual relations with Satan himself
- Eve had sexual relations with a fallen angel, and Cain was a Nephilim (giant)
- The forbidden fruit was a tribe or race of people.
- The forbidden fruit was given to Adam, which would indicate a homosexual act (this is how they knew they were naked)

> "37 He that soweth the good seed is the Son of man: 38 The field is the world; the good seed

> are the children of the kingdom; but the tares are the children of the wicked one; The enemy that sowed them is the devil..." [Matthew 13:37-38]
>
> "¹² Not as Cain, who was OF THAT WICKED ONE, and slew his brother. And wherefore slew he him? Because his own works were evil, and his brother's righteous." [I John 3:12]

The theories are far, broad, and for lack of a better word, unbelievable to orthodox Bible believers. Those that hold to this theory believe it is the thread that binds the entire Word of God together.

The Bible records the story of a people that came from Adam. These people would eventually be known as the 12 Tribes of Israel. Throughout the Bible, YAH consistently warned His people about intermixing with outside tribes or gentiles.

Cain was wicked, that was for sure, but how did he become corrupted? The Scripture in I John states, "Cain was of that wicked one" those that uphold the serpent seed doctrine believe it is spiritually irresponsible to ignore the parentage of Cain as the source of his wickedness.

"If the woman's seed is a biological family line, then the serpent's seed MUST also be a biological family line. To say otherwise would be wholly inconsistent with Gen. 3:15."

"There is no mention of Cain at all in Adam's genealogy listed in Genesis 5. Now an argument could be made that he was removed from the genealogy because he was banished from the family for murdering Abel. That's not an unreasonable argument. But considering all the other evidence the only thing that makes sense is that Cain was *not* a **son begat in Adam's own likeness,** like Seth was, but was rather a son in the image of *his* father-Satan." (Heath)

According to serpent seed proponents, even Jesus the Lord Himself acknowledges this lineage;

> "³⁴ Wherefore, behold, I send unto you prophets, and wise men, and scribes: and some of them ye shall kill and crucify; and some of them shall ye scourge in your synagogues, and persecute them from city to city: ³⁵ That upon you may come all the righteous blood shed upon the earth, FROM THE BLOOD OF RIGHTEOUS ABEL unto the blood of Zacharias son of Barachias, whom ye slew between the temple and the altar. ³⁶ Verily I say unto you, All these things shall come upon this generation." [Matthew 23:34-36]

And this parable by Jesus is perhaps one of the most convincing for the serpent seed doctrine;

> "24 Another parable put he forth unto them, saying, The kingdom of heaven is likened unto a man which sowed GOOD SEED in his field: 25 But while men slept, his enemy came and sowed TARES among the wheat, and went his way. 26 But when the blade was sprung up, and brought forth fruit, then appeared the tares also. 27 So the servants of the householder came and said unto him, Sir, didst not thou sow good seed in thy field? From whence hath it TARES? 28 He said unto them, An ENEMY hath done this. The servants said unto him, Wilt thou then that we go and gather them up?" [Matthew 13:24-28]

Although we reviewed the opponents of the serpent seed doctrine in the first volume, let's review a few arguments;

"The Serpent Seed idea appears with third century Gnostics and then in a 9th century book called *Pirke De-Rabbi Eliezer.* Who on Genesis 1 Ch. xii.-xxiii. Identifies the serpent with Samael who is an archangel in Talmudic writings, a accuser, seducer and destroyer, *regarded as both good and evil.* This teaching is not just wrong, it is destructive. It leads directly and logically to racism: believing that certain races are irredeemable. The only possible outcome of such a worldview is prejudice and bigotry." (Curtis)

"Also, since there is an immutable principle given in Genesis 1 that all forms of life reproduce "after their kind," any seed of Satan would bear Satan's hereditary traits. Since Satan is referred to as "a serpent," a "dragon," and a "covering cherub," any progeny of his would bear reptilian features."

"Since Genesis 3:20 also states Eve "was the mother of all living," there is no room in the Biblical accounts for some men to have been survivors of the pre-Adamic era either, as any such beings would not have come via Eve's lineage. Genesis 1:26-27 clearly states that God decided to make man "in His own image" and this applies to both males and females."

"Those who teach or believe the serpent seed doctrine ought to take sober warning from God's word in Mark 3:28-29. This passage states that all blasphemies will be forgiven except blasphemy against the Holy Spirit. To declare that the work of God's Holy Spirit is the work of Satan is perilously close to (if it is not indeed) blasphemy against the Holy Spirit." (Collins)

The serpent seed doctrine is attributed to the *Gnostic Book of Thomas*; however, this is also a premise taught in the *Babylonian Talmud.*

The serpent seed doctrine is an authentic source of serious contention that lies at the heart of the entire story of mankind, the source of evil and humanity in general. This doctrine does pit various races at odds with each other. However, the Bible doesn't speak of black, white, yellow, or brown; the Word of God tells of families, lineages, tribes, and territories.

Many theologians have also discussed that many such tribes were Nephilim (fallen ones) or giants and thus not fully human. The tribes of Israel were forbidden to intermarry with these tribes and were constantly in battles with these nations.

To others, the serpent seed line didn't denote Cain but that a race of people of Satanic origin would eventually emerge. The theories are far and wide. The serpent's identity is so critical. Is this enemy of GOD a metaphor, a race of aliens, hybrid DNA, Nephilim giants, or something else? *The debates will continue.*

Leviathan

Leviathan is a mysterious serpent monster that many consider the serpent of Genesis and the dragon of Revelation. Satanic invocations use the name Leviathan in certain rituals.

> "¹ In that day the Lord with his sore and great and strong sword shall punish Leviathan the piercing serpent, even Leviathan that crooked serpent; and he shall slay the dragon that is in the sea." —Isaiah 27:1

Leviathan-West-Water, a Satanic invocation;

"Satan does have a watery aspect too, especially insofar as Satan is a god of magick. The things you need most in order to do magick, such as intuition, primal emotion, and access to your subconscious mind, are all associated with the element of Water. And, in the Biblical book of Revelation/Apocalypse, Satan is portrayed as both a serpent and a red dragon who spews a river of water out of his mouth (Revelation 12:17)." (Vera)

"In lore, the sea creature *Leviathan* which appears in the book of Job in the Old Testament was an original totem deity of the **Levite clan,** whose name means *son of Leviathan.* Medallions from the 1st century AD portrayed *Jehovah as a serpent god* and so Leviathan may have been a dual deity with Jehovah each ruling half of the year. In the Genesis account, the equal creature was *Behemoth* who was a male creature who roamed the earth and Leviathan was a female sea creature who roamed the sea." (Gardiner and Osborn Appendix III. Page 307-308)

Dogon People of Mali
Ceremonial masks

"The Dogon people of central Africa who say they descend from the ancient pre-dynastic Egyptians have a sacred serpent called *Leve* who is the first or head-member of the "living dead" that neutral "alive-dead" state which exists between the opposites of life and death and is related to the positive and negative halves of a cycle. It is this serpent that first had the power to overcome actual death." (Gardiner and Osborn Chapter Seven The Serpent in Classical Myth. Page 114)

"The Ocean in Babylonia as well as in Hebrew mythology is conceived as a serpent; *Tiamat* is a marine serpent and *Tehom-Leviathan* is in Isaiah XXVII, 1 expressed called, serpent." (Wensinck The Navel and the Universe. Page 62)

"Here again is a peculiarity of Leviathan. Psalms LXXIV, 12, "Though Yahweh hast crushed the heads of Leviathan. In the *Odes of Solomon* the dragon has seven heads (XXII, 5). Further the Mekkan traditions maintain the sanctuary was built upon the serpent. Here a Jewish tradition may be compared: The Ocean surrounds the world as a vault surrounds a large pillar. And the world is placed in its circular form on the fins of Leviathan." (Wensinck The Navel and the Universe. Page 62)

Plumed Serpent

Kukulcan Pyramid
Archeological Site of Chichen Itza

"*Quetzalcoatl* comes out of the golden age of the Toltecs. Quetzal means *bird* and co atl *serpent*, and putting those words together gives us the name of this South American god. The plumed serpent god of Central America also known as the *Lord Don* or **morning star** but more importantly as the master of life."

Note: Lucifer is also referred to as the morning star (Venus).

"The Maya had an equivalent god-like hero in *Kukulcan* and *Gucumatz*. Quetzalcoatl is also known as *Votan*. It is said that Votan visited *King Solomon* and returned with strange jars with unknown contents. Votan then buried the jars and the Spanish claimed to have found them with no material value and burned them in 1691." (Gardiner and Osborn Chapter 10 American Myths. Page 185)

"The fabled *Tezcatlipoca* was the son of a mother serpent who presented himself as a physician to the physically ill Quetzalcoatl and gave him a mysterious beverage that would restore his health. The native people of South America who follow the order of *Montezuma* their lost King, looks towards Quetzalcoatl for extended life because of this reference to the healing power of the serpent.

The myth also says that this *elixir of life* was given to the serpent god by the son of a serpent, that he might gain immortality and then bestow it to others. It is said that Quetzalcoatl left the country on a raft supported by snakes and floated across the water promising to return as the future King."

"Although this Quetzalcoatl had been a man, they respected him as a god." Indeed, he was the creator, for "He made the heavens, the Sun, the earth. The Toltecs claim that in the beginning their race knew only one god: Only one god did they have, and they held him as the only god, they invoked him, they supplicated him; his name was Quetzalcoatl." (Talbott The Age of Kronos)

"Osiris, who ruled over the First Time, was able to walk over (or in) the oceans and traveled around the globe bringing civilization to many nations. Thus, we may conclude that *Viracocha = Osiris = Adam = Orion.*

"As a celibate demi-god, Quetzalcoatl invented the Mayan and Aztec calendar and bequeathed the secret doctrine to his priests, who were also celibate. Quetzalcoatl was driven away on a *serpent boat* by his evil twin, Tezcatlipoca (the black twin), but is expected to return from the East (where he spread his knowledge of science and the arts) to reclaim his power among the Mesoamerican people."

"Does Quetzalcoatl not compare to Osiris, who was also murdered by his evil twin, taught the Hermetic doctrines to the Egyptians, and is regarded as Egypt's once and future King? A promo for a book titled "The Return of the Serpents of Wisdom," by *Mark Amaru Pinkham*, reveals that the various supreme deities **were all indigenous serpent-gods!**" (The Book of Secrets – Reflections and Notes on the Royal Families of the Grail Page 71)

Serpents of Wisdom

"According to ancient records, the patriarchs and founders of the early civilizations in Egypt, India, China, Peru, Mesopotamia, Britain, and the Americas were the **Serpents of Wisdom**—spiritual masters associated with the serpent—who arrived in these lands after abandoning their beloved homelands and crossing great seas. While bearing names denoting snake or dragon (such as *Naga, Lung, Djedhi, Amaru, Quetzalcoatl, Adder,* etc.), these *Serpents of Wisdom* oversaw the **construction of magnificent civilizations** within which **they and their descendants served as the priest Kings and as the enlightened heads of mystery school traditions.** *The Return of the Serpents of Wisdom* recounts the history of these *Serpents*—where they came from, why they came, the secret wisdom they disseminated, and why they are returning now." (The Book of Secrets – Reflections and Notes on the Royal Families of the Grail Page 71)

Seraph as the Serpent

Many scholars claim that the Seraphim class of angels are the serpents of which Lucifer was the highest-ordered member. We know from the book of Isaiah that the Seraphim had six wings. Two covered the face, two covered the feet, and two were for flight. (Isaiah 6:2)

"In the sense given to them in the Holy Bible, he would hardly like to connect the sacred name of his Saviour with the "Brazen Serpent" incident. The *Seraphim* (fiery winged serpents) are no doubt connected with, and inseparable from, the idea " of the serpent of eternity — God," as explained in Kenealy's Apocalypse. But the word **cherub also meant serpent**, in one sense, though its direct meaning is different." (Blavatsky Egg-Born Logos. Page 364)

"Unrelated to the Bible, an ancient tractate from the 3rd-century Alexandria, entitled "The Origin, Tales of the Immortal Sophia," and of the ruler *Saboath* who created a great throne on a four-face chariot called *Cherubim*...And on that throne he created some other **dragon-shaped seraphims.** Interestingly, it is narrated in Genesis 3:24 that the Lord stationed Cherubims (chariots of mobile thrones) and a revolving sword of fire to protect the Garden of Eden. The Cherubim appears again in an ancient Greek work called "The Hypostasis of the Archons," which deals with the *Rulers of Entirety* and the Creation of Adam." (Gardner Chapter Four The Early Mission. Page 44)

"*Agathodaemon*- in Gnosticism "**the seven-voweled serpent [seraph], the Christ**. Derived from the Egyptian serpent Agathodaemon, the good spirit, as opposed to *Kakadaimon*, the evil spirit. Agathodaemon has also been designated a guardian angel or genius and identified with *Hermes*, the bringer of good, the angel standing by the side of *Tyche*."

Serpent Symbology

Ouroboros

"The Gnostic ouroboros or circular serpent is half black and half white and encloses the Sun. The Muslim circular serpent, enclosing the Ka'ba and constituting the world ocean, "glitters" in the Sun and is half white and half black. But the same twofold serpent will be found from China to the Americas." (Talbott The Two Cords)

"The Persian winged "griffins" — the guardians of the golden mountain — are the same, and their compound name shows their character, as it is formed of (kr) circle, and "aub," or ob — serpent — therefore, a "serpent in a circle" And this settles the phallic character of the Brazen Serpent and justifies Hezekiah for breaking it (See II Kings, 18, 4)." (Blavatsky Egg-Born Logos. Page 364)

"Another Mayan myth is that of *Chac*, a dragon beast. He ruled over bodies of water and was also known as the rain bringer, he required sacrifices from his people. In exchange for people's sacrifices he shared his blood so that there would be rain. The sacrifice being the element of death and the blood being the element of life. Rain symbology is most always connected to or attributed to the serpent in the mythos of the Americas. In both North and South America as well as Australia and Africa there is a connection between the serpent the water and the rainbow. The serpent is also considered to be a bringer of peace, a culture hero, the creator, the healer, and the giver of immortal life. The serpent is said to guard the treasure that is at the end of the rainbow.

- "All of the Saturnian gods—Atum-Re, An, Yama, Huang-ti, Quetzalcoatl, Kronos—reside within the fold of a serpent (dragon, fish, crocodile, etc.).
- But this symbol cannot be evaluated in isolation from the celestial earths, eggs, wheels, temples, crowns, and eyes which fill the ancient lexicon.

- In the general mystic tradition, reports *Cirlot,* "the dragon, the serpent or the fish biting its tail, is a representative of time."
- Father Time, of course, is Saturn.
- Thus the Greeks placed in the hands of Cronos a snake which formed a ring by holding its tail in its mouth, and this circular serpent is clearly that which the Hindus called *Kali* ("Time").
- The Zoroastrians represented Zurvan ("Time") by an enclosing serpent.
- A serpent encircles a Nahuatl calendar wheel (wheel of time) published by *Clavigero.*
- On the famous Mexican calendar stone twin serpents form a single enclosure around the stone.
- The Egyptians associated the circular serpent with Atum (god of Time), identifying the serpent with the cosmic waters erupting from the creator: "I am the outflow of the Primeval Flood, he who emerged from the waters," the serpent announces.
- The serpent was the circle of the mother goddess and defined the limits of the All (i.e., the cord, egg, shield, or belt of Saturn's Cosmos).
- The serpent enclosed the world-wheel, city, throne, earth-navel and celestial ocean.
- The same serpent formed the wall of the cosmic temple, encircled the god-King as a crown, enclosed the celestial waters as a vase, and defined the circle of the all-seeing eye.

"Here is a fact which linguists and comparative mythologists overlook: in several lands the word for "mountain" is the same as the word for "serpent" or "dragon," though our natural world offers no basis for the equivalence. In Mexico, *Nahuatl* can mean "serpent" but also "mountain," so that one might term the polar Mount Colhuacan a cosmic "serpent-mountain." "Serpent-Mountain" is indeed the title of the Mexican primeval hill Coatepelt."

"The Egyptian *Set* is the primordial serpent or dragon but set also means "mountain." The mythical *Mountain of Set,* in fact, is the acknowledged Egyptian counterpart of the Hebrew *Zaphon* in "the farthest reaches of the north. And like the Mexicans, the Egyptians knew the "Serpent Mountain," a figure of the pole, according to Massey." (Talbott The Serpent/Dragon)

"As the prince of the underworld, Baal was also associated with snakes and serpents, which were symbols of Satan and the demons. So "Baal Zbl" became transliterated to "Beelzebub" and "Baalzebub" which are Biblical titles of Satan." (Sorenson)

"The symbol of the *Therapeutae* healers was a serpent-the same as is shown (along with the Rosy Cross Grail emblem) to denote St. John in the *Rosslyn-Hay Manuscript* of *King Rene d'Anjou, The Gnostic Serpent of Wisdom* is used as part of the *caduceus insignia* of many medical associations today." (Gardner Chapter 21 Heresy and Inquistion. Page 260)

"Lightning was known as the sky serpent or lightning snake, while thunderstorms were believed to be the mating of the sky father and the earth mother, which brought forth fertilizing rains. The sight of the lightning strike was thus considered to be a place of power designated an abyss or forbidden place. The lightning flash corresponds to the flash of bright light in the center of the head during the enlightenment experience (third eye)."

"In the *Dionysian mysteries,* a serpent representing the god was carried in a box called a "cista" on a bed of vine leaves. The cista was said to contain the *phallus* of Dionysus. The system mentioned in the mysteries of Isis is also said to have held the serpent which represented the missing phallus of Osiris." (Gardiner and Osborn Chapter Five The Hidden Wisdom in Arthur's Grail. Page 74)

"Serpent imagery is connected with current witchcraft rituals; in the early rituals of the mother goddess she was imagined as the Moon and the serpent dragon as the Sun, also symbolizing the *red and the white*. In the Roman ritual *drawing down the moon* which many in witchcraft still practice today, the great mother moon goddess would sink down from the heavens as a serpent. The power of this serpent then was utilized for all manners of cures potions and love spells." (Gardiner and Osborn Chapter 12 Archaeology and Imagery. Page 229)

Virgin Mary is often depicted as trampling the serpent underfoot.

"*Zervan,* [in the] Mithraic mysteries, is depicted as having the body of a man, the head of a lion being wrapped in the cosmic serpent. The serpent is shown with the Sun god Mithras along with his horse and dog, licking the blood of the sacrificed bull." (Gardiner and Osborn Appendix III. Page 307-308)

Draco

Draco constellation

Draco constellation- The serpent itself is in the stars as the constellation Draco.

"The famous rabbi, Ibn Ezra, taught in the Talmud that, "Serpents stand as servants to do your will." The serpents represent various astral deities, stars, and planets, including Draco, the dragon and serpent constellation." (Marrs, Holy Serpent of the Jews: The Rabbis Secret for Satan to Crush Their Enemies and Vault the Jews to Global Dominion)

"Venus has always been identified, since the establishment of Roman Catholic dogmatism, with Satan and Lucifer, or *the great Dragon*, contrary to all reason and logic. As shown by the symbologists and astronomers, the association between the **serpent and the idea of darkness** had an astronomical foundation. The position which the constellation of *Draco* at one time occupied showed that the great serpent was the ruler of the night. This constellation was formerly at the very centre of the heavens, and is so extensive that it was called the *Great Dragon*. Its body spreads over seven signs of the Zodiac and *Dupuis*, "who," says *Staniland Wake*, "sees in the **Dragon of the Apocalypse** a reference to the celestial serpent," remarks that " it is not astonishing that a constellation so extended should be represented by the author of that book as a Great Dragon with seven heads, who drew the third part of the stars from heaven and cast them to Earth " (Dupuis, tome III , p 255). (Blavatsky The Horses' of Sukra's Car. Page 31-32)

Serpent and Divine Feminine

- Throughout all of ancient Egypt the circular serpent was the symbol of the *Great mother*.
- In the hieroglyphs, the Uraeus serpent, often used in conjunction with an egg, means "goddess."
- "The goddess *Uatchet* cometh unto thee in the form of the living Uraeus, to anoint thy head," reads the *Book of the Dead*.
- A Karnak Temple inscription states that the goddess *Nut*, in the form of a serpent, encircled "her father *Re* and gave birth to him as *Khonsu*."
- The Babylonians knew the great goddess as "the mother python of heaven."
- The Cosmos, according to *Jeremias*, was represented as the womb of the "**shining Tiamat,**" the enclosing serpent or dragon of the primeval sea.
- So also did the Hindus, Cretans, Celts, Greeks, Romans, and Mexicans represent the mother goddess as a serpent or dragon.
- The serpent itself was the rope which the creator stretched round about, gathering the primeval waters or primeval matter into an organized enclosure.
- The Babylonian Esharra, the circle of created "earth," is identified as the primordial beast Tiamat, the world-enclosing serpent-dragon which the Hebrews called *Tehom* and the Muslims the "Mysterious Serpent." (Talbott The Circular Serpent)

"According to ancient mythology, **the snake was originally the symbol of the virgin goddess** who birthed the cosmos unaided by any masculine principle and was *androgynous* in nature. The connection of the snake with both male and female traits meant the *serpent was the symbol of duality*, dividing itself into. The coiled spiral serpent also represented the *womb of the virgin* goddess, with the opening of the vortex symbolizing the *vagina of the goddess*. In the *Pelagian* creation myth, the goddess created the giant serpent *Ophion*, from the air. **She then became a female serpent and mated with her son,** giving birth to the world egg or cosmic egg, which is seen the world over. *The goddess then became a dove* and floated on the primordial ocean while her son/lover Ophion, coiled around the egg three times like the *Kundalini* serpent at the base of the spine. This continued until the egg hatched thus forming the heavens, the earth and the underworld. The dove later becomes a symbol for the spirit of god and the human, both of which are seen as female." (Gardiner and Osborn Appendix III. Page 307)

In a 1916 document from Amsterdam, this little known feature of the Holy Shekhinah is found;

"Finally it is to be noted the *Mekkan* serpent in the main part of the traditions is either the *Shekhinah*, the divine Presence, or a being sent by Allah, not a demoniac but a divine being." (Wensinck The Navel and the Universe. Page 65)

Serpent Father

"Of the mythic serpent is its **phallic powers**, "Even today it is said in the *Abruzzi* that the **serpent copulates with all women**. The Greeks and Romans also believed it. *Alexander the Great*'s mother, *Olympia*, played with snakes. The famous *Aratus of Sicyon* was said to be a son of *Aesculapius* because, according to *Pausanias*, his mother **conceived him of a serpent**. *Suetonius* and *Dio Cassius* tell how the mother of *Augustus* conceived from the embrace of a serpent in Apollo's temple. A similar legend was current about the elder *Scipio*. In Germany, France, Portugal and elsewhere, women used to be afraid that a snake would slip into their mouths when they were asleep, and they would become pregnant, particularly during menstruation." (Gardner Chapter Four The Early Mission. Page 44)

"The claim that several ancients of royalty were fathered by a serpent or a god in serpent form, connects with the royal lineages in the country of India. Indian royals claim descent from the Naga serpents of antiquity."

"In other serpent paternity mythos, the *Emperor Augustus* was said to have been fathered by a snake and his mother never lost the marks of that encounter. A serpent was said to have been found beside Olympias (sleeping), she is the mother of *Alexander the Great* whose life was based partly on pre-existing myths her husband *Philip of Macedon* who is reputed never to have coupled with the bride of the serpent again. " (Gardiner and Osborn Chapter Six The Cauldron of the Head of the Underworld. Page 90)

Jewel in Serpent's Head

"The power that resides within the head of a serpent is known in lure as the *jewel in the head*. The jewel in the serpent's head is said to be *green like an emerald*. Lucifer, the serpent god of the sky, came down to earth and **brought the emerald jewel,** which became the *Philosopher's stone*. According to many Gnostics, *Lucifer* is the true savior and any research into ancient secret societies will reveal this belief, which is one of the secrets of Freemasonry. The jewel is known as the dew drop essence of the *Rose, the Ros* or *moon dew* of *the Alchemist*. (Gardiner and Osborn Chapter 9 Celtic and European Myths. Page 181)

Note: The emerald seems like a connection to The Emerald Tablet of Hermes Trismegistus and the Egyptian God Thoth.

"During a monumental conflict the *Archangel Michael* struck the stone from *Lucifer's* crown. Some accounts say that the stone was transformed into a *golden cup*, while others say that Michael incarnated himself into *the Grail* and descended to earth to prepare the way of redemption-not only for a fallen human race, but also for Lucifer as well. The legendary capstone of the great Giza pyramid was suggested to be a clear crystal, a candidate for the so-called "stone of light" knocked from the crown of Lucifer by the mighty Michael." (Church Chapter Two What is the Grail. Page 34-35)

Serpent Seasons

In ancient mythology the seasons were divided upon *three aspects of the goddess*, the seasons were ruled and represented by;
the lion,
the goat
and the serpent.
The serpent represented autumn and the *death of the goddess. The Python at Delphi* is said to have been slayed by the Sun ray arrows of the Sun god *Apollo*. The snake may also be seen as;

- *Lord of the waning year*
- *Dark twin of the Sun lord* with the two lords fighting for rulership of the land at the beginning of summer and again at the beginning of winter.

"According to pagan mythology, all slain lords rise again every year and the light and dark winter, along with the summer day and night, rule and balance. The Sun lord also dies nightly and passes through the underworld **realm of the serpent or dragon**." (Gardiner and Osborn Appendix III. Page 307-308)

Subtil Serpent

One of the significant end times deceptions is to reverse everything you know about YAH, His Word, and character. Believe it or not, twisted doctrines teach YAH as the serpent and dragon; therefore, Christ was the serpent King on earth. This Luciferian lie attempts to paint Christ as a "serpent King" to connect His Royal lineage with the European "Dragon" bloodline. Thereby claiming European royalty with "the divine right to rule."

As proof, Lucifer and his ilk equate Christ shedding his garments after the resurrection to a snake shedding its skin.

"There are possible links here with the story of Jesus, especially when we consider that the Hindus influence the Essenes. The Essenes, a group who encoded information regarding the Grail who had their own old fight cult and medicine text. It could be that *Jesus was seen as the serpent King who resulted from the union of a serpent and a snake Princess,* who theoretically would be a virgin or serpent mother. The date of AD 33 fits remarkably well with the time that Jesus is said to have gone to the heavenly Kingdom which after all is also the realm of the Nagas." (Gardiner and Osborn Chapter 8 Asian Myths. Page 146)

"In Ethiopia a strange oral tradition known as the *snake in the grove* is connected to *Mary* who is called the *Queen of the snakes.* The legend says that when Mary came to Ethiopia with Joseph and baby Jesus after leaving Egypt, they stayed for many years at Axum, the capital of Ethiopia (said to hold the *Ark of the Covenant).* Before returning to their homeland Mary ordered the snakes to never hurt the women of the area, she was thus mythically said to be Queen of the snakes."

In actual pagan mythos, the enemy has tried to link Mary, the mother of Jesus, with being a serpent queen. This deplorable un-biblical fable connects Mary with the serpentine form of the goddess Isis, the mother of Horus. Isis was also the wife and sister of Osiris, Horus' father in his previous incarnation. Reference *Thy Queendom Come Chapter 13-Egyptian.*

The Gnostic Sophia has recently seen a surge in popularity, although this mother goddess figure goes back to antiquity. It's critical to understand Gnostic teaching in these last days. It is one of the primary foundations for the enemy's lies.

"*Sophia* meaning wisdom or the *virgin of light* comes from the light of Ophis, the serpent. The light of the serpent is thus synonymous with wisdom and according to the apocryphal *Wisdom of Solomon,* it is Wisdom (Sophia), who grants immortality. The Ophite (Gnostic worshipers of snakes) taught that Sophia and *the Christ* entwined together like serpents in the person of Jesus and thereafter, he became *Jesus the Christ* that is the anointed or Christ One. In this context Sophia represents the sacrificial blood offering of the mother goddess or world mother while the Christ represents the male positive energy force, *the conscious self*. When the serpentine or subtle serpent energizes Sophia and the Christ fused together in the person of Jesus, they were embodied in him (symbolically speaking) he became the *Serpent of Wisdom*." (Gardiner and Osborn Chapter 11 The Serpent in Religion. Page 199)

Shining Ones

"Osiris the Egyptian King" was also known as *Ob-El* meaning *shining serpent* or *Pytho Sol* (serpent Sun). Great pillars of stone were dedicated to the worship of Osiris in Grecian times, these were called obelos or obeliscus. Commonly known now as obelisk pillars and related to the Basilisk."

"*Imhotep* (Egyptian) is said to have been a scribe, poet, astrologer, doctor and physician-priest. He was revered for his scientific knowledge that even the Greeks held in high esteem. Imhotep is equated with the Greek *Aesculapius* the man-god who knew how to revive the dying using the blood or venom of a snake. Imhotep was [not only] the **son of Horus** but... he was in receipt of the knowledge of the *Shining Ones*." (Gardiner and Osborn Chapter Seven The Serpent in Classical Myth. Page 125-127)

"In ancient Sumeria for it was there that the *Shining Ones*-the fish deities led by *Oannes* or Dagon-were said to have first emerged from the sea and educated the people of the area." (Gardiner and Osborn Chapter Seven The Serpent in Classical Myth. Page 111)

"The teachings surrounding Aesculapius spread, and he was seen not just in association with but actually as *Apollo, Hermes, Thoth* and *Mercury*, who all held the Caduceus-styled staff (the rod of Arcadia) the symbol of the *Shining Ones*. These gods either collectively or individually became known as the god Thoth, the initiator of wisdom, writing, art and greatest of all healing who in later centuries became known as Hermes Trismegistus." (Gardiner and Osborn Chapter Seven The Serpent in Classical Myth. Page 129)

"The *Tuatha De Danann* were called the Shining Ones, an ancient pre-Celtic Irish tribe, the fifth one that invaded the island in ancient times. They would later be associated with Elven or Fairy Folk. This tribe was not human but described as elegant, beautiful, and even shining with light. These mysterious beings arrived with the secret knowledge of the gods. When you begin to look into their story, you begin to see a dizzying array of connections to ancient mythologies in other parts of the world. These demi-gods arrived on ships descending from the heavens in a great mist that blocked out daylight for three days and nights. Then, they burned the ships, forcing themselves to take up residence permanently. Tuatha Dé Danann is translated to "people of the goddess Danu," a primordial mother goddess." (Ancient Code Team)

"As the Ocean, it assumed the form of a circle. As the Ocean, the Mekkan serpent is glittering in the Sun and as the Ocean it is black and white. As Tehom it is connected with the nether world. It has however not only the natural features of Tehom, but also, it's mythological ones. Just as Tehom in the form of Leviathan, so the Mekkan serpent will reappear at the resurrection. There is another, constantly returning characteristic of the serpent, viz. it's having the head of a he-goat, of course this is also a mythological feature." (Wensinck The Navel and the Universe. Page 64)

Serpents of Renown

"*The Grail* is a stone that is said to be brought from heaven to earth by the "neutral angels" the ones that refused to take sides in the *war in heaven*. The Grail therefore is said to go back in time to a mysterious priesthood of gods and demigods known as **"the Shining Ones."** The Egyptians gods of pre-dynastic period were known as the *Nete*r or *Neteru*. The Neter gods were *Osiris, Horus and Thoth*. According to the *Turin Papyrus* which list the names of these gods and the later pharaohs, and the long reign of the Neter followed by a mysterious priesthood known as the *Shemsu Hor* (the followers of Horus). Horus having been the last Neter god. This priesthood was also known as the Akhu, which means "the Shining Ones." (Gardiner and Osborn Chapter One Alpha-Omega. Page 17)

"*Thoth* is said to have incarnated as a serpent. *Apep* or *Apophis* the great primoradial serpent of death and chaos, who said to live in the Nile and who represented the black void. Apep was worshiped by the Israelite's as the *Golden Calf* and is etymologically closely related to Pope/Papa. He appears in another form as *Typhon, the dragon*." (Gardiner and Osborn Chapter Seven The Serpent in Classical Myth. Page 114)

"Known to the Greeks as *Dionysus*, who was **born as a serpent**, *Bacchus* is represented a bearded man crowned with vines and ivy two plants associated with the serpent. He is essentially a serpent god, and the sign of the serpent was *Ichthus* which became a fish when taken up by the followers of Jesus. Bacchus is also the guardian spirit of Islam." (Gardiner and Osborn Chapter Seven The Serpent in Classical Myth. Page 120)

"*Zeus* takes the form of a serpent to attend the spring rites of the *mother goddess,* earth. This ability to shape shift if he personified the ability to control the serpent energy of the cosmos. He also took on the form of the serpent *Ophion* to avoid the wrath of his father Cronos, the god of time from whom is derived the word chronology. (Gardiner and Osborn Chapter Seven The Serpent in Classical Myth. Page 129)

"*Zeus* also had his own angels, the invisible beings known in Greek as daemons, which have become our Westernized demons. They appeared as handsome youths or wise serpents, and Zeus assigned them as guardian spirits to guide and give wise counsel." (Gardiner and Osborn Chapter Seven The Serpent in Classical Myth. Page 130)

"Now *Ea* is the god of *Apsu*, Tehom and Leviathan is a fish as well as a serpent." (Wensinck The Navel and the Universe. Page 65)

Serpent Etymology

Europe is derived from *Aur-ab* (the solar serpent) which is etymologically linked to the word "aura" and contains the word *ab*, meaning "wisdom" as attained from the underworld. The original inhabitants of Europe were said to have descended from a mother goddess of serpentine form.

"The original Hebrew word relating to "the deep" was *tehom*, which has a similar root to *Tiamat*. Tehom in the plural becomes *tehomot* but as pointed out by Semitic scholars, the association between the Hebrew word tehomot and the Akkadian name Tiamat was purposely suppressed for doctrinal reasons. In the *Enuma Elish* epic, the Babylonia god *Marduk* is said to have fought a great battle to overcome the primordial salt waters of Tiamat, who is portrayed in the account as the great Dragon Queen." (Gardner, Genesis of the Grail Kings Chapter Four The Chaldean Genesis. Page 41)

"Mendes is a place in the Egyptian Nile Delta, we discovered that *Mendes* was also a ram-headed god as well as the dwelling place of the *Ba* where *Re* and *Osiris* met, uniting in their ba or soul. Taking the world *Baphomet* backwards, we get Tem, Oph (ohp), Ab.

Tem could come from the root word for time or it could mean to proclaim.

*Ohp, or Op*h is the *winged serpent or dragon* of the Ophites.

Ab means father, the creator or great one. It also means wisdom, intelligence or will and is a root word for "shake or serpent."

"Our conclusion is that Baphomet means to **proclaim the wisdom of the serpent**. Another decoding of Baphomet through an atbash Ciperit reads Bet Pe Vav Mem Taf, this becomes Shin Vav Pe Yud Alef, which in English reads as *Sophia* a word with both serpent and wisdom connotations." (Gardiner and Osborn Chapter Six The Cauldron of the Head of the Underworld. Page 103-104)

"The name "Ethiopia" may come from *Thoth* and *Athoth* or a mistaken translation of *Ath-Ophion*, a sacred title for *followers of the serpent deity*. Or it could be that "Ethiopia or "Athiopia" came directly from terms such as *Athe-Ope* and *Ath-Opis* (worshiper of the snake) an obvious link with the Egyptian serpent Apophis or Apep. (Gardiner and Osborn Chapter Seven The Serpent in Classical Myth. Page 110)

"In Benin, the Dahomey or Fon people have a great serpent that is seen as a rainbow named *Danh*, a name that is similar to that of the Celtic god *Dana*, which spawned the names "Danube" and "Denmark." This serpent symbolizes the life-force and encircles the world as the Ouroboros." (Gardiner and Osborn Chapter Seven The Serpent in Classical Myth. Page 114)

"*Viracocha* is also analogous to Quetzalcoatl of the Aztecs; to the Queshua, Aymara, and other tribes of South America, he is known as *Ameru,* which means 'serpent'. It will come as a shock to many Americans that the name 'America' is probably derived from '**Ameru', the serpent-god, and not the Italian voyager 'Amerigo' Vespucci!**" (The Book of Secrets – Reflections and Notes on the Royal Families of the Grail Page 71)

"America is not named after the explorer *Amerigo Vespucci*, let's examine the true and hidden etymology and history of the continents name. *America came from Amaruca.*

Manly P. Hall gives more insight in *The Secret Teachings of All Ages*: "These Children of the Sun adore the *Plumèd Serpent*, who is *the messenger of the Sun.* He was the god *Quetzalcoatl* in Mexico, *Gucumatz* in Quiché; and in Peru he was called *Amaru*. From the latter name comes our word *America.* A*maruca* is, literally translated, '**Land of the Plumèd Serpent.**' The priests of this [flying dragon], from their chief center in the *Cordilleras*, once ruled both Americas."

Nagas

Nagas

"The country of India has always overflowed with serpent mythology and ideology. The Hindu goddess *Kali* originally came from Sumeria and by tradition was said to be the **sister of the Biblical Cain's wife Luluwa**. Kali was a primary *Princess of the Dragon House* who had for a consort the Hindu god *Shiva*. Kali is also an avatar of the goddess *Durga*, we covered Kali in *Thy Queendom Come*, Chapter 15 Hinduism. As the *World Mother*, Kali was the controller of immortality and was worshiped by the *Thugees* who the Assassins were descendants."

"The royal dynasty of India was said to be descended from serpents and that their blood possessed immortality like the snake. The Hindu serpent goddess *Kadru* is said to be the progenitor of the *cobra people* or *serpent people*, more commonly known as the Nagas. Their blood was called *lunar blood* in connection with the moon and the feminine principle, the venom of the serpent was considered the masculine principle, these masculine and feminine expressions gives birth to the **Kundalini serpent power**. It is Kadrus blood that gives immortality to the Naga".

"The Sanskrit term *naga* simply means *serpent or cobra*, this term became more commonly known as the name for the serpent deities and demigods that dwelt in the underworld or Patalas in the city of Bhogravati and the Naga were the guardians of great treasures. Like so many other serpent legends and mythologies, the Naga were said to be **underwater serpents and fish deities** who came by the way of Mesopotamia from the sea. Likewise the *Merovingian Kings* also claimed descent from the sea serpent." (Gardiner and Osborn Chapter 8 Asian Myths. Page 141-148)

Note: there is no coincidence that the latest Black Panther movie featured these native Indian serpent beings that were blue like Hindu gods and lived as a lost tribe under the water.

The Nagin are the women of the Naga race and were said to be alluringly beautiful and had the ability to **shapeshift**. The Nagin have precious **gems (emeralds)** that grant them magical powers which are embedded in their skulls. These female snakes marry earthly princes.

The hero of the *Mahabharat*, marries the Nag *Princess Ulupi*, who provides him protection from all the underwater threats and beasts. Their marriage is also connected to the Chinese and Japanese myths of royal dragon descent.

In fact several royal families in India claim descent from the Naga. The royalty of Manipur in northeastern India trace their lineage back to A.D. 33, their progenitors who in legend were a serpent Princess and a human man, the same story and myth is accounted to the southern India PALAVAS.

"In both the Egyptian shrines of Isis as well as Hindu Temples legend to this day claim that cobras haunt these shrines. When the cobras hear the priests, the cobras supposedly stick their head in a hole to accept offerings of milk. These serpents are said to be guardians of treasures that go back hundreds of years. The idea of a serpent guardian guarding treasures is a part of mythology worldwide. The sleeping guardian dragon must be overcome by a hero before the hero can receive the treasure. But here is the real secret, **the sleeping dragon is really only a reflection of the sleeping hero or the hero within** the dragon represents their unconsciousness of the source of their power which is itself the treasure that they must win in order to awaken." (Gardiner and Osborn Chapter 8 Asian Myths. Page 141-148)

Connecting the Dots

Nachash=divination, magic spell, shining ones, resembled man, stood upright, wanted to be most high, divine celestial beings

Samael=Satan, Seraphim, Archangel, accuser, seducer, destroyer, good and evil

Cain= Samael (Satan) and Eve's son, father is Enki (Masda, Mazdao)

Enki=Masda=one who prostrates like a serpent, Ohrmazd (Serpent of the Night)

Good Seed = Woman's Seed, Tares = Serpent's Seed, Enemy = Satan / The Serpent

Satan= serpent, dragon, covering cherub, reptilian features

Eve= mother of all living

Ocean in Babylonia=serpent

Tiamat=marine serpent

Leviathan=seven heads, world is placed in its circular form on the fins of Leviathan, Levite clan

Quetzalcoatl=feathered serpent, lord Don, morning star, creator

Osiris=civilization to many nations, celibate, bequeathed secret doctrine to his priests, evil twin, Tezcatlipoca (the black twin), will return from the East, Quetzalcoatl

Supreme deities=indigenous serpent-gods

Serpents of Wisdom=construction of magnificent civilizations, descendants served as the priest Kings and as the enlightened heads of mystery school traditions.

Seraphim=fiery winged serpents, serpent of eternity, cherubim, dragon shaped

Cherubim=four faced chariot, archons

Ouroboros=circular serpent, half black and half white, encloses the Sun

Griffins=guardians of the golden mountain, serpent in a circle, phallic

Serpent=bringer of peace, a culture hero, the creator, the healer, giver of immortal life, guards the treasure that is at the end of the rainbow, time, cosmic waters, circle of the mother goddess, the cord, egg, shield, or belt of Saturn's Cosmos, encircled the god-King as a crown, celestial waters as a vase, circle of the all-seeing Eye, ruler of the night

Saturnian gods=reside within the fold of a serpent

Snake=symbol of the virgin goddess, androgynous, duality

Coiled spiral serpent=womb of the virgin goddess,

Dove=goddess, spirit of god and the human (female)

Shekhinah=Mekkan serpent

Royals=fathered by serpent

Mountain=serpent, dragon
The Egyptian Set =serpent, dragon, mountain
Baal=prince of the underworld, associated serpents, Beelzebub, Baalzebub
Lightning=sky serpent, lightning snake
Thunderstorms=mating of the sky father and the earth mother
Lightning flash=third-eye
Head of a serpent=jewel in the head, green emerald
Lucifer=serpent god of the sky, emerald jewel, Philosopher's stone, true savior,
Lucifer's jewel (crown)=dew drop essence of the Rose, the Ros or moon dew of the Alchemist, Michael Archangel struck down, formed golden cup, capstone Giza (stone of light), Nagin
Goddess seasons =the lion, the goat, serpent
Serpent=autumn, death of the goddess, head of he-goat
Underworld=realm of serpent, dragon
Sophia=virgin of light, light of Ophis, the serpent, wisdom, blood offering, mother goddess
Sophia and the Christ= entwined serpents became Jesus the Christ
The Christ=male positive energy force, the conscious self, serpent of wisdom
Jesus (their belief) =parents are serpent father and serpent mother
Imhotep= scribe, poet, astrologer, doctor and physician-priest, son of Horus, knowledge of the Shining Ones
Shining Ones= fish deities, Oannes, Dagon, educated the people, Caduceus, gods became known as the god Thoth, Hermes Trismegistus, demi-gods, priesthood, Watchers or Nephilim (come from the sea, Atlantis), Tuatha Dé Danann
Thoth=incarnated as a serpent
Apep=great primordial serpent of death and chaos, Golden Calf, etymologically closely related to Pope/Papa, Typhon, the dragon
Dionysus= born as a serpent
Bacchus=bearded man, serpent god, guardian spirit of Islam
Zeus=transforms to serpent, controls serpent energy of the cosmos, daemons (handsome youths, wise serpents, guardian spirits)
Baphomet= proclaim the wisdom of the serpent, Sophia
Venus=Satan, Lucifer, great Dragon
Kali =sister of the Biblical Cain's wife Luluwa, Princess of the Dragon House
God of time= Atum (Egyptian), Cronos (Greek), Saturn
Mother goddess=serpent or dragon

7

The Little Mermaid

Starbucks cup with Melusine's image of two tails

The most well-known serpent, dragon, or mermaid in lore belongs to a name most people have never heard of, MELUSINE. While this name is unfamiliar, indeed, the following three things are not,

The Little Mermaid

The Starbucks mermaid

The movie *Splash*

The Royal House of Windsor

How are all four of these seemingly unconnected things connected? The answer is in a very forgotten story about a *Serpent Queen* with two double tails named *Melusine*. Melusine is also a form of *Melissa*, a form of *Isis*.

Melusine's story starts with her parents; her mother, a fairy (a form of serpent/dragon), and her father, the King of Scotland. Mischievous as a youth, young Melusine trapped her father in a mountain! As punishment for her deed, her mother put a horrible curse upon her. This curse also ensured no man would ever marry her. Every Saturday, she would transform into a serpent creature with two tails for the rest of her life. As a half-human/half-creature, Melusine was then regarded as a shapeshifter or werewolf, sealing her fate as a maiden forever.

During the Knight's Templars era, the *Count of Anjou* was a bachelor looking for a wife. During this time, he crossed paths with a mysterious woman named Melusine. That's where her mother was wrong! They fell in love, and Melusine agreed to marry the Count on one condition: on Saturdays all day, she would be left alone in her room, not to be disturbed by anyone, including him and the staff. The Count agreed to her demands, and they lived a wonderful life and ruled the Kingdom in harmony.

The couple went on to have children, and everything was fine for a while until the townspeople became suspicious of Melusine's absence. There are two separate legends about the vanishing Melusine. One, of course, every Saturday, she would lock herself away to be confined to water. But the second absence was on Sundays during church service. Melusine would disappear and never partake of the Eucharist, representing the body and blood of Christ. Before the Eucharist on Sunday, she would miraculously disappear; according to legend, one of these issues sealed Melusine's eventual fate.

Melusine's bathing ritual

One legend regarding the Eucharist explains that on a particular Sunday, a priest stopped Melusine to administer the holy rite before she made her usual exit. Melusine then let out a terrifying shriek, turned into the form of a dragon, and flew off with her children, never to appear again!

The second account unfolds during the secret Saturdays. On this day, the curse of Melusine's mother turned her into a horrifying two-tailed serpent from the waist down. On Saturdays, Melusine would remain in a tub of water all day long with her doors locked. Her husband and his staff become suspicious of Melusine's activities. Despite his agreement to honor her on Saturday, he decided to spy on her. To the Count's detriment, he was horrified to see the love of his life and the mother of his children was a half woman, half serpentine creature. The Count, startled and mortified, let out a scream! Once his presence was known to Melusine, she let out a shriek and flew off with her children.

Some traditions recount later years; the Count would remarry. On his wedding day, Melusine showed up as a dragon! In this serpentine form, she perched on top of the cathedral; blood began dripping from the ceiling, and that's how the Count knew she was there.

Melusine's children and transformation

Note: Melusine is also said to have given birth to at least ten children who were the roots of European nobility.

There are many stories and variations of the Melusine myth. However, this is where the tail (pun intended) gets separated from the myth. Melusine is considered the matriarchal progenitor of most European nobility! Historically the founder of a small European country called Lusignan (near western France), the inhabitants are called Mélusins and Mélusines. *The* Lords of Anjou were members of the Plantagenet family who became rulers of much of Europe.

"Through *Jacquetta of Luxembourg's* descendants, Melusine's fairy blood allegedly flows in the veins of all British monarchs dating back to the 15th century."

"*Elizabeth Woodville* was the link between the British Royal family and Melusine. In 1464, during the *War of the Roses, King Edward IV* secretly married Elizabeth, who came from a *Lancastrian family* without royal rank. Rather than securing his rule by marrying into another European royal family, as most Kings did. Edward followed his heart, choosing a widow as his bride."

"But Elizabeth did have a claim to royal blood through her mother, Jacquetta of Luxembourg, a member of the powerful Ducal Luxembourg Dynasty. Jacquetta traced her family back to the myth of Melusine, arguing that she was a descendant of the fairy princess, as she had - according to legend - married Jacquetta's ancestor, *Siegfried*. In short, this means that the current British royal family is allegedly descended from Melusine, a tempting water goddess and the inspiration for the mermaid on the Starbucks cup." (Carlton)

Melusine's lineage connects to the Grail families or the "Holy Grail," which we will reference in this book as, *the unholy grail*. The secret of the Grail family is in what "secret" they protect. The secret is said to be the venom and blood of the serpent, the elixir of life. This elixir of life colors is red and white, signaling the bloodline of the Royal families of Europe.

Connecting the Dots

Melusine = form of *Melissa*, a form of *Isis*, 10 children, 10 kings, House of Windsor, country of Lusignon, Grail families, Ducal Luxembourg Dynasty
Grail secret=serpent venom, elixir of life, red and white, blood and venom of serpent

SECTION III

Unholy Grail

UNHOLY GRAIL

8

Illuminati Bloodlines

Rothschild Family Crest

The average Believer doesn't think of their lineage in terms of a bloodline. Believers focus on the *Blood of the Redeemer*. This line of thinking is not how the people in power run the world. Believers would be shocked to learn the entire ruling class claims the right to rule based on their bloodline heritage which traces back to a few places;

- 12 Tribes of Israel
- Fallen Angels
- Sea creatures (as shown in the Melusine epoch)
- A prominent religious figure such as the founder of Islam, *Prophet Mohammad,* whom *Queen Elizabeth* and *King Charles* claim lineage
- King David (House of Judah)

The family crest that the Royals wear tells the story of their bloodline. The Royals' bloodlines worldwide give them the "Divine Right to Rule." This "right to rule" comes from *god* and their genealogy. These bloodlines stretch to every area of world power, including, The Vatican, celebrities, world politicians, corporate executives, and even United States Presidents! Many U.S. Presidents are said to be bloodline descendants.

These bloodlines are one of the secrets of secret societies. I can't stress enough; these bloodlines control the entire world's power system. The controversy, of course, is the legitimacy of many who claim heritage. The danger in these bloodlines is the outward appearance of religious sanctity, but these families are Luciferians and generational Satanists. Much work and research have gone into this area, and there is no need to repeat that work. This book aims to give a general overview of the leading bloodlines and their anti-Christ, world-domination agenda.

The Illuminati was covered extensively in *Thy Queendom Come* over several chapters. The Illuminati is, in fact, the concealment of the bloodline families that rule the world. Often these families rule under other names and may or may not be the ruling elite of a particular nation; they are, however, the secret power behind the scenes (Kings without a Kingdom).

> "¹² And the ten horns which thou sawest are ten kings, which have received no kingdom as yet; but receive power as kings one hour with the beast. [Revelation 17:12]

The Illuminati operate in several secret societies, and each association represents the interest of various bloodlines. The public secret societies are far removed from the actual purpose and aim; world domination.

"Illuminati--The Illuminati are 13 elite bloodlines that have maneuvered themselves into control over this planet. They lead double lives, one for society and a hidden one which is based on a Gnostic Luciferian philosophy which consists of lots of blood rituals." (Springmeier and Wheeler Page 13)

"It should also be mentioned that ex-Illuminati members have explained how planned births are coincided to have the child be born on particular special occult dates. The Illuminati have a intense lifestyle of secrecy, so **most of their members do not carry the last name of the bloodline they belong to.** Some members are given significant occult names for their legal name, and others use legal names which have no significance. Having a legal occult-significant name is not essential, because the alter system will receive a secret Illuminati occult name." (Springmeier and Wheeler Chapter 1. Science No. 1 - Selection and Preparation of the Victim. Page 24)

"This is the secret hierarchy level. It is secret by virtue of almost all (if not all) its members being programmed multiples from elite powerful bloodlines- This is hardcore generational Satanism that believes in a Gnostic Luciferian doctrine; hence, they may be called your elite Luciferians."

"This level of activity is secret by virtue of its secret ties. It includes the anarchy level of the

Illuminati, the various criminal syndicates, the music industry, the various fraternities, new age institutions and people in power all over the globe." (Springmeier and Wheeler Page 76)

"*Baron Guy de Rothschild,* of France, has been the leading light of his bloodline. The Baron is an Illuminati Kingpin and slave programmer. For those who have bought the cover story that the Catholic Church is not part of the Illuminati's NWO, I would point out that the Baron has worked with the Pope in programming slaves." (Springmeier and Wheeler Chapter 1. Science No. 1 - Selection and Preparation of the Victim. Page 31)

"AN ASSOCIATION [Illuminati] HAS BEEN FORMED for the express purpose of ROOTING OUT ALL THE RELIGIOUS ESTABLISHMENTS AND OVERTURNING ALL THE EXISTING GOVERNMENTS OF EUROPE. I have seen this Association exerting itself zealously and systematically, till it has become almost irresistible." (Robison Pages 6-7)

"The Illuminati consist of many of the world's richest families including the Rothschilds, the Rathskellers and the Windsors. While they pay lip service to religion, **they worship Lucifer**. Their agents control the world's media, education, business and politics. These agents may think they are pursuing success, but success often literally means serving the devil." (Makow PhD The Conspiracy is Against God. Page 66)

"The Illuminati are the movers and shakers of the world. **They are an elite group of bloodlines**—I call these tribes or families—there are 13 major bloodlines. They are what are called "generational Satanists." That means that they have practiced their secret witchcraft for many centuries and they have passed their religion down from one generation to the next. They lead double lives. They have one life that the world sees and then they have a hidden life that the world doesn't see." (Makow PhD Movers and Shakers. Page 70)

Jewish/European Nobility

"In the meantime, let us just remember, that the plain tale of Brotherly love had been polished up to protestations of universal benevolence, and had taken place of loyalty and attachment to the unfortunate Family of Stuart, which was now totally forgotten in the English Lodges. The Revolution had taken place, and *King James,* with many of his most zealous adherents, had taken refuge in France." (Robinson Chapter I Schisms in Free Masonry. Page 15)

"The confluence of Jewish and British interest extended to marriage. "Marriages began to take place, wholesale, between what had once been the aristocratic territorial families of this country and the Jewish commercial fortunes. After two generations of this, with the opening of the twentieth century, those of the **great territorial English families in which there was no Jewish blood was the exception**."(Makow PhD Are the Jews Responsible? Page 38)

"In tracking the bloodlines, it became apparent that the **European Illuminati bloodlines were trying to integrate some of the American Indian bloodline**s into their own bloodlines. Why? They wanted the **occult power that these bloodlines contributed**." (Springmeier and Wheeler Chapter 1. Science No. 1 - Selection and Preparation of the Victim. Page 22)

Khazarians

Map of Ancient Khazarian Empire
Dr. Henry Makow

Benjamin H. Freedman an influential Jewish businessman and researcher writes in his book *Facts are Facts*;

"Relentless research established as equally true that the so-called or self-styled "Jews" in eastern Europe at no time in their history could be correctly regarded as the direct lineal descendants of the legendary "lost ten tribes" of Bible lore. The so-called or self-styled "Jews" in eastern Europe in modern history cannot legitimately point to a single ancient ancestor who ever set even a foot on the soil of Palestine in the era of Bible history. Research also revealed that the so-called or self-styled "Jews" in eastern Europe were never "Semites", are not "Semites" now, nor can they ever be regarded as "Semites" at any future time by any stretch of the imagination. Exhaustive research also irrevocably rejects as a fantastic fabrication the generally accepted belief by Christians that the so-called or self-styled "Jews" in eastern Europe are the legendary "Chosen People" so very vocally publicized by the Christian clergy form their pulpits." (Freedman)

"What secret mysterious power has been able for countless generations to keep the origin and the history of the Khazars and Khazar Kingdom out of history textbooks and out of classroom courses in history throughout the world? The origin and history of the Khazars and Khazar Kingdom are certainly *incontestable historical facts.* These incontestable historic facts also establish beyond any question of doubt the origin and history of the so-called or self-styled "Jews" in eastern Europe. The origin and history of the Khazars and Khazar kingdom and their relationship to the origin and early history of the so-called or self-styled "Jews" in eastern Europe was one of history's best-kept secrets until wide publicity was given in recent years to my research on this subject." (Freedman Page 51)

The mysterious Kingdom of the Khazars is a historical secret; you won't find it in your high school history textbooks or universities. I have the same question as Mr. Freedman, why would the history of the Khazars be a secret? The Kingdom was a huge nation covering approximately 1,000,000 square miles and occupied the region of the Caucasus mountains near modern-day Ukraine, the Black Sea, and the southern part of Russia. The Khazars were people of Turkish origin and a nomadic tribe with a desire for plunder and revenge. The Khazars' origins are unknown, and their history dates back to around the First century BC. The Khazar Kingdom was constantly at war.

The Khazars were pagan in nature, and their religion was a mix of phallic worship and other idolatrous practice. The Khazar's religious beliefs included vial sexual excess and indulgence. The lewdness of the people caused the country to go into moral decay, and the Khazar *King Bulan* could no longer endure his people. Due to the constant threat of outside invaders, King Bulan decided that his entire country would turn to a new monolithic religion. He decided against Christianity and Islam and instead agreed on Talmudism, now known as Judaism.

Babylonian Talmudic rabbis converted King Bulan and four thousand nobles. The King abolished phallic worship and all other forms of idol worship. The Khazar kings brought rabbis to open synagogues and schools and educate their population on their new Talmudic religion. "Converted Khazars were the first population of so-called or self-styled Jews in Eastern Europe. By the 7th century, the entire Kingdom of the Khazaria was Talmudic Jews."

On page 141 in his "History of the Jews" Professor H. Graetz states;

"According to a *fundamental law of the state* only Jewish rulers were permitted to ascend the throne...for some time the **Jews of other countries had no knowledge of the conversion of**

this powerful kingdom to Judaism, and when at last a vague rumor to this effect reached them, they were of the opinion that Khazaria was peopled **by the remnant of the former ten tribes."**

These rumors grew, and no doubt gave way that Palestine was the homeland of the Khazars. When the Russians conquered the Khazars and the Khazar Kingdom disappeared, the language of the Khazars became known as Yiddish. Yiddish is still used today by European Jews, also those in Russia, Poland, Lithuania, Romania, Hungary, and even in America. The Yiddish language is not a German dialect, but Yiddish borrowed many words from the German language.

"Approximately 90% of the world's so-called or self-styled "Jews" living in 42 countries of the world today are either emigrants from eastern Europe, or their parents emigrated from eastern Europe. "Yiddish" is a language common to all of them as their first or second language according to where they were born. It is an "international" language to them." (Freedman Page 60)

Excerpts from a lecture by Islamic scholar and Historian Sheikh *Imran Hosein*;

- "Something very mysterious happened in that part of the world that historians have chosen to bury."
- "So the world witnessed for the first time the very strange phenomenon of non- Semitic people becoming Jews, non-Semitic, becoming Jews."
- "These people chose to convert to Judaism but they did so not for any religious reason. They were not so much interested in following the law. They embraced Judaism for purposes of political expediency." (Metro Examiner)

"The Khazars grew wealthy as a result of trade, which was greatly facilitated by their geographical position. The east-west route linking the Far East and the Byzantine Empire, as well as the north-south route linking the Slavic tribes and the Caliphate, both had to pass through the lands of the Khazars. The Khazars collected customs fees from the caravans carried along these routes, thereby contributing to the prosperity of the Khaganate." (DHWTY)

"Definitive DNA studies have now been conducted, and the results are clear and indisputable. The people who today call themselves "Jews" and reside both in the Middle East and around the world are not descendants of the ancient Israelites. They are not the seed of Abraham and have no blood connection to the prophets of ancient Israel. Instead, DNA shows these people to be descendants of the Kingdom of Khazaria, a country that formerly existed in the Caucasus, south of Russia.... From there they emigrated throughout Europe and into the United States and, in 1948, the Khazarian Jews established the new nation of Israel." (Marrs, DNA Science and the Jewish Bloodline Introduction)

"Scientific DNA studies were conducted first in 2001 by *Dr. Ariella Oppenheim*, a Jewish genetics researcher of Hebrew University in Tel Aviv. Her finding: Almost all who today identify themselves as "Jews" are not the descendants of Abraham but are, in fact, of Turkish/Mongol stock. The Jews are Khazarians, not Israelite."

"Then, in 2012, *Dr. Eran Elhaik*, an Israeli-born, Jewish researcher from prestigious Johns Hopkins Medical University in Baltimore, Maryland, published his findings. They confirmed those of Oppenheim: "Those who today identify themselves as "Jews" are not the descendants of Abraham but are, in fact, of Turkish/Mongol stock. The Jews are Khazarians, not Israelites."

"According to Dr. Elhaik's research, those who identify themselves as today's Jew and as descendants, therefore, of Abraham, are mistaken." (Marrs, DNA Science and the Jewish Bloodline Chapter 2 The Evidence is Clear—Today's Jews are Khazars)

Why is the history of the Khazars vital today? It is one of the greatest deceptions in all of world history, revealing the indisputable background and genetic testing of the true origin of today's "chosen people."

The Khazarian bloodline has since intermarried with other bloodlines and still holds to the claim of their divine lineage. The Khazars are spread throughout European nobility and comprise a significant portion of the Illuminati bloodline families.

> 9 I know thy works, and tribulation, and poverty, (but thou art rich) and I know the blasphemy of them which say they are Jews, and are not, but are the synagogue of Satan. [Revelation 2:9]

"In his book, Livingstone traces the genealogies of these Khazar bloodlines, which include the Rothschilds, the Hapsburgs, the Sinclairs, the Stuarts, the Merovingians, the Lusignans, and the Windsors. "The great secret of history is this story of the ascent of heretical Cabalists to world power," says Livingstone. "Ordinary Jews and people in general have no idea how they are being manipulated." (Makow PhD Independent Historian Unveils Cabala Conspiracy. Page 97)

"From the early centuries of the first millennia, the Khazars of Eastern Europe were known as the diabolical "Serpent People," and now, the nation of Israel has admitted that its people are indeed, the Khazars." (Marrs, Serpent People Return to Ukraine)

Anthropologist Robert Sepehr makes reference to the ancient Khazars in relation to the serpent;
"Historic tribes such as the ancient people of Ukraine from the earliest centuries in the first millennia, the Khazars of eastern Europe were known as the *Serpent People* which use snake or dragon symbolism and were not reptilian themselves." (Sepehr)

Desposyni

Merovingian Dynasty
Known for their long red hair

"Following the Jewish Revolt in Jerusalem during the 1st century AD, the Roman overlords were reputed to have destroyed all records concerning the Davidic legacy of Jesus the Messiah's family. As confirmed by the Ecclesiastical History of *Eusebius*, the 4th century Bishop of Caesarea, these heirs were called the **Desposyni** (ancient Greek for "of the Master", theirs was the sacred legacy of the *Royal House of Judah-* a dynastic bloodline that lives on today." (Gardner Chapter One Origins of the Bloodline. Page 1)

"It was the Desposynic Vine of Judah perpetuated in the West through the blood of Jesus. This lineage included the Fisher Kings and Lancelot del Acqs. It descended to the Merovingian Kings of France and the Steward Kings of Scots. In descent from Jesus's brother James /Joseph of Arimathea, the Grail Family founded the House of Camulod (Colchester) and the *Princely House of Wales*. The Sangreal was perpetuated in the sovereign and most noble houses of Britain and Europe and it is still extant today. (Gardner Chapter 17 The Grail Hallows. Page 202)

"During the latter years of the declining Empire, the greatest of all threats to the Roman Church arose from a desposynic royal strain in Gaul. They were the **Merovingian** dynasty-male line descendants of the Fisher Kings with a Sicambrian female heritage. The Sicambrians took their name from *Cambra* a tribal Queen of about 380 BC. Originally from Scythia **north of the Black Sea and were called the Newmage (New Covenant)."**

Note: The area of the Sicambrians of the Black Sea is perhaps a connection to the Khazarians.

"Despite the carefully listed genealogies of his time, the heritage of *Meroveus* was strangely obscured in the monastic annals. Although the rightful son of *Clodion* he was, nonetheless, said by the historian *Priscus* to have been sired by an arcane sea creature, the Bistea Neptunis. There was evidently something very special about King Meroveus and his priestly successors, for they were accorded special veneration and were widely known for their esoteric knowledge and occult skills." (Gardner Chapter 12 Religion and the Bloodline. Page 144-145)

Note: You read that correctly! History records the paternal father of Clodion a sea monster. How could this demonic lineage that claims actual ancestry from a sea creature also claim heritage from the House of Judah?

"The series of 13 poems published under the title LE SERPENT ROUGE date January 17, 1967 contains a Merovingian genealogy and two maps of France in Merovingian times, in addition to a commentary to the Merovingian bloodline. The poems represent a symbolic or allegorical pilgrimage through the signs of the zodiac beginning with Aquarius and ending with Capricorn. They appear to be the story of a **red snake representing a bloodline or lineage uncoiling across the centuries- the bloodline of the Grail family**." (Church Chapter Four The Myth of Mary Magdalene. Page 74-77)

"There were 21 Kings of the Merovingian dynasty reigning over a Germanic tribe known as *the Franks,* from 447 to 751 a total of 304 years, they were called "the long-haired Kings" From there the dynasty became weakened, deposed and overtaken. Later the bloodline of the Merovingians became connected with the Spanish Visigoths. In 751 *Pepin,* the son of *Charles Martel,* deposed *Childeric III* considered by most historians to be the last Merovingian King. "(Church Chapter Five The Merovingian Bloodline. Page 81-84)

"Regardless of their ultimately Jewish heritage, the Merovingians were not practicing Jews, but neither were other non-Roman Christians whose beliefs had sprung from Judaic origins. **In practice their spiritual cult was not dissimilar to that of the Druids and they were greatly revered as esoteric teachers, judges, faith-healers and clairvoyants."**

"The Merovingian Kings did not rule the land, nor were they politically active; governmental functions were performed by their Mayors of the Palace (Chief Ministers) while the Kings were more convened with military and social matters. Among their primary interest were education, agriculture and maritime trade...their revered model was King Solomon, son of David." (Gardner Chapter 12 Religion and the Bloodline. Page 144-145)

"From the 5th to the 8th centuries, the Merovingian dynasty of kings ruled Europe and, **from the Middle Ages until the present day, most of Europe's monarchs have been of Merovingian lineage.** In 679 A.D., the Roman Catholic Church collaborated with the Carolingian dynasty to assassinate the Merovingian *King, Dagobert II*. The removal of the Merovingian kings culminated with the coronation of *Charlemagne*, who became the Holy Roman Emperor in 800. Ironically, Charlemagne and the Carolingians *married Merovingian wives in order to guarantee the continuation of their dynasty.* This would account for the perpetuity of the Merovingian bloodline in the royalty of Europe." (Aho, The Merovingian Dynasty; Satanic Bloodline of the Anti-Christ and False Prophet)

"It is hard for people to grasp that the Illuminati controlled Russia, Great Britain, Germany and France during World War II, but they did. *Churchill, Roosevelt* and *Stalin* were all Masons. *DeGaulle* of France was closely linked with several esoteric groups, and the Prieuré de Sion and Grand Orient Masons helped him to power in the 50s... the people of the world weren't ready for a world government, and most not even a united Europe. W.W. II was carried out to adjust people's thinking toward wanting European unity." (Springmeier, The Top 13 Illuminati Bloodlines)

Connecting the Dots

Khazar Bloodlines = Jews-European Nobility-called Serpent people
Illuminati=13 bloodline families, Luciferians, generational Satanists
Merovingian = Kings of France, Steward Kings of Scots, ancestor sea creature, Bistea Neptunis, Jewish heritage, occultists, esotericist, clairvoyants, all European nobility
Jesus's brother James /Joseph of Arimathea=House of Camulod (Colchester), Princely House of Wales, King Arthur

9

Our Lady of Secrets

Desposyni Jesus, Mary Magdalene, Chalice, Apostle

The *DaVinci Code*, a best-selling novel and blockbuster movie by author *Dan Brown* was a public relations campaign. This massive campaign introduced the world to the idea that Jesus Christ had a wife, Mary Magdalene, and they had children. Of all the end times deception, this Gnostic based, heresy, is the basis for one aspect of the Holy Grail. The Holy Grail is said to be; the chalice Jesus drank out of at the last supper, his holy garments, various relics, and the list goes on. Secret societies protect the Grail. Regardless of the "item" which they are holding for "proof" of this Royal lineage, the unholy grail (which we will call it) is the bloodline descendants of the "children" of Jesus. Believers in Christ do not be deceived. This bloodline is a lie from the pit of hell and the father of lies. This falsehood must not fool you because this Desposyni bloodline will come forward in tribulation, claiming the *Divine Right to Rule* the entire world. However, these

Illuminati bloodlines are here and have never stopped working towards their goal. The irony, they hate Christ and are out to destroy HIS followers.

The following are some of the blatant lies from Lucifer;

"In their attempts to constrain the royal birthright of Judah, the High Christian movements have installed various figurehead regimes, including Britain's own **House of Hanover-Saxe-Coburg-Gotha.**"

"*Chalice*, a chalice that once contained the lifeblood of Jesus. The Grail has additionally been portrayed as a vine, weaving its' way through the annals of time. The fruit of the vine is the grape and from the grape comes wine." (Gardner Chapter One Origins of the Bloodline. Page 2)

"It is now generally acknowledged that the opening chapters of the Old Testament do not represent the early history of the world as they suggest. More precisely, **they tell the story of a family**, a family that became a race comprising various tribes-a race that in turn became the Hebrew nation. If Adam was the first of a type, then he was seemingly a progenitor of the Hebrews and the tribes of Israel….a predestined line of priestly governors." (Gardner Chapter One Origins of the Bloodline. Page 8)

"David of Bethlehem married *Saul's* daughter to become King of Judah (corresponding to half the Palestinian territory) in around 1008 BC. Subsequently, he also acquired Israel (the balance of the territory) to become overall King of the Jews."

"A dynasty of Priest Kings of, as Jesus's descendants became aptly known in Grail lore as Fisher Kings." (Gardner, Bloodline of the Holy Grail Page 111)

"Mary Magdalene died in AD 63 aged sixty at the place now called Saint Baume in southern France. According to the Gnostics, Mary Magdalene was associated with Wisdom (Sophia) represented by the Sun, Moon and a halo of stars. The female gnosis of Sophia was deemed to be the Holy Spirit thus represented on earth by the Magdalene who fled into exile bearing the child of Jesus. John in Revelation 12:1-17 describes Mary and her son and tells of her persecution, her flight into exile and of the continued Roman hounding of the remnant of her seed (her descendants)."

"Mary's mother *Eucharia* was related to the house of Israel (that was the Hasmonaean royal house, rather than the Davidic House of Judah). The Notre Dame cathedrals of Europe which were wholly Cistercian-Templar instigated were dedicated not to Jesus's mother Mary, **but to Our Lady, Mary Magdalene.**"

Mary Magdalene

Depiction of Mary Magdalene holding the skull of "Christ"

"Mary (Magdalene) is remembered as *la Dompna del Aquae*: the *Mistress of the Waters*. To the Gnostics (as indeed to the Celts), females who were afforded religious veneration were often associated with lakes, wells, fountains and springs. Indeed, gnosis (knowledge) and wisdom were attributed to the female Holy Spirit which "moved on the face of the waters" [Genesis 1:2].

"On both occasions, the anointing was carried out while Jesus was seated at the table (as defined in The Song of Solomon). This was an allusion to the ancient rite by which a royal bride prepared her bridegroom's table. To perform the rite with spikenard was the express privilege of a Messianic bride and was performed solely at the First and Second Marriage ceremonies. Only as the wife of Jesus and as a priestess in her own right could Mary have anointed both his head and his feet with the sacred ointment." (Gardner Chapter Five The Messiah. Page 54)

"Mary Magdalene reportedly fled Jerusalem in AD 70 with her "sacred" children. She sailed across the Mediterranean to France bringing *the cup* from which Christ drank the Last Supper and in which her alleged uncle, Joseph of Arimathea, had caught the blood of Christ. Some accounts say that Joseph took the Grail on to England, while other accounts hold that Mary Magdalene kept the Grail in France. The question remains, what was the holy Grail? In *Wolfram von Eschenbach's* epic poem on the subject, published around 1200, the Grail represents **a "stone of light" (similar to a crystal ball)."**

"But the cup and the stone appear to only be symbolic of a deeper esoteric meaning. Now, take a deep breath and consider what I believe to be the greatest heresy of history. These so-called guardians of the Grail have made the cup to become symbolic of another "vessel" that supposedly contained and preserved the bloodline of Christ, namely the body **(or perhaps I should say the womb) of Mary Magdalene**!

"In an esoteric sense, the womb of Mary Magdalene becomes the Grail-preserving the bloodline or lineage of Jesus. Her offspring supposedly married into the royal family of the Franks, eventually producing a King to sit upon the throne -Merovee, from whom has come the so-called sacred Merovingian bloodline." (Church Chapter Four The Myth of Mary Magdalene. Page 74-77)

"A few years ago a booklet was published in France entitled LE SERPENT ROUSE (The Red Serpent). It contained 13 prose poems and thirteen signs, with the thirteenth, *Ophiuchus* or the Serpent Holder, inserted between Scorpio and Sagittarius. Under the astrological sign of Leo was this paragraph;

"From she whom I desire to liberate, there wafts towards me the fragrance of the perfume which impregnates the sepulcher. Formerly some named her: Isis, Queen of all sources benevolent. Come unto me all ye who suffer and are afflicted and I shall give ye rest. **To others, she is Magdalen**e, of the celebrated vase, filled with healing balm. The initiated know her true name: *Notre Dame des Cross*."

The implications of this paragraph are extremely interesting. **Mary Magdalene is lined with the Egyptian goddess of fertility, Isis, whose Babylonia name was Ishtar.**

Black Madonna

Virgin of Montserrat and Black Madonna Statue
Montserrat Monastery, Catalonia, Spain

"[Mary Magdalene] as a Head Sister of the Nazarite Order (the equivalent of a Senior Bishop) was entitled to wear black. A cult known as the *Black Madonna* emanated from Ferrieres in Ad 44. Among the many Black Madonna representations that still exist, one of the finest statues is displayed at Verviers, Liege, she is totally black with a golden scepter and crown, surmounted by Sophia's halo of stars. Her infant child also wears a golden crown of royalty."

Note: The statue above has tons of esoteric symbolism. The mother statue has a ball with a ring around it. Is this Saturn? At the bottom, the two pine cones represent "the third eye" or illumination; the child is doing the "As above, So below" hand signal and holding a pine cone (pineal gland).

Saint Mary Magdalene Fesco
Piero della Francesca

In contrast to the Black Madonna, Mary's high clerical status also portrayed her as wearing a red cloak, often over a green dress (representing fertility).

Note: notice the red and green colors as representative of Christmas

"The church was battling in the early years with the universal goddess image and worship, such as *Cybele, Diana, Demeter* and *Juno*. Whatever the name, **they were all identified with Isis** (the universal mother, mistress of all the elements, primordial child of time, sovereign of all things and the manifestation of all)."

"To the ancient Egyptians Isis was the sister/wife of Osiris, the founder of civilization and the judge of souls after death. Isis was specially a maternal protectress and her cult spread far and wide. She was frequently portrayed holding her child Horus, whose incarnations were said to be the Pharaohs themselves. It is a well-established fact that the image of the **White Madonna is founded upon the depictions of Isis, the nursing mother. She too inspired the Black Madonna**. The Black Madonna and child have black faces, hands and feet although **they are not negroid** in character.

"The Black Madonna according to Alexandrine doctrine "transmitted the true secret of Jesus."

"She is black because Wisdom (Sophia) is black, having **existed in the darkness of chaos before the creation**. To the Gnostics of Simon Zelotes, Wisdom was the Holy Spirit-the great and immortal Sophia who brought forth the first father, *Yaldaboath*, from the depths. Sophia was held to be incarnate as the Holy Spirit in Queen Mary Magdalene and it was, she who was said to bear the ultimate observance of the faith."(Gardner Chapter 9 Mary Magdalene. Page 97-105)

"The Black Madonna is revered throughout the world, particularly in France, Poland, Italy and Spain. She is the Blessed Virgin Mary of the Crusades and holy pilgrimages. The **Black Madonna is honored as a true goddess figure** and has been since Christianity entered Europe. She is honored by many as Isis, Gaia, Kali, Mary, "the Other Mary" (Mary Magdalene), Diana, Sheela Na Gig, and the Ancient Primal Earth-Mother goddess. For many European Christians, the blending of their ancient goddesses with the Blessed Virgin Mary has been a well-accepted fact of their faith for centuries, there is no conflict. The Black Madonna, be she called Isis, or Mary, or Kali, or Diana, embodies all the aspects of Female Divinity for many millions of people." (Finney)

Connecting the Dots

Grail= Jesus and Mary Magdalene lineage, Fisher Kings, House of Judah, vine, fruit of the vine, grape, womb of Magdalene

Chalice=life blood of Jesus

Mary Magdalene=Wisdom (Sophia), Sun, moon, halo of stars, holy spirit, tower, mistress of the waters, moved on the face of the waters,

Black Madonna= Isis, universal goddess, Lilith, true secret of Jesus, Sophia, chaos before creation, Gaia, Kali, Mary, "the Other Mary" (Mary Magdalene), Diana, Sheela Na Gig, Ancient Primal Earth-Mother goddess. For many European Christians, the blending of their ancient goddesses

10

Order of the Dragon

T*hy Queendom Come* extensively researched four secret societies; Rosicrucians, Knights Templar, Freemasons, and the Illuminati. To avoid duplicating the work, we have included new information or relevant information about the secret societies in relation to the royal bloodlines. For the history, beliefs and in-depth study on secret societies, please revisit our first volume.

Order of the Dragon

Societas Draconistarum
Order of the Dragon Insignia

"**The Typhonian or Draconian Tradition** refers to the secret doctrine of the Ordo Draconis, the Order of the Dragon which is associated with the Rosicrucians.

"In 1408...the Dragon Court was formally reconstituted as a sovereign body at a time of wars and general political turmoil. The Court's reemergence was instigated by *Sigismund von Luxembourg*, King of Hungary, a descendant of **the Lusignan Dragon Kings of Jerusalem.**"

"Having inherited the legacy in 1397 he drew up a pact with twenty-three nobles who swore to observe 'true and pure fraternity' within the Societas Draconis (later called Ordo Draconis)."

"The Draconian Current refers to the **demonic bloodline which is represented by the Dragon Order**. The Dragon Court was constituted in 1408 for the express purpose of preserving the **ancient Vere bloodline.**"

"The most important of all of these ancient groups is the **Brotherhood of the Snake, or Dragon, and was simply known as the Mysteries.** The snake and dragon are symbols that represent wisdom. *The father of wisdom is Lucifer, also called the Light Bearer.* The focus of worship for the Mysteries was **Osiris, another name of Lucifer.** Osiris was the name of a bright star that the ancients believed had been cast down onto the earth. The literal meaning of Lucifer is "bringer of light" or "the morning star." After Osiris was gone from the sky, the ancients saw the Sun as the representation of Osiris, or more correctly, Lucifer. Osiris was represented by the sun. (Albert Pike)

> "How art thou fallen from heaven, O Lucifer." [Isaiah 14:12]

It is claimed that, after Lucifer fell from Heaven, he brought with him the power of thinking as a gift for mankind." (Copper Chapter 2 Secret Societies and the New World Order. Page 71)

"An organization that was once headed by the one and only Aleister Crowley, this tradition is part of a current of magical force and occult lore dating back to Sumeria and pre-Dynastic Egypt. Originally known as the Draconian Tradition it is a magical current "based on initiated knowledge" or gnosis of the Fire Snake. The Fire Snake is also known as the Kundalini or the Ophidian Current; the basis of all true initiation."

"Who is Typhon? According to *Mr. Grant,* Typhon is "The feminine aspect of Set; sometimes typified as the Mother of Set in her role of goddess of the Seven Stars, of which Set is the Eighth." Set is the brother of Osiris in the Egyptian Pantheon. Set, Osiris' dark brother, chopped Osiris up into many pieces, leaving him for dead. Set means black and "he who is below" and Set was also the prototype for Satan." (Vulgarian)

Freemasonry

"The British and Jewish goal of world domination was synonymous and used **Freemasonry** as an instrument. *Belloc* writes, "Specifically Jewish institutions, such as **Freemasonry** (which the Jews had inaugurated as a sort of bridge between themselves and their hosts in the seventeenth century) were particularly strong in Britain, and there arose a political tradition, active, and ultimately to prove of great importance, whereby the British state was tacitly accepted by foreign governments as the official protector of the Jews in other countries." (Makow PhD Are the Jews Responsible? Page 38)

"If they aren't Jewish by intermarriage, **many European aristocrats consider themselves descendants of Biblical Hebrews.** The Hapsburgs are related by marriage to the Merovingians who claim to be descendants of the Tribe of Benjamin. In addition, many aristocrats belong to the "British Israel" movement that believes the British sovereign is the head of the Anglo-Saxon "Lost Tribes" of Israel and that the **Apocalypse will see the full reconstitution of the British Empire.**"

"According to *Barbara Aho*, Rosicrucians and Freemasons, who believe in British Israelism, have a plan to place one of their bloodlines on the throne of the rebuilt Temple in Jerusalem. **This positioning of a false messiah whom the world will worship as Christ has been carefully planned and executed over many centuries.**"

"*Barry Chamish* writes, "there would be no modern state of Israel without British Freemasonry. In the 1860s, the British-Israelite movement was initiated from within Freemasonry. Its goal was to establish a Jewish-Masonic state in the Turkish province of Palestine... Initially, **British Jewish Masonic** families like the **Rothschilds and Montefiores** provided the capital to build the infrastructure for the anticipated wave of immigration. However, luring the Jews to Israel was proving difficult. They liked European life too much to abandon it. *So Europe was to be turned into a nightmare for the Jews.*" (Makow PhD British Israel. Page 34)

Priory of Sion

Priory of Sion logo (note the Hexagram)
Priory of Sion Official Website (Italy)

"The Priory of Sion appears to be the guardians of a "holy bloodline" and the Holy Grail-the holy bloodline being the lineage of Mary Magdalene and the Holy Grail being the cup from which Jesus drank the Last Supper. The Holy Grail, therefore, was believed to contain the holy blood, or in a mystical sense, the holy bloodline from the "harlot," Magdalene. We are told in Revelation 17 of a woman guiding the governments of the world- and in her hand was seen a golden cup. It may well represent what I consider to be the Unholy blood and the Unholy Grail." (Church Chapter One Who Are the Guardians? Page 29)

"These are indisputable facts regarding the Priory of Sion;

- There was a secret order behind the Knights Templar, which created the Templars as its military and administrative arm. This order functioned under the name of the Prieure de Sion (Prior of Sion).
- Although the Templars were disbanded between 1307-1314 the Prior of Sion has continued to function through the centuries.
- It has orchestrated certain critical events in Western history.
- The Priory of Sion exists today and is still operative.
- It plays an influential role in high-level international affairs as well as in the domestic affairs of certain European countries."

"The avowed objection of the Priory of Sion is the **restoration of the Merovingian dynasty and bloodline to the thrones of certain European nations.** The restoration of the rule of the Merovingians is considered "justifiable, both legally and morally.

Although it became deposed in the eight century, it did not become extinct, some of those family lines include;

- Saint Clair (Sinclair)
- Montesquiou
- Plantard
- Habsburg (ruled the Holy Roman Empire since the 13th century), *Franz Joseph* of the Merovingian-Habsburg dynasty, **launched WWI**

The Merovingian bloodline presently claims a so-called" "legitimate claim to rightful heritage."

"The Order of Sion was founded in 1099 by *Godfroi de Bouillon* just after his conquest of Jerusalem. The headquarters were at the Abbey of Notre Dame du Mont de Sion, Mt Sion (Zion) the famous "high hill" upon which the city of Jerusalem is built. Godfroi was offered the title "King of Jerusalem" but declined, asking to be known only as *Defender of the Holy Sepulcher*. Godfroi was of Merovingian blood." (Church Chapter Five The Merovingian Bloodline. Page 85-89)

Mount Hermon is also called Sion…Priory of Sion.

Note: Mount Hermon is the location of the fallen angels. We will cover this in an upcoming chapter.

Rosicrucian

"The Priory of Sion came to be known as the Rose-Croix or Rosicrucians. One of the first Grand Masters of the Prior of Sion *Guillaume de Gisors* (1266-1307) was said to have organized the body into an "Hermetic Freemasonry." The word evolved from the Greek god Hermes, who was called (Mercury by the Romans). **Mercury, bore the two symbols of the Israelite tribe of Dan- the eagle and serpen**t. He was also called *Odin* (a form of the word Dan) by the Merovingians who claimed ancestry from him. He was considered the god of science, eloquence and cunning, and also the guide of departed souls of Hades." (Church Chapter Five The Merovingian Bloodline. Page 86-87, 91)

Knights Templar

'The Prieure de Sion was a religious order founded upon Mount Sion in Jerusalem. The Order set for itself the goal of **preserving and recording the bloodline of Jesus and the House of David**. Through every means available to them, the Prieure de Sion had found and retrieved the remaining relics. These relics were entrusted to the **Knights Templar** for safekeeping. I am amazed at the authors of *Holy Blood, Holy Grail* and the information that they have unearthed. Most of all I am amazed at their inability to put the puzzle together. The treasure hidden in France is not the treasure of the Temple of Jerusalem. It is the Holy Grail itself, the robe of Jesus, the last remaining pieces of the Cross of Crucifixion, and, according to my sources, someone's bones. I can tell you that the reality of the bones will shake the world to its very foundations if I have been told the truth." (Copper Chapter 2 Secret Societies and the New World Order. Page 76)

"During the crusading era, various knightly Orders emerged include the Ordre de Sion (Order of Sion) founded by Godefroi de Bouillon in 1099. Others were the Knights Protectors of the Sacred Sepulcher and the **Knights Templars**." (Gardner Chapter 18 Guardians of the Sacred Relic. Page 211)

> ### *Connecting the Dots*
>
> **Order of the Dragon**= Priory of Sion, Rosicrucian
> **Osiris**=Lucifer=sun=light bearer, fallen star cast down to earth
> **Mercury**=Tribe of Dan, eagle, serpent, Odin (a form of the word Dan), Merovingians, guide of departed souls of Hades
> **Typhon** = feminine aspect of Set; Mother of Set, Goddess of the Seven Stars, of which Set is the Eighth

11

Symbology

Unicorn

In esoteric lore, **the womb** was identified as the "vessel of life" and was represented by a cup or chalice. Prehistoric shrines dating from 3500 BC associate the figure with the womb of the Mother goddess. The reverse male symbol was **a blade or horn,** ordinarily symbolized as a **sword**, although its **most powerful representation was in the fabulous mythology of the Unicorn**. Psalm 92:10 my horn shalt thou exalt like the horn of an unicorn. Along with the Lion of Judah the legendary **Unicorn remained synonymous with the Kingly line of Judah**. (Gardner Chapter 17 The Grail Hallows. Page 200)

Bees

Napoleon bee adornment

"The Great Mother goddess of the Merovingian bloodline was Diana, who was a lesbian. "[Diana] devoted herself to hunting, always accompanied by a band of young women, who, like herself, abjured marriage. She is depicted with a quiver and attended by dogs. her most famous temple was at Ephesus and was one of the seven wonders of the world."

"Among Diana's sacred animals are the bear, **the bee** and the crab, which all point to the sign of Cancer. **The bee is also a symbol of Set or Satan.** There are eleven bees on the arch of the Plantard crest; eleven, of course, is an occult number."

"There are eleven bees because eleven is the number of magick and of the sephirah on the *Tree of Life* [Kabbalah], which is the 'Gateway' to the backside of the Tree and to the Gods." (The Book of Secrets – Reflections and Notes on the Royal Families of the Grail Page 7-8)

"To the Merovingians, the bee was a most hallowed creature and having been a sacred emblem of Egyptian royalty, it became a symbol of wisdom. Some 300 small golden bees were found stitched to the cloak of Childeric I (son of Meroveus) when his grave was unearthed in 1653. *Napoleon* had these attached to his own coronation robe in 1804. The Merovingian bee was adopted by the exiled

Stuarts in Europe, and engraved bees are still to be seen on some Jacobite glassware." (Gardner Chapter 12 Religion and the Bloodline. Page 147)

"The model for the Merovingian Kings was King Solomon himself, perhaps the mystical priest-King Melchizedek, and even before them the sorcerer Kings of Atlantis. Their disciplines were largely based on Old Testament scripture. The Magi were another group also admired by the Merovingians, the Merovingians becoming noted sorcerers in the same manner as the Samaritan Magi which stemmed from *Simon (Magus) Zelotes*. They firmly believed in the hidden power of the honeycomb, the basis for cellular structure, and now a central image of the **Mormon Church-a central image seemingly for all cultures based on a rule by the elite over a 'worker colony."** (The Book of Secrets – Reflections and Notes on the Royal Families of the Grail Page 45)

"In *The Two Babylons,* Alexander Hislop associated the bee with the **Essenes, Diana and also with Mithraism**. It seems that this insect typified the 'Word' and the 'Seed of the Woman' in the various pagan religion." (The Book of Secrets – Reflections and Notes on the Royal Families of the Grail Page 19-20)

"Found in the grave of King Childeric I was a special set of 300 miniature solid gold bees. The bees were given to *Leopold Wilhelm von Hapsburg*, military governor of the Austrian Netherlands, who was considered a descendant of the Merovingian dynasty."

"By 1804, when Napoleon was crowned emperor, those 300 golden bees had been returned to France. Having special importance to Napoleon, he had them affixed to his coronation robes. Napoleon of course had a special interest in the Merovingian dynasty. In 1810 Napoleon married *Marie-Louise,* the daughter of *Francis II,* the last Hapsburg to sit upon the throne of the Holy Roman Empire." (Church Chapter Five The Merovingian Bloodline. Page 81-84)

"The symbol of the bee is also used in Mormon temples today. The bee is the state symbol for Utah. Furthermore the Mormon doctrine teaches that Mary Magdalene was the wife of Jesus Christ. The religion of the Mormon Church of the LDS is replete with Merovingian ideology." (Church Chapter Five The Merovingian Bloodline. Page 81-84)

Beehive

State of Utah State Emblem

"*The Beehive* would be a veiled reference to the **multitude of the offspring of the Merovingian** bloodline. *Fritz Springmeier* stated in The Top 13 Illuminati Bloodlines:

"Family trees subdivide over the centuries until the Merovingian family tree has become a forest." He added: "Be Wise as Serpents revealed for the first time...how all the heads (presidents) of the [Latter Day Saints] and [Reformed Latter-Day Saints] have been descendants of the Merovingian dynasty, and they and the Masons have both used the Merovingian symbol of the bee. This would explain why Utah is called 'the Beehive State.' J. R. Church confirms the Mormon-Merovingian connection in Guardians of the Grail." (The Book of Secrets – Reflections and Notes on the Royal Families of the Grail Page 19)

- The Mother goddess, under her various names, was known as the Queen Bee
- The priests who ministered in her temples were called Essenes or King Bees
- Her priestesses were Melissae, the Bees (Melissa is an ancient title referring to a priestess of the Great Mother or to a nymph (the full-grown larva of bees are called nymphs)

"The Cretan Zeus was born in a cave of bees and was fed by them, and Zeus also had the title of Melissaios, Bee-man; he fathered a son, the hero *Meliteu*s, by a nymph who hid the child from *Hera* in a wood, where Zeus had him fed by bees. Dionyous was fed on honey as a babe by the nymph *Makris,* daughter of *Aristaeus,* protector of flocks and bees."

Bear

Plantard family crest
Priory of Sion official website

"¹ And I stood upon the sand of the sea, and saw a beast rise up out of the sea, having seven heads and ten horns, and upon his horns ten crowns, and upon his heads the name of blasphemy. ² And the beast which I saw was like unto a leopard, and his feet were as the feet of a BEAR, and his mouth as the mouth of a lion: and the dragon gave him his power, and his seat, and great authority." [Revelation 13:1-2]

"The Plantard family crest is regarded as the key to the Typhonian/Draconian Current, which is the **demonic lineage of the Merovingian bloodline**. The Typhonian Current refers to the *Dragon lineage of Satan.*

> "9 And the great dragon was cast out, that old serpent, called the Devil, and Satan, which deceiveth the whole world." [Revelation 12:9]

"The two bears denote the Mother (Typhon) and her son (Set) [Satan]" (The Book of Secrets – Reflections and Notes on the Royal Families of the Grail Page 2-3)

"In the Typhonian Tradition the bear is the constellation of Ursa Major. The stars must be aligned in a specific way in order for Set [Satan] to be properly invoked." (The Book of Secrets – Reflections and Notes on the Royal Families of the Grail Page 7-8)

Ursa Minor, the Lesser Bear, Ursa Major the Greater Bear.

Ursa Minor (lesser bear)

> "2 And the beast which I saw was like unto a leopard, and his feet were as the feet of a Bear." [Revelations 13:2]

"Associated in esoteric knowledge with this role of high Kingship is the symbol of the North Pole Star - the *crown of the world* - and the circumpolar constellations. Of these, the Lesser and the Greater Bear are the most important: the former providing the present North Pole Star. The 'Bear' is a veil to the real name, which means Dove, or Sheepfold, or Chariot." (The Book of Secrets – Reflections and Notes on the Royal Families of the Grail Page 14)

Red Cross

"One of the prime symbols for the Holy Grail is **the red cross placed over the circle**, supposedly the sign of *u*nity or the original Creator. The Merovingians were regarded as priest-Kings, embodiment of the divine. They did not rule simply by God's grace but were apparently deemed the living embodiment and incarnation of God's grace, a status usually reserved for Jesus. **Here, however, it only makes sense that they ARE indeed the bloodline of the incarnations of Lucifer - their `divine."** (The Book of Secrets – Reflections and Notes on the Royal Families of the Grail Page 45)

Connecting the Dots

Unicorn= male symbol was a blade or horn, sword, Kingly line of Judah.

Bear=and the beast which I saw was like unto a leopard, and his feet were as the feet of a Bear." [Revelations 13:2], North Pole Star, veil to the real name which means Dove, or Sheepfold, or Chariot, Diana sacred animal

Two Bears=The two bears denote the Mother (Typhon) and her son (Set) [Satan]

Bees= Diana's sacred animals, sign of Cancer, symbol of Set or Satan. There are eleven bees on the arch of the Plantard crest; eleven, of course, is an occult number, emblem of Egyptian royalty, wisdom, Mormons and Masons (used symbol), Zeus (born in cave of bees Bee-man), son Meliteus (by nymph hid from Hera Zeus fed him by bees), Dionysus (feed honey by nymph), symbols of Demeter, Cybele, Diana, Rhea and the Ephesian Artemis, bees are lunar and virgin. The bee appears on statues of Artemis, State of Utah

Merovingian Kings= (model), King Solomon himself, priest-King Melchizedek, sorcerer Kings of Atlantis, The Magi, hidden power of the honeycomb, Lucifer's incarnation

Mormon's=honeycomb, bee rule by the elite over a "worker colony"

Beehive=multitude of the offspring of the Merovingian bloodline
Goddess Diana=Merovingians, Essenes (King Bee), Queen Bee, Priestesses (Melissae) the bees (nymph), Mithraism
Typhonian current=lineage of Satan
Holy Grail = red cross placed over circle

SECTION IV

Babylon Rising

12

The Lost Tribe

The Apostate Tribe of Dan

In the apostate tribe of Dan, many of the ideas and themes discussed thus far will begin to converge and make a complete picture.

Mary Magdalene was attached to the regional Order of Dan.

"The tribe of Dan later became involved *in the worship of false gods* when they relocated from their inheritance by the seacoast of Israel to the northern area of **Palestine at Mount Hermon** [location of the fallen angels covenant]. Considering Samson's apostasy and the idolatrous history of the tribe of Dan, it may be that Samson's riddle was an end-time prophecy revealing Dan's alliance with pagan cultures **whose agenda was *to reestablish a future Golden Age*. A restoration of the Golden Age of Saturn**, the pre-flood civilization which God judged, would be accomplished on the ruins of the tribe of Judah, the bloodline of Jesus Christ, or more likely, **the overthrow of Jesus Christ by Satan's demonic bloodline**. This future coup may have been typified by Samson as honey (gnosis/ancient wisdom) in the carcass (dead body) of the Lion of Judah (Jesus Christ). J.

R. Church states that the apostate tribe of Dan specifically engaged in the worship of the Mother goddess, Diana, which they adopted from the indigenous Canaanites who had occupied the northern area of Palestine at Mt. Hermon. Church also posits that the Danites exported this goddess worship to Greece after the Assyrian invasion in 722 B.C." (The Book of Secrets – Reflections and Notes on the Royal Families of the Grail Page 21)

"Just as the Messiah has His roots in the tribe of Judah, **the antichrist may have his roots in the tribe of Dan.** " (Church Chapter Six The Roots of the Merovingians. Page 116)

"The founder of Troy was named *Dar-dan-us*. It contains the name of Dan! **Dardanus was the son of Zeus**. Dardanus had a son named *Erichthonius*, who had a son named *Tros*, who was the namesake of the ancient Trojans and of their capital city, Troy. Tros had three sons, *Ilus, Ganymede* and *Assaracus. Priam,* the reigning King of the Trojans, was in the line of Ilus. *Aeneas,* founder of the Roman Empire, was a prince of the royal house of Assaracus. Ganymede was the great-grandson of Dardanus, the founder of Troy."

"According to *Homer's Iliad (Book V)* Zeus kidnapped the prince, Ganymede. Zeus wanted Ganymede to be a special **cupbearer to the gods** (which may be a clue to the origin of the legend of the so-called Holy Grail). In the kidnapping epic, **Zeus turned into an eagle**! This is a possible connection to the *progenitors of the ancient Trojans with the tribe of Dan,* who had adopted the eagle as their insignia. **Zeus has been pictured as an eagle as well as a serpent** to **whom offerings of honey were made!**"

"Merovingian French royalty claimed **descent from the Trojans**. The story of the Trojan horse brought the downfall of Troy, Trojan royalty then scattered throughout Europe." (Church Chapter Six The Roots of The Merovingian. Page 101-110)

"When Jacob who later became Israel the father of the 12 tribes of Israel was dying, he gathered his twelve sons around his bed to give proper prophecies on what their fate and their future would be. He spoke of *Judah* as a lion and said that *the scepter shall not depart from Judah until Shiloh came* which is taken to be a prediction of the coming Messiah. But then he spoke of Dan,

> **"Dan shall be a serpent** by the way, an adder in the path, that biteth the horse heels, so that his rider shall fall backward." [Genesis 49:17].

"Here we see on the trail of the serpent a reminder of the prophecy to Adam and Eve, **that the serpent shall bruise the heel of the Messiah, the seed of the woman**. The dying Jacob referred to Dan under the **insignia of the serpent**.

"These symbols take us back to the ancient Zodiac, to Judah was given the Insignia of Leo the lion, and *to Dan was given the Insignia of Scorpio, the seed of the serpent.* The reference by the dying Jacob could be a prediction that the offspring of **Dan may one day produce Mr. 666** who would attempt to sit upon the throne of the world. In Revelation 7 the 144,000 Israelites are listed. All of the tribes are given but the tribe of Dan. By the time we reach that point in world history, the time of Revelation Chapter 7, the tribe of Dan is missing. The implication is that Dan will produce the great usurper, the Antichrist." (Church Chapter Six The Roots of the Merovingians. Page 101-128)

> "4 And I heard the number of them which were sealed: and there were sealed an hundred and forty and four thousand of all the tribes of the children of Israel.
> 5 Of the **tribe of Juda** were sealed twelve thousand.
> Of the **tribe of Reuben** were sealed twelve thousand.
> Of the **tribe of Gad** were sealed twelve thousand.
> 6 Of the **tribe of Aser** were sealed twelve thousand.
> Of the **tribe of Nepthalim** were sealed twelve thousand.
> Of the **tribe of Manassas** were sealed twelve thousand.
> 7 Of the **tribe of Simeon** were sealed twelve thousand.
> Of the **tribe of Levi** were sealed twelve thousand.
> Of the **tribe of Issachar** were sealed twelve thousand.
> 8 Of the **tribe of Zebulon** were sealed twelve thousand.
> Of the **tribe of Joseph** were sealed twelve thousand.
> Of the **tribe of Benjamin** were sealed twelve thousand.
> [Revelation 7:4-8]

Excerpts from the apocryphal book of the *Testament of Dan*;

Chapter 5; 1 Observe, therefore, my children, the commandments of the Lord, And keep His law; Depart from wrath, And hate lying, That the Lord may dwell among you, And Beliar may flee from you." (The Testament of Dan)

Beliar: "lord of the forest," Beliar, a name of Satan, Definition: "lord of the forest", Beliar, a name of Satan. Usage: Belial, a demon, and in fact a name for Satan. (955.Beliar)

2 Speak truth each one with his neighbour, So shall ye not fall into wrath and confusion; But ye shall be in peace, having the God of peace, So shall no war prevail over you. 3 Love the Lord through all your life, And one another with a true heart. 4 **I know that in the last days ye shall depart from the Lord, And ye shall provoke Levi unto anger, And fight against Judah; But ye shall not prevail against them, For an angel of the Lord shall guide them both; For**

by them shall Israel stand. 5 **And whensoever ye depart from the Lord, ye shall walk in all evil and work the abominations of the Gentiles, going a-whoring after women of the lawless ones, while with all wickedness the spirits of wickedness work in you. 6 For I have read in the book of Enoch, the righteous, that your prince is Satan**, and that all the spirits of wickedness and pride will conspire to attend constantly on the sons of Levi, to cause them to sin before the Lord. 7 And my sons will draw near to Levi, And sin with them in all things; And the sons of Judah will be covetous, Plundering other men's goods like lions. 8 **Therefore shall ye be led away with them into captivity, And there shall ye receive all the plagues of Egypt.** And all the evils of the Gentiles. 9 And so when ye return to the Lord ye shall obtain mercy, And He shall bring you into His sanctuary, And He shall give you peace. 10 And there shall arise unto you from the tribe of Judah and of Levi the salvation of the Lord; And he shall make war against Beliar and execute an everlasting vengeance on our enemies: 11 And the captivity shall he take from Beliar the souls of the saints, And turn disobedient hearts unto the Lord, And give to them that call upon him eternal peace. 12 And the saints shall rest in Eden, And in the New Jerusalem will the righteous rejoice, And it shall be unto the glory of God for ever. 13 And no longer shall Jerusalem endure desolation, Nor Israel be led captive; For the Lord shall be in the midst of it living amongst men, And the Holy One of Israel shall reign over it in humility and in poverty; and he who believeth on Him shall reign amongst men in truth.

CHAPTER 7 1 And when he had said these things, he kissed them and fell asleep at a good old age. 2 And his sons buried him. And after that they carried up his bones, and placed them near Abraham, and Isaac, and Jacob. **3 Nevertheless, Dan prophesied unto them that they should forget their God and should be alienated from the land of their inheritance and from the race of Israel, and from the family of their seed.** (The Testament of Dan)

"In the book of Numbers when the Tabernacle was being built and the various tribes were placed at various locations, **on the north side were Asher, Neftali, and Dan.**" [Numbers 2:25].

The specific position of the Danites on the north side of the camp may be prophetic of their eventual location at the extreme North End of the nation at the Lebanon border. It may also be connected to the prophecy given by Isaiah concerning *the fall of Lucifer*;

> "How art thou fallen from heaven O Lucifer son of the morning how art thou cut down to the ground which did this weaken the nations for thou hast said in thine heart I will ascend it to heaven I will exalt my throne above the stars of God I will sit also upon the mount of the **congregation in the sides of the north**." [Isaiah 14:12 -13]

Notes from the Open Bible say; *the north side means in the place of control*. Could it be that the

tribe of Dan who was situated on the north side of the congregation was the target of Lucifer? (Church Chapter Six The Roots of the Merovingians. Page 101-128)

> [1] These are the sons of Israel; Reuben, Simeon, Levi, and Judah, Issachar, and Zebulun, [2] Dan, Joseph, and Benjamin, Naphtali, Gad, and Asher. [I Chronicles 2:1-2].

"Dan was the largest tribe in Israel in the days of the tabernacle. Their population was numbered 157,600. After conquering Canaan, Dan was the last tribe to receive any land. Though they were the largest tribe they received the smallest amount of territory, west of Jerusalem, down to the Mediterranean coast."

"After the death of Samson however they were deprived even of that land and had to migrate north to southern Lebanon. There they captured the city of Laish and changed its name to Dan. Thus we have the term in the Old Testament, from *Dan to Beersheba*. The ancient name *Laish means a lion* which fulfills the prophecy of Moses in Deuteronomy 33: 22 when he said, *Dan is a lion's well, he shall leak from Bashan*. In I Chronicles 1-8, the Israelite tribes are listed, all that is but the tribe of Dan. The date for writing the first eight chapters of the Chronicles has been placed at 1056 BC. By then Dan had become a lost tribe." (Church Chapter Six The Roots of the Merovingians. Page 101-128)

Chronicles goes on to list the genealogy of the sons of Israel;
I Chronicles 4:1 – Judah
I Chronicles 4:24 -Simeon
I Chronicles 5:1 -Reuben
I Chronicles 6:1 – Levi
I Chronicles 6:77- Zebulun
I Chronicles 6:80 – Gad
I Chronicles 7:1 Issachar
I Chronicles 7:6 – Benjamin
I Chronicles 7:13 – Naphtali
I Chronicles 7:20 – Ephraim (son of Joseph)
I Chronicles 7:30 -Asher

The sons of Dan are missing from this list.

Dan Symbology

"The standard of the tribe was of *white and red*, and the crest upon it, and *eagle, the great foe to serpents*, which had been chosen by the leader instead of a serpent, because Jacob had compared

Dan to a serpent. It may prove worthwhile to consider the possible connection to the tribe of **Dan whenever an eagle is used as the symbol of a subsequent leaders or nations.** Here are the clues which could connect the tribe of Dan with the political leaders of the Greeks, the Romans, the Germans, the French, and all of the thrones of Europe including leaders of ancient czarist Russia. Not only have those nations displayed the symbol of the eagle, but their colors have primarily been white and red, the colors of the Danites. It may be more than a coincidence that the Knights Templar wore white uniforms displaying a red cross on the chest." (Church Chapter Six The Roots of the Merovingians. Page 101-128)

"Four symbols are used in the Bible concerning the Danites — a serpent, an eagle, a lion, and the bees. In the story of *Samson* [In the Book of Judges], we find the famous riddle of the bees who made honey in the carcass of a lion which had been killed by Samson. The symbolic nature of the bees could represent the concept that the descendants of the tribe of Dan would one day try to bring about the destruction of the tribe of Judah, whose symbol was the lion, and from the carcass of the lion the tribe of Dan would attempt to produce the golden age of a world empire, symbolized by the honey. The Merovingians claim of coming from the tribe of Judah (through Mary Magdalene and Jesus Christ) is not true. The lie may have been advanced because the symbol of Judah was the lion. However, I believe the Merovingians were from the tribe of Dan." (The Book of Secrets – Reflections and Notes on the Royal Families of the Grail Page 20-21)

"According to historian *Flavius Josephus* the symbol of the ancient Spartans *was an eagle with a dragon in his claws.* The dragon by the way was synonymous with the snake among the early cultures. This is an incredible clue linking the tribe of Dan with the Spartans of southern Greece. It is curious to note that the *Spartans claim to be brothers to the tribes of Israel of the stock of Abraham,* displaying the symbol of an eagle and its enemy, the snake. When *Herod the Great* built the magnificent temple in the years before the birth of Christ, he placed a huge eagle above the gate."

Spartans

"Aside from the fact that the Spartans wore long hair like Samson there is a legend about the son of *Belus*, King of the Spartans who arrived in Greece with his daughters by ships. According to the legend his daughters called themselves *Danades*, they introduced *the cult of the Mother goddess* which became the established religion of the Arcadians and developed over the years until the worship of Diana. Diana may be another form of Dan."

"The Spartans so love their King that they called themselves *Danaans,* long before they adopted the name of Spartans. The symbol of imperial Rome was a single headed eagle but after Constantine divided the empire in the 4th century AD and moved his throne to Constantinople, a two headed eagle evolved as a symbol of the Byzantine Roman Empire. "

(Church Chapter Six The Roots of the Merovingians. Page 101-128)

Note: Recall the Merovingians were called "the long-haired Kings."

Khazars

"In the 9th century, most of the Thrones of Europe were established including the huge Jewish Kingdom known as the *Khazarian Kingdom of the Caesars*. It was located above the Black Sea and offered a refuge for all of the tribes of the diaspora. **Could the Khazars have been Danites?** Strangely enough, there are four major rivers that ran through the Kingdom of the Khazars emptying into the Black Sea. There is the Danube, the Dnister, the Dnieber, and the Don. It appears to have been a common theme for the people of Dan to name their rivers by their ancient forefathers. The Jordan river weaves like a snake along the eastern border of the land of Israel and is named after the ancient tribe of Dan. **Jordan means *the going down of the Dan.*"** (Church Chapter Six The Roots of the Merovingians. Page 101-128)

Caesars

"The Caesars ruled under the symbol of the two-headed eagle (same as the Habsburgs). So the tribe of Dan could possibly go as follows the Romans came from the Trojans came from the Spartans admit to being brothers to the Jewish people and sack of Abraham." (Church Chapter Six The Roots of the Merovingians. Page 101-128)

Various flags with eagles
Note; not necessarily connected to "Dan"

Connecting the Dots

Mary Magdalene=Tribe of Dan

Tribe of Dan=idol worship, seacoast, Mt. Hermon, Samson, Long hair, golden age of Saturn, pre-flood world, ruin Judah, overthrow Christ, goddess Diana, anti-Christ, serpent, eagle, lion, bees, Scorpion (seed of serpent), white and red, Merovingians, alienated from the land of their inheritance, race of Israel, family of their seed, north

Samson=Dan, honey, lion

Red and White=Danites, Knights Templar, European nations, czarist Russia

Trojans=Dardanus (son of Zeus) grandson Tros (Trojans) three sons, Ilus, Ganymede and Assaracus, Merovingians, scattered Europe

Aeneas=founder Roman Empire, prince of Assaracus.

Eagle=Zeus, tribe of Dan, Greeks, Romans, Germans, French, all of the thrones of Europe, czarist Russia

Zeus=eagle, serpent, honey

Spartans=eagle with dragon in claws, Dan, claim lineage of Abraham, eagle, serpent, Herod the Great

Khazria=thrones of Europe, black sea, Danites, Danube, Dnister, Dnieber, Don, Jordan (going down of the Dan)

Double headed eagle=Caesars, Hapsburg, Freemasons,

Romans=Trojans=Spartans=Dan

13

X-Man

Nimrod the Mighty Hunter
Ancient Assyrian relief

In *Thy Queendom Come*, our focus was on the "illusive" Queen of Babylon, *Semiramis*, who in legend purports to be the wife and mother of Nimrod. Please review our comprehensive writings on Semiramis. In this account, we must study Nimrod. Nimrod, the founder of Babylon and many other cities, was considered the firstly earthly ruler. Nimrod departed from God, and all evil workings originated from Babylon and spread across the world from the division at the Tower of Babel.

"Historians have never been able to place Nimrod into the history of Mesopotamia, but many believe that the name "Nimrod" (meaning "rebellious one") was a description of his character, and that his real name was, or later became *Gilgamesh*. Sumer was the first civilization of the ancient world, and Gilgamesh is mentioned as an early King of Sumer in the Sumerian King list. The Epic of Gilgamesh describes him as very large, aggressive, and sexually obsessed; therefore, may well have had Nephilim genes from his ancestors." (Sorenson)

Babel

> [10] And the beginning of his kingdom was Babel, and Erech, and Accad, and Calneh, in the land of Shinar. [11] Out of that land went forth Asshur, and builded Nineveh, and the city Rehoboth, and Calah, [12] And Resen between Nineveh and Calah: the same is a **great city.** [Genesis 10:10-12]

This scripture denotes a great city, the same as Revelation 17, which is the chapter that speaks about Mystery Babylon.

> 18 And the woman which thou sawest is that **great city**, which reigneth over the kings of the earth. [Revelation 17:18]

"Now it was Nimrod who excited them to such an affront and contempt of God. He was the grandson of ham, the son of Noah, a bold man, and of great strength of hand. He persuaded them not to ascribe it to God as if it was through his means they were happy, but to believe that it was their own courage that procured that happiness. **He also gradually changed the government into tyranny**, seeing no other way of turning men from the fear of God, but to bring them into constant dependence upon his power. He also said he would be revenged on God, if he should have a mind to drown the world again, for that he would build a tower too high for the waters to be able to reach, and that he would avenge himself on God for destroying their forefathers. Now the multitude were very ready to follow the determination of Nimrod, and to esteem it a piece of cowardice to submit to God, and they built a tower neither sparing any pains nor being in any degree negligent about the work, and, by reason of the multitude of hands employed in it grew very high sooner than anyone could expect." (Hislop Chapter IV. Book 2 Concerning the Tower of Babylon, and the Confusion of Tongues)

Cush

"If Ninus was Nimrod, who was the historical Bel. He must have been Cush for "Cush begat Nimrod " (Gen. 10. 8); and Cush is generally represented as having been a ringleader in the great apostasy. But, again, Cush, as the son of Ham, was Her-mes or Mercury; for Hermes is just an Egyptian synonym for the "son of Ham."

"Now, Hermes was the great original prophet of idolatry; Cush, the son of Ham, was the divider of the speeches of men. He, it would seem had been the ringleader in the scheme for building the great city and tower of Babel, and as the **well-known title of Hermes**, interpreter of the gods. He caused the language of men to be divided and themselves to be scattered abroad on the face of the earth. That Cush was known to Pagan antiquity under the very character of belle Bel, *the confounder*, chaos is just one of the established forms of the name of Cush. Associated with the two-headed Janus." (Hislop)

Power

What was the source of Nimrod's great power, one may ask? According to the ancient book of Jasher and many historical records, the clothes of skin that covered Adam and Eve in the garden were that source of power. This account parallels the Masonic tradition of the aprons, one of the secret interpretations in Freemasonry. These garments or relics were said to hold supernatural abilities that gave the possessor extraordinary strength and might.

"The first among the leaders of the corrupt men was Nimrod. His father Cush had married his mother at an advanced age, and Nimrod, the offspring of this belated union, was particularly dear to him as the son of his old age. **He gave him the clothes made of skins with which God had furnished Adam and Eve at the time of their leaving Paradise**. Cush himself had gained possession of them through Ham. From Adam and Eve they had descended to Enoch, and from him to Methuselah, and to Noah, and the last had taken them with him into the ark. When the inmates of the ark were about to leave their refuge, Ham stole the garments and kept them concealed, finally passing them on to his first-born son Cush. Cush in turn hid them for many years. When his son Nimrod reached his twentieth year, he gave them to him." (Ginzberg, Legends of the Jews Nimrod. Page 77)

"[30]And Nimrod became strong when he put on the garments, and God gave him might and strength, and he was a mighty hunter in the earth, yea, he was a mighty hunter in the field, and he haunted the animals and he built altars, and he offered upon them the animals before the Lord." [Jasher 7:30]

"[45] **And all nations and tongues heard of his fame, and they gathered themselves to him, and they bowed down to the earth, and they brought him offerings, and he became their lord and king,** and they all dwelt with him in the city of Shinar, and **Nimrod reigned in the earth over all the sons of Noah**, and they were all under his power and counsel. [46] And all the earth was of one tongue and words of union, but Nimrod did not go in the ways of the Lord, and he was more wicked than all the men that were before him, from the days of the flood until those days. [47] And he made gods of wood and stone, and he bowed down to them, and he rebelled against the Lord, and taught all his subjects and the people of the earth his wicked ways, and Mardon his son was more wicked than his father." [Jasher 8:45-47] (Johnson, Ken, Th.D.)

> "¹³ These have one mind, and shall give their power and strength unto the beast." [Revelation 17:13]

The Word of God always sets up parallels and prototypes, the nations of the earth at that time, all yielding their power to Nimrod. The same event will occur during the end times.

Mardon, his son, is reflective of Marduk, the son of the Babylonian god Baal, who conquered the great monster Tiamat. These myths are always reflective of actual historical figures. Mardon=Marduk. (Lynn Chapter 27 Babylonian gods. Page 308)

"Patron deity of the capital, the great conqueror. Babylon is the beloved city of Marduk, *great lord*, the king of heaven and earth. Bel expressly transfers his title, *lord of lands* of Marduk. Bel and Marduk blend and he takes control over kings, the land and its inhabitants. On his head rests a crown of high horns. Life and death are in his hands.(Jastrow, The Pantheon in the Days of Hammurabi. Page 115-121)

X-Man

> ¹⁰ Cush begot Nimrod; he began to be a giant [gigas] hunter on the earth" [1 Chronicles 1:10].

1. In Genesis, the *gibbor* were giants/Nephilim
2. Nimrod became a *gibbor* in Genesis
3. Therefore, per Genesis, Nimrod became a giant/Nephilim

"Nimrod began to be something he was not before—a giant (i.e., a Nephilim). Pure linguistical and contextual analysis yields this result. One does not need to resort to myth and legend to make this deduction. **Nimrod is linked by the word gibbor to the Nephilim of Genesis**. But how did the giants (i.e., Nephilim) in Genesis 6:4 come about? *By fallen angels mating with humans.* By the same process of reasoning, one would deduce that the contextual inference is that if Nimrod is a giant (i.e., Nephilim) like the those in Genesis 6:4, then he became a giant/Nephilim in the same way: by the matting of fallen angels with humans."

Nimrod's mother, rather than his father, is the more plausible source of Nimrod becoming a Nephilim. Many theologians have come to these conclusions;

- Nimrod was a Nephilim
- His mother was a fallen female angel who also became his wife
- His wife instituted the Babylonian Mystery Religion

> "8 The beast that thou sawest was, and is not; and shall ascend out of the bottomless pit, and go into perdition: and they that dwell on the earth shall wonder, whose names were not written in the book of life from the foundation of the world, when they behold the beast that was, and is not, and yet is." [Revelation 17:8]

- Nimrod is the Assyrian beast of the sea

> " 5 Then the angel that talked with me went forth, and said unto me, Lift up now thine eyes, and see what is this that goeth forth. 6 And I said, What is it? And he said, This is an ephah that goeth forth. He said moreover, This is their resemblance through all the earth. 7 And, behold, there was lifted up a talent of lead: and this is a woman that sitteth in the midst of the ephah. 8 And he said, This is wickedness. And he cast it into the midst of the ephah; and he cast the weight of lead upon the mouth thereof. 9 Then lifted I up mine eyes, and looked, and, behold, there came out two women, and the wind was in their wings; for they had wings like the wings of a stork: and they lifted up the ephah between the earth and the heaven. 10 Then said I to the angel that talked with me, Whither do these bear the ephah? 11 And he said unto me, To build it an house in the land of Shinar: and it shall be established, and set there upon her own base. " [Zechariah 5:5-11]

- The woman carried in the *ephah (measure)* to the land of Shinar by the two-winged female was Semiramis.
- Entities that represent this Babylonian Mystery Religion come back home to roost [Zechariah 5:9-11] (Cauley)

"All tradition from the earliest times bears testimony to the apostasy of **Nimrod, and to his success in leading men away from the patriarchal faith and delivering their minds from that awe of God and fear of the judgments of heaven that must have rested on them while yet the memory of the flood was recent**. And according to all the principles of depraved human nature, this too, no doubt, was one grand element in his fame; for men will readily rally around anyone who can give the least appearance of plausibility to any doctrine which will teach that they can be assured of happiness and heaven at last, though their hearts and natures are unchanged, and though they live without God in the world. How great was the boon conferred by Nimrod on the human race, in the estimation of ungodly men, by emancipating them from the impressions of true religion."

"Although Nimrod [aka Orion/Saturn/Tammuz] as a type of the Anti-Christ who will soon be revealed, *this false messiah* was able to draw the multitudes into his one-world religion." (The Book of Secrets – Reflections and Notes on the Royal Families of the Grail Page 61-62)

"The esoteric interpretation of the myth of Isis and Osiris is disclosed in Spiritual Politics: Changing the World From the Inside Out: "Like the goddess Isis, who found and restored all of the lost pieces of her husband, Osiris, many are restoring the unity of all life, bringing together the separate parts of humanity — different races, religions and cultures."

"From this understanding, we may infer that **Osiris was Nimrod—the great hunter of men and unifier of mankind under a pagan religious system**—who, as stated by Hislop, '**was the prototype, the grand original**'. Nimrod was simply venerated in various cultures under different names: Osiris, Tammuz, Wotan, Viracocha, Quetzalcoatl, Varuna, etc. All were priest-Kings who taught mankind the ancient mysteries as well as academic disciplines. By reason of the supernatural powers and intellectual prowess of these divine beings, the civilization of mankind was greatly advanced. All are expected to return to earth to revive the ancient pre-flood mysteries and culture." (The Book of Secrets – Reflections and Notes on the Royal Families of the Grail Page 70)

"**The legendary symbol for Nimrod is "X:** the use of this symbol denotes witchcraft. When X is used as a shortened form for Christmas it actually means "to celebrate the feast of Nimrod." The double X means to cross or betray, indicating *one's betrayal into the hands of Satan.* Nimrod also introduced the practice of genocide and cannibalism It was said that when Abraham's birth was announced that Nimrod called for the execution of all children but Abraham was hid in a cave." (Eddie)

"**Fish were originally worshiped as a symbol of Nimrod**; Each priest is depicted wearing a fish-head mitre. One of the names of this god in Babylon and Philistia was Dagon (dag=fish, on=Sun). The head of the fish formed a mitre above that of a man, while it's scaly, fin-like tail fell as a cloak behind, leaving the human feet and limbs exposed."

Dagon with a Fish Mitre – Pope Francis with a Fish Mitre
Headdress from Babylon

"**When Nimrod died, he became the "Sun**." Semiramis claimed that she gave birth to Nimrod (reborn) who was called Tammuz. This story has traveled down through time. Nimrod worshipers believed that when he was going through this transformation that the Fish God was protecting him." (Eddie)

"In *The Two Babylons*, Hislop elucidates the reason for the lamentation for Osiris/Tammuz/Nimrod et al. The untimely death of this false messiah, known in other cultures as Tammuz, Nimrod, Wotan, Viracocha, Quetzalcoatl and Varuna, meant **the dissolution of the global religious system established by this demi-god**. Because God put an end to Nimrod's 'unity in diversity' experiment, He is forever labeled as the Scorpion in the Zodiac."

"The infant by the *serpentine goddess* is not yet a Nephilim (giant) but has Nephilim DNA and will eventually grow into a Nephilim (giant). Semiramis, who even had the children of Israel fooled into (Tammuz), who is a hybrid that also would grow to be a giant like his father, Nimrod." (Cauley)

Semiramis

"Semiramis, that beautiful but abandoned queen of Babylon was not only herself a paragon of unbridled lust and licentiousness, but in the Mysteries which she had a chief hand in forming, she was worshiped as Rhea, the great "Mother" of the gods, with such atrocious rites as identified her with Venus, the Mother of all impurity, and raised the very city where she had reigned to a bad eminence among the nations, as the grand seat at once of idolatry and consecrated prostitution. Apocalyptic emblem of the Harlot woman with the cup in her hand was even embodied in the symbols of idolatry derived from ancient Babylon. The Roman Church has actually taken this very symbol as her own chosen emblem." (Hislop Distinctive Character of the Two Systems. Page 5-11)

"Thus from Assyria, Egypt, and Greece, we have cumulative and overwhelming evidence, all conspiring to demonstrate that the child worshiped in the arms of the goddess-mother in all these countries in the very character of **Ninus or Nin, 'The Son,' was Nimrod, the son of Cush**. A feature here, or an incident there, may have been borrowed from some succeeding hero; but it seems impossible to doubt, that of that child Nimrod was the prototype, the grand original." (The Book of Secrets – Reflections and Notes on the Royal Families of the Grail Page 60)

Mystery Religion

"The *Mystery Religion of Babylon* might be better described as the unfinished work of Semiramis. Historically, the Babylonian Mystery Religion was her baby. Mystery Babylon was started by a woman and will end with a woman."

> " [5] And upon her forehead was a name written, Mystery, Babylon the Great, The Mother of Harlots and abominations of the earth." [Revelation 17:5]

"The Anti-Christ (the beast who comes out of the bottomless pit a few verses later in Rev 17:8) is Nimrod."

> " [8] The beast that thou sawest was, and is not, and shall ascend out of the bottomless pit, and go into perdition, and they that dwell on the earth shall wonder, whose names were not written in the book of life from the foundation of the world, when they behold the beast that was, and is not, and yet is." [Revelation 17:8]

"If the beast is Nimrod, a mere demi-god, why not allow the possibility that the woman in Chapter 17 is Semiramis, a fallen angelic goddess? After all, she is depicted as the *Queen of Heaven*, spanning the pages of Scripture from Genesis to Revelation."

Nimrod's Legacy

- Nimrod was the actual father of the gods
- First deified mortal
- Nimrod as Cronos/Saturn meant *the horned one*
- The Assyrian *Hercules* is Nimrod the giant as he is called in the Septuagint
- He sets the bull's horns on his head as a trophy of victory and a symbol of power
- Nimrod pictured as a bull with wings means;
- Nimrod's army or *mighties* were under his "wings' or his command

- Nimrod's *mighties* or *winged ones* were often represented as winged serpents

Fate of the god

If Osiris was Nimrod, as we have seen, that violent death that the Egyptians so pathetically deplored in their annual festivals was just the death of Nimrod. The accounts in several mysteries of the different countries all adhere to the same effect. The statement of Plato shows that in his day, the Egyptian Osiris was identical to Tammuz. Tammuz is well known to have been the same as Adonis, the famous huntsman, for whose death Venus is fabled to have made such bitter lamentations. As the women of Egypt wept for Osiris, as the Phoenician and Assyrian women wept for Tammuz, so in Greece and Rome, the women wept for Bacchus, whose name, as we have seen, means " The bewailed," or "Lamented one.

Killed by Shem

"Now when *Shem* had so powerfully wrought upon the minds of men as to induce them to make a terrible example of the great Apostate, and when that Apostate's dismembered limbs were sent to the chief cities, were no doubt his system had been established, it will be readily perceived that, in these circumstances, if idolatry was to continue–if, above all, it was to take a step in advance, it was indispensable that it should operate in secret. The terror of an execution, inflicted on one so mighty as Nimrod, made it needful that, for some time to come at least, the extreme of caution should be used. In these circumstances, then, began, there can hardly be a doubt, that system of "Mystery," which, having Babylon for its centre, has spread over the world. **In these Mysteries, under the seal of secrecy and the sanction of an oath, and by means of all the fertile resources of magic, men were gradually led back to all the idolatry that had been publicly suppressed, while new features were added to that idolatry that made it still more blasphemous than before. That magic and idolatry were twin sisters, and came into the world together, we have abundant evidence.**" (Dumond)

Killed by Esau

" ⁴And on a certain day Esau went in the field to hunt and he found Nimrod walking in the wilderness with his two men...⁶ and Nimrod and his men that were with him did not know him, and Nimrod and his men frequently walked about in the field at the cool of the day, and to know where his men were hunting in the field. ⁷ and then brought in two of his men that were with him came to the place where they were, when Esau started suddenly from his lurking place, and drew his sword and hastened and ran to Nimrod and cut off his head. ⁸ and Esau fought a desperate fight with these two men that were with Nimrod and when they called out to him, he saw turned to them as smote them to death with his sword...¹⁰ and when Esau saw the mighty men of Nimrod coming at a distance, he fled, and thereby escaped, and **Esau took the valuable**

garments of Nimrod, which Nimrod's father had bequeathed to Nimrod, and with which Nimrod prevailed over the whole land, and he ran unconcealed them in his house. [Jasher 27:4, 6-8, 10] (Johnson, Ken, Th.D.)

The story then goes on to say that Esau went to his home, he was exhausted and ready to die from the fierce battle. At this juncture, he makes the fateful decision to "sell his birthright" to Jacob. The book of Jasher does not explain the fate of those magical relics. In legend, the garments are supposedly in the "safe keeping" of a secret society.

[17] And at the death of Nimrod his Kingdom became divided into many divisions, and all those parts that Nimrod reigned over were restored to the respective kings of the land, who recovered them after the death of membrane, and all the people of the House of Nimrod were for a long time enslaved to all the other kings of the land". [Jasher 27:17](Johnson, Ken, Th.D.)

The account of Nimrod's death at either the hand of Shem or the hand of Esau is fascinating in deed considering their fate. Keep in mind the history of Nimrod's death does not occur in the canon of Scripture. So there is no actual data to validate either account.

Jasher is a book of antiquity that puts the end of Nimrod solely at the hands of Esau. The later account given by Reverend Hislop and others puts the killing at the hands of Shem, which issues the 12 tribes of Israel in which Esau=Edom are perpetual enemies.

> " [23] The Lord said to her, "Two nations are in your womb; And two peoples will be separated from your body; And one people shall be stronger than the other; And the older shall serve the younger." [Genesis 25:23]

Connecting the Dots

Nimrod=Gilgamesh, Bel, mighty hunter, rebellious one, gibbor, Nephilim, the Assyrian beast, Orion, Saturn, Tammuz, Wotan, Viracocha, Quetzalcoatl, Varuna, priest-King, supernatural powers, Scorpion, genocide, cannibalism, X, child worshiped on lap of mother goddess, beast of the sea, anti-Christ, fish (symbol), became the sun, first deified mortal, father of gods, horned one, bull, Hercules, bull horns, wings, army "winged serpents", head cut off, chopped in pieces, Shem, Esau

Adam and Eve garments =Ham, survived flood, Cush, Nimrod, Esau (took garments)

Cush=Hermes, Mercury, Bel (the con-founder),chaos, Janus, taught Atlantean doctrine

Semiramis=serpentine goddess, Rhea, Diana, harlot, cup of abominations, Venus, fallen angel, husband Saturn, Isis, Nana, Eve, Ishtar, Demeter, Hecate, Themis, Hera, Astraea, Diana, Cybele, Fortuna, Erigone, Sibylla, Virgin Mother, whore of Babylon.

Tammuz=hybrid, Adonis, Marduk, Jupiter, Horus

Osiris cut up=tower of Babel
Roman church = harlot, Semiramis, mystery religion
Magic=idolatry

14

Cain's Mark

Esoteric Mark of Cain
This should not be confused with the BIBLICAL Mark of Can

It is at this juncture we must revisit Cain, who was the first human murderer on earth, and many scriptures attribute him as being the "wicked seed."

"In "Starfire: Gold of the Gods", Gardner elucidates the ancient pedigree of the **Dragon succession, which began with Cain,** supposedly the offspring of Eve and Satan. Gardner's revision of the Genesis account traces **the genealogy of Jesus back to Cain, who was therefore an offspring of the Anunnaki."**

"One of the interesting items from the archives of the Dragon Court was the origin of the word "Kingship." It derives from the very earliest of Sumerian culture wherein Kingship was identical with *kinship* and kin means *blood relative*. In its original form, kinship was *Kainship*. And the **first King of the Messianic Dragon succession was the biblical 'C(Kain)',** head of the Sumerian House of Kish." (The Book of Secrets – Reflections and Notes on the Royal Families of the Grail)

"According to the Dragon tradition, the importance **of Cain was that he was directly produced by Enki [Satan] and Ava [Eve], so his blood was three quarters Anunnaki**. His half-brothers *Hevel* and *Satanael* (better known as Abel and Seth) were less than half Anunnaki, being the offspring of Ateba and Ava (Adam and Eve)." (The Book of Secrets – Reflections and Notes on the Royal Families of the Grail Page 5)

"*Cain* was an advancement on the **earlier cloning experiments**, with *Hawah's* ovum further enriched with Enki's Anunnaki blood. That means that Q'ayin (Cain) emerged as the most advanced product of the Royal seed." (Gardner, Genesis of the Grail Kings Chapter Ten The Tree of Knowledge. Page 129)

"*The Mark of Cain* is defined as being an upright centered cross within a circle. It was in principle a graphic representation of Kingship, which the Hebrews called the *Malkhut*. This was a legacy of **Tiamat**, the great matriarch of the Grail bloodline. In accordance with the history of the *Imperial and Royal Court of the Dragon* an ancient fraternity with Egyptian origins from about 2170 BC the outer circle of the Mark of Cain was emblematic of a serpent-dragon clutching its own tail, a symbol of wholeness and wisdom known as the Ouroboros."

"Cain has often been called the first *Mr. Smith*. Because the term q'aying also means "smith" as in metal-smith or blade-smith, a required skill for early Kings. In the alchemical tradition he was indeed a q'ayin as were his descendants, particularly Tubal-cain (Genesis 4:22) who is revered in scientific Freemasonry. Tubal-Cain was the great Vulcan of the era, the holder of Plutonic theory and was therefore a prominent alchemist."

"The letter Q as in *Q'ayin* and Queen is metaphysically assigned to the Moon, and the *khu* (Q) was perceived as the monthly lunar female essence of the goddess. The divine menstruum constituted the purest and most potent life-force and it was venerated as *Star fire*. Its representation was the All-seeing eye (ayin) whose hermetic symbol was a pot centered within a circle, the *kamakala* of the Indian mystics, the *tribindu* of the oriental school and the Egyptian symbol for light." (Gardner, Genesis of the Grail Kings Chapter Ten The Tree of Knowledge. Page 132)

The **Mark of Cain becomes the familiar symbol of Venus**. When set about with the cross above the circle the representation is that personified by the Orb of sovereign regalia.

It is also associated with the symbolic all-seeing eye, that of *Enki* who was called *lord of the Sacred Eye*. Given that Kingship (Malkhut) was perceived as a matrilinear inheritance through *Tiamat and Lilith*, the name of Q'ayin (Kain is identified with King) was also directly associated with the definition Queen." (Gardner, Genesis of the Grail Kings Chapter Ten The Tree of Knowledge. Page 130-131)

"The letter **Q derives from the Venus symbol**, which was equally attributed to *Isis, Nin-khursag, Lilith* and *Kali* all of whom were deemed "black but beautiful" (Song of Solomon 1:5) Lilith and Kali were both titular names, with Kali appropriated from kala (the periodic time of the female lunar cycle), while Nin-khursag was the ultimate *Lady of life*. Hers was the genus that constituted the true beginning of the **sacred bloodline-the genesis of the Grail Kings**. In the Rosicrucian tradition this genesis has long been identified with the transcendent *gene of Isis*. (Gardner, Genesis of the Grail Kings Chapter Ten The Tree of Knowledge. Page 132)

"While the descendants of *Cain* resembled their father in his sinfulness and depravity, the descendants of *Seth* led a pious, well-regulated life, and the difference between the conduct of the two stocks was reflected in their habitations. The family of Seth was settled upon the mountains in the vicinity of Paradise, while the family of Cain resided in the field of Damascus, the spot whereon Abel was slain by Cain." (Ginzberg, Legends of the Jews The Generation of the Deluge. Page 15)

"God placed a mark on Cain to identify him in perpetuity for murdering Abel and lying. Occultists believe that Cain's father was not the "bad" Jehova-God but the "good" serpent Lucifer-Samael. The Mark of Cain, or cross, symbolizes a hammer, for Cain was a Worker in Metals, which is what a **practitioner of Alchemical Sorcery** is called. The Qenites tribal mark **was a tattoo on their foreheads in honour of their progenitor,** for they were and are itinerant goldsmiths, blacksmiths, carpenters, potters, peddlers, medicine men, entertainers, craftsmen, and magicians. **They also did not shear their hair**, often braiding it in the Nazorites fashion. Cain's direct descendant today whether Tubal-Cain himself, or someone else of whom we know not, has this Mark of Cain, **the cross, as a red birthmark on his chest or back.**" (Freemasonry Watch)

"**Moloch means in Hebrew the same as Cain - "King" or "Possession"**. He is also known as Baal and was part of the Phoenicians Trinitarian Deity which included Ashtoreth "our dear lady of the sea," and the handsome but fierce son who died and was reborn." (Freemasonry Watch)

"Nay, even while Adam was alive, it came to pass that the posterity of Cain became exceedingly wicked, **everyone successively dying one after the other, more wicked than the former**. They were intolerable in war, and vehement in robberies; and if anyone were slow to murder people, yet was he bold in his profligate behavior, in acting unjustly, and doing injury for gain." (Josephus)

"HP Blavatsky says that the causes which precipitated the Atlantean disaster, under the evil and simulations of their demon the vetted the Atlantis race became a nation of wicked magicians. And consequence of this war was declared the story of which will be too long to narrate is substance may be found in the **disfigured allegories of the race of Cain, the giants and that of Noah**

and his righteous family. (Hall, The Secret Teachings of All Ages The Scheme of the Universe according to the Greeks and Romans. Page 34)

> ## Connecting the Dots
>
> **Cain**=Dragon succession, Eve and Satan, Jesus lineage, Anunnaki, King, Enki (Satan) father, three quarters Anunnaki, Clone, royal seed, Mr. Smith, metal-smith (blade-smith), letter Q (Q'ayin), associated with Queen, serpent Lucifer-Samael (father), sorcery, alchemy
>
> **Mark of Cain**=upright centered cross, the Malkhut, legacy of Tiamat, ouroboros, symbol of Venus, all-seeing eye, hammer,
>
> **Tiamat=** Lilith=matriarch grail bloodline
>
> **Tubal-cain**=Vulcan, alchemist
>
> **Mother goddess**=cup (womb), King's consort
>
> **Enki**=lord of sacred eye, Cain's father,
>
> **Q**=Venus symbol, Isis, Nin-khursag, Lilith, Kali (all black but beautiful)
>
> **Nin-khursag**= Lady of life, true beginning of the sacred bloodline-the genesis of the Grail Kings.
>
> **Grail king** = gene of Isis.
>
> **Descendant tribes**=nomads, Cainites, Canaanites, Kenites, Qenites, Midianites, Sleb, Salubim, Rekhabites, Nasoreans, Mandeans, Johanites, or Nazorites, Essenes, the Druze, secretive ruling sect of Syria and Turkey known as the Alawites, Gypsies, tribal mark was a tattoo on their foreheads, goldsmiths, blacksmiths, carpenters, potters, peddlers, medicine men, entertainers, craftsmen, and magicians, didn't cut hair, braided, the cross, as a red birthmark on his chest or back."
>
> **Moloch**=Cain - "King" or "Possession", Baal, Phoenicians Trinitarian Deity
>
> **Atlantis=** disfigured allegories of the race of Cain, the giants and that of Noah and his righteous family, Babylonian

SECTION V

Lucifer's Legions

15

Fallen Angels and Nephilim

Mt. Hermon, Lebanon
Location of fallen angels descent

Fallen Angels! Are they human spiritual hybrids? As the sons of God, many have equated them to the line of Seth versus Cain. The Biblical, Apocryphal, and historical records paint a much different picture. These invisible beings have captivated our imaginations, haunted dreams, and are the source of endless debates.

"[1]And it came to pass when the children of men had multiplied that in those days were born unto them [2] beautiful and comely daughters. And the angels, the children of the heaven, saw and lusted after them, and said to one another, "Come, let us choose us wives from among the children of men [3] and beget us children." And Semjaza, who was their leader, said unto them" "I fear ye will not [4] indeed agree to do this deed, and I alone shall have to pay the penalty of a great sin. And they all answered him and said, "Let us all swear an oath, and all bind ourselves by mutual imprecations ⁵ not to abandon this plan but to do this thing." Then sware they all together and bound themselves ⁶ by mutual imprecations upon it. And they were in all two hundred; who descended in the days of Jared on the summit of Mount Hermon, and they called it Mount Hermon, because they had sworn ⁷ and bound themselves by mutual imprecations upon it. And these are the names of their leaders: Samiaza, their leader, Arakiba, Rameel, Kokabiel, Tamiel, Ramiel, Danel, Ezeqeel, Baraqijal, ⁸ Asael, Armaros, Batarel, Ananel, Zaqiel, Samsapeel, Satarel, Turel, Jomjael, Sariel. These are their chiefs of tens. [Enoch 6:1-8]

Mt Hermon is also called Sion...Priory of Scion

⁶...Thou seest what Azazel hath done, who hath taught all unrighteousness on earth and **revealed the eternal secrets which were (preserved) in heaven**, which ⁷ men were striving to learn: And Semjaza, to whom Thou has given authority to bear rule over his associates. And they have gone to the daughters of men upon the earth, and have slept with the ⁹ women, and have defiled themselves, and revealed to them all kinds of sins. And the women have ¹⁰ borne giants, and the whole earth has thereby been filled with blood and unrighteousness. [Enoch 6-10]

"The 64,800 is the number of the fallen angels, and the last one year signifies the **liberation of Lucifer and return to his original estate.**" (Hall, The Secret Teachings of All Ages Page 145)

"Schnoebelen believes that when angels initially fall, they are exceeding handsome or beautiful Nordics. Over the passage of time, however, fallen angels become serpentine, reflecting the nature of their new leader—Satan." (Cauley)

"In that hour three of the ministering angels, Uzza, Azza, and Azzael came forth and brought charges against me in the high heavens, saying before the Holy One, blessed be He "Said not the Ancient Ones (First Ones) rightly before Three: "Do not create man!" The Holy One, blessed He, answered and said unto them: "I have made and I will bear, yea, I will carry and will deliver." (Is. 46:4) (Ben Elisha Chapter 4. Page 156)

"The Angels fallen into generation are referred to metaphorically as *Serpents and Dragons of Wisdom.*" . (Blavatsky The Mysteries Among the Mayas. Page 230)

"The fall of Azazel and Semyaza came about in this way. When the generation of the deluge began to practice idolatry, God was deeply grieved. The two angels Semyaza and Azazel arose and said: "O Lord of the world! It has happened, that which we foretold at the creation of the world and of man, saying, 'What is man, that Thou art mindful of him?' " And God said, "And what will become of the world now without man?" Whereupon the angels: "We will occupy ourselves with it." Then said God: "I am well aware of it, and I know that if you inhabit the earth, the evil inclination will overpower you, and you will be more iniquitous than ever men." The angels pleaded, "Grant us but permission to dwell among men, and Thou shalt see how we will sanctify Thy Name." God yielded to their wish, saying, "Descend and sojourn among men!"

"When the angels came to earth and beheld the daughters of men in all their grace and beauty, they could not restrain their passion." (Ginzberg, Legends of the Jews The Punishment of the Fallen Angel. Page 10)

Female Fallen Angels

"Schnoebelen describes his sexual experience as a "congress (meaning sexual introitus)." Sexual introitus would be expected to refer to entrance into the vaginal tubular opening. He says that he had "sexual introitus, sexual intercourse" with this fallen angel. Would this not be sex with a fallen female angel? He says that, in doing so, he became one flesh with the entity, and the Biblical passage to which he alludes is describing sexual relations between a male and a female: "Do you not know that the one who joins himself to a harlot is one body with her? For He says, 'The two will become one flesh'" (1Cor 6:16). Schnoebelen says, "You are becoming one with a fallen angel." But the implications of his terms and citation are more explicit: If you are a male, you are becoming one with a fallen female angel. "A satanic wedding was performed, where I was married to the arch goddess Lilith." And she actually came down. And how many of you have heard of Lilith? She is a very nasty, very ancient demoness, strongman type being."(Cauley)

"One reason I am open to the possibility of fallen female angels impersonating other well-known fallen female angels is that I suspect that they would do so in order to give the illusion that these fallen female angels are omniscient, spanning history in time and space. For example, *Our Lady of Fatima* is based on the apparitions of the Blessed Virgin Mary in the village of Fatima in 1917. Actually, in my opinion, **these were apparitions of Semiramis** who was probably locked away in Tartarus at the time. In my working model, Semiramis was not released from her imprisonment until 1946. **Semiramis was (and still is) assisted in her impersonating the Virgin Mary by other fallen female angels performing these apparitions**. Semiramis knew the Biblical prophesies of the virgin who would give birth to the Messiah and, as the wife of Nimrod and Queen of Babylon, **Semiramis created a false religion in which she made herself out to be that virgin.** Therefore, very early in human history, she imitated the blessed virgin while in her earthbound mortal form. After her death, Semiramis was imprisoned in Tartarus. *Aspirations of Mary* would have had to be performed by other fallen female angels until Semiramis was released. The spirit of the mystery religion of Babylon and the worship of Our Lady (actually of Semiramis under the guise of Mary) has been kept alive and well on planet Earth, even during Semiramis' imprisonment, by the assistance of other fallen female spirits." (Cauley)

Nephilim

Pan's Grotto (satanic council)
What Christ' calls "The Gates of Hell"

Enoch has the most comprehensive details on the fallen angels. *The Book of Enoch* disappeared from mainstream texts between 300 and 400 AD. In 1773 scripts from the book of Enoch were discovered in Ethiopian monasteries by Scottish explorer *James Bruce*.

"Unfortunately, at the time of Methuselah, following the death of *Adam*, the family of Seth became corrupted after the manner of the Cainites. The two strains united with each other to execute all kinds of iniquitous deeds. **The result of the marriages between them were the Nephilim**, whose sins brought the deluge upon the world. In their arrogance, they claimed the same pedigree as the posterity of Seth, and they compared themselves with princes and men of noble descent." (Ginzberg, Legends of the Jews The Generation of the Deluge. Page 13)

[1]And all the others together with them took unto themselves wives, and each chose for himself one, and they began to go in unto them and to defile themselves with them, and they taught them charms [2] and enchantments, and the cutting of roots, and made them acquainted with plants. And they [3] became pregnant, and they bare great giants, whose height was three thousand ells: Who consumed [4] all the acquisitions of men. And when men could no longer sustain them, the giants turned against [5] them and devoured mankind. And they began to sin against birds, and beasts, and

reptiles, and [6] fish, and to devour one another's flesh, and drink the blood. Then the earth laid accusations against the lawless ones. [Enoch 7:1-6]

"Nephilim really means "those who came down" those who descended, or those who were cast down. Given that the so-called "sons of God were reputed to have caused their own dishonour by consorting with earthly women, they were said in the 2nd century BC book of Enoch and in various apocryphal writings, to have fallen from grace." (Gardner, Genesis of the Grail Kings Chapter Five Realm of the Angels. Page 52)

"A solemn council forthwith to be held at Pandemonium the high capital of Satan and his peers, their summons called from every band and squared regiment by place or choice the worthiest, they anon with hundreds and with thousands trooping came attended. Behold a wonder! They but now who seemed in bigness to surpass **earth's giant sons**, now less than smallest dwarfs in narrow room. The **great Seraphic lords and Cherubim** in close recess and secret conclave sat, a thousand demi-gods on golden seats, frequent and full. After short silence then and summons read, the great consult began." (Milton Book I)

"The Grail is a stone that is said to be brought from heaven to earth by the "neutral angels" the ones that refused to take sides in the war in heaven. The Grail therefore is said to go back in time to a mysterious priesthood of gods and demigods known as **"the Shining Ones."** The Egyptians gods of pre-dynastic period were known as the *Neter* or *Neteru*. The Neter gods were Osiris, Horus and Thoth. According to the Turin Papyrus which list the names of these gods and the later pharaohs, and the long reign of the Neter followed by a mysterious priesthood known as the *Shemsu Hor* (the followers of Horus). Horus having been the last Neter god. This priesthood was also known as the Akhu, which means "the Shining Ones." By all accounts, these gods and their priests or militant arm, who were known as the **Watchers or Nephilim** (the angels who were said to have come down from heaven). This mysterious class of beings were also said to have come from the sea. More specifically they were said to have come from a submerged land, which invokes thoughts of Atlantis." (Gardiner and Osborn Chapter One Alpha-Omega. Page 17)

"Baal was also referred to as a "prince" and called "prince and lord of the underworld," which was the place of the **"Rephaim" ("the dead ones").** Rephaim is a general term for the Nephilim in Canaan and may refer to the fact that the Nephilim were fathered by sons of God who were judged and imprisoned in Hades for their actions (i.e. they are the dead ones). The presence of the Rephaim/Nephilim in Canaanite societies thus seems to have been a significant factor in Canaanite and eventually Philistine culture. This is the heritage of the Nephilim through the person of Canaan – **a revival of the evil that existed prior to the flood.** (Sorenson)

> "Hear, O Israel! You are crossing over the Jordan today to go in to dispossess nations greater

> and mightier than you, great cities fortified to heaven, a people great and tall, the sons of the Anakim, whom you know and of whom you have heard it said, 'Who can stand before the sons of Anak?' Know therefore today that it is the Lord your God who is crossing over before you as a consuming fire. He will destroy them, and He will subdue them before you, so that you may drive them out and destroy them quickly, just as the Lord has spoken to you." [Deuteronomy 9:1-3]

"When the Israelites first entered Canaan, they attacked and destroyed the Amorites in Heshbon, north of Moab, and then proceeded farther north to Bashan. This area includes the **Mount Hermon region where the sons of God who produced the Nephilim** were said to have first appeared, so it is Nephilim "ground zero." ibid

> "Concerning Bashan, it is called the land of Rephaim." [Deuteronomy 3:13]

"It is impossible to know how many Nephilim there were, or what percentage of the population they represented, but they were apparently scattered among the Canaanite regions. They are also variously referred to as the Emim ("the dreaded ones" from Moab), the Zamzummim ("schemers" also from Moab) the Anakim (sons of Anak who lived throughout the land), and the Rephaim, discussed above."

"One of the main cites of Bashan was named Ashtaroth after the Canaanite goddess of sex and fertility, as discussed above, and an Ugaritic text places the god Rpu, the patron deity of the Rephaim in Ashtoreth. Other Ugaritic literature indicates that the Bashan cites of Ashtaroth and Edrei **were gateways to the underworld**, and the city of Ashtoreth was associated with Molech."

The Emim and the Zamzummin were annihilated before the Israelites arrived, but the Anakim were widely spread throughout the land. *Anak* was a son of *Arba*, the man who founded or more likely conquered and/or reoccupied the city of Hebron. There is a valley to the east of Jerusalem called the "Valley of the Rephaim" which was populated by Anakim, and that area also connects with the Valley of Hinnom mentioned above where children were sacrificed."

"Many have been shocked by the fact that God commanded Moses and Joshua to conduct a war of extermination against the Canaanites, where not only the men were killed, but also the women and children. How could a loving God have commanded such a thing? But this policy was only ordered and carried out against **Nephilim/Anakim/Rephaim** areas, which were the source of the evil described above. If the descendants of the Nephilim were also psychopathic, it is even more understandable why God would command this. Sentencing a psychopathic killer to death is done for the benefit of society and is an act of mercy, rather than cruelty."

"Given the fact that Nephilim characteristics of height, musculature, and psychopathology are heritable, it seems likely that they were passed via genetics. **The fact that they appeared especially in the person of Canaan, one of Ham's sons, would point to either Ham – or more likely to his wife – as the source.** Genetics is complex, and the genes controlling both extreme height and psychopathology may be recessive; like other recessive characteristics, it not certain which children of a couple will receive the genes for a given set of traits, and to what extent those traits will ultimately be exhibited by the descendants." ibid

"Unlike Ishtar, the pious maiden, *Naamah*, the lovely sister of Tubal-Cain, led the angels astray with her beauty, and from her union with *Shamdo*n sprang the devil, *Asmodeu*s. She was as shameless as all the other descendants of Cain, and as prone to bestial indulgences. Cainite women and Cainite men alike were in the habit of walking abroad naked, and they gave themselves up to every conceivable manner of lewd practices. Of such were the women whose beauty and sensual charms **tempted the angels from the path of virtue.** The angels, on the other hand, no sooner had they rebelled against God and descended to earth than they lost their transcendental qualities, and were invested with sublunary bodies, so that a union with the daughters of men became possible. The offspring of these alliances between the angels and the Cainite women **were the giants**, known for their strength and their sinfulness; as their very name, the Emim, indicates, they inspired fear. They have many other names. Sometimes they go by the name Rephaim, because one glance at them made one's heart grow weak; or by the name Gibborim, simply giants, because their size was so enormous that their thigh measured eighteen ells; or by the name Zamzummim, because they were great masters in war; or by the name Anakim, because they touched the Sun with their neck; or by the name Ivvim, because, like the snake, they could judge of the qualities of the soil; or finally, by the name Nephilim, because, bringing the world to its fall, they themselves fell." (Ginzberg, Legends of the Jews The Punishment of the Fallen Angels. Page 12)

"In their arrogance, they rose up against God. A single sowing bore a harvest sufficient for the needs of forty years, and by means of magic arts they could compel the very Sun and moon to stand ready to do their service. The raising of children gave them no trouble. They were born after a few days' pregnancy, and **immediately after birth they could walk and talk**; they themselves aided the mother in severing the navel string. Not even demons could do them harm." (Ginzberg, Legends of the Jews The Generation of the Deluge. Page 15)

"Nephilim were called the "people of the shem." The word *shem* along with the term shamaim meaning heaven derives from the root word shamah, which means "that which is highward." To the Sumerians, shems were called an-ru-"stones that rise, and to the Amorites they were fiery objects. **A shem was made of stone**, but in some form or another the Nephilim used shems and they were associated with heaven. Some writers have said that **shems were a form of transport**

akin to the fiery chariots of the Bible." (Gardner, Genesis of the Grail Kings Chapter Nine Shepherds of the Royal Seed. page 106-109)

Fallen Angel Knowledge

[1]And Azazel taught men to make swords and knives, and shields, and breastplates, and made known to them the metals of the earth and the art of working them, and bracelets, and ornaments, and use of antimony, and the beautifying of the eyelids, and all kinds of costly stones, and all [2] colouring tinctures. And there arose much godlessness, and they committed fornication, and they [3] were led astray and became corrupt in all their ways. Semjaza taught enchantments, and root-cuttings, Armaros the resolving of enchantments, Baraqijal (taught) astrology, Kokabel the constellations, Ezeqeel the knowledge of the clouds, Araqiel the signs of the earth, Shamsiel the signs of the Sun, and Sariel the course of the moon. And as men perished, they cried and their cry went up to heaven…[Enoch 8:1-3]

[1]And after this judgment they shall terrify and make them to tremble because they have shown this to those who dwell on the earth. [2] And behold the names of those angels [and these are their names]

- The first of them is Semjaza
- The second Artaquifa,
- And the third Armen,
- The fourth Kokabel,
- The fifth Turael,
- The sixth Rumjal,
- The seventh Danjal,
- The eight Neqael,
- The ninth Baraqel,
- The tenth Azazel,
- The eleventh Armaros,
- The twelfth Batarjal,
- The thirteenth Busasejal,
- The fourteenth Hananel,
- The fifteenth Turel,
- And the sixteenth Simapesiel,
- The seventeenth Jetrel,
- The eighteenth Tumeel,
- The nineteenth Turel,
- [3] The twentieth Rumael,
- The twenty-first Azazel.

And these are the chiefs of their angels and their names, and their chief ones over hundreds and over fifties and over tens.

- [4] The name of the first Jeqon: that is, the one who led astray [all] the sons of God, and brought them [5] down to the earth, and led them astray through the daughters of men.
- And the second was named Asbeel: he imparted to the holy sons of God evil counsel and led them astray so that they defiled [6] their bodies with the daughters of men.
- And the third was named Gadreel: he it is who showed the children of men all blows of death, and he led astray Eve, and showed [the weapons of death to the sons of men] the shield and the coat of mail, and the sword for battle, and all the weapons [7] of death to the children of men. And from his hand they have proceeded against those who dwell [8] on the earth from that day and forevermore.
- And the fourth was named Penemue: he taught the [9] children of men the bitter and the sweet, and he taught them all the secrets of their wisdom. And he instructed mankind in writing with ink and paper and thereby many sinned from eternity to [10] eternity and until this day. For men were not created for such a purpose, to give confirmation [11] to their good faith with pen and ink. For men were created exactly like the angels, to the intent that they should continue pure and righteous, and death, which destroys everything, could not have taken hold of them, but through this their knowledge they are perishing, and through his power [12] it is consuming me.
- And the fifth was named Kasdeja: this is he who showed the children of men all the wicked smitings of spirits and demons, and the smitings of the embryo in the womb, that it may pass away, and [the smitings of the soul] the bites of the serpent, and the smitings [13] which befall through the noontide heat, **the son of the serpent, named Taba'et**.
- And this is the task of Kasbeel, the chief of the oath which he showed to the holy ones when he dwelt high [14] above in glory, and its name is Biqa.
- This (angel) requested Michael to show him the hidden name, that he might enunciate it in the oath, so that those might quake before that name and oath who [15] **revealed all that was secret to the children of men.** And this is the power of this oath, for it is powerful and strong, and he placed this oath Akae in the hand of Michael. [Enoch 69:1-15]

[6] And a command has gone forth from the presence of the Lord concerning those who dwell on the earth that their ruin is accomplished because they have learnt all the secrets of the angels, and all the violence of the Satan's, and all their powers – the most secret ones-and all the power of those who practice sorcery, and the power of witchcraft, and the power of those who make molten images [7] for the whole earth; And how silver is produced from the dust of the earth, and how soft metal [8] originates in the earth. For lead and tin are not produced from the earth like the first; if is a foundation [9] that produces them, and an angel stands therein, and that angel is preeminent[10]...Because of the sorceries which they have searched out and learnt, the earth and those [11] who dwell upon it shall be destroyed. And these they have no place of repentance forever, because they have

shown them what was hidden, and they are the damned, but as for thee, my son, the Lord of Spirits knows that thou art pure, and guiltless of this reproach concerning the secrets. [Enoch 65:6-11]

"The legacy of Ha Qabala dates back well beyond Adam and Eve, to whom its secrets were disclosed by **Enki (Samael) and Lilith who were jointly defined as the Tree of Knowledge.** The Qabalah emphasizes the intuitive grasp of the absolute truth of the ancient Masters-the great Archons who brought forth the world out of primeval chaos. One of those archons was female, Wisdom. Wisdom was Tiamat, Sophia, Ashtoreth-Anath and in general terms, Wisdom was the Shekhinah who embodied them all." (Gardner, Genesis of the Grail Kings Chapter Eleven The Queen of Heaven. Page 140-144)

Black Magic

The theory of black magic can be derived by several themes, first the visible universe has invisible counterparts and higher planes which are occupy with good and beautiful spirits, the lower planes however are dark foreboding and are inhabited by evil spirits and demons which are under the rulership of the fallen Angel and his twin Princess.

Second by means of secret processes and ceremonial rights it is possible to contact these spirits in order to assist in your human undertaking and request. Good spirits will lend their help to any worthy request but the evil spirits only to perversion and destruction.

Contractual agreements are possible between these entities and the magician for fixed periods of time.

Pure black magic is performed with the assistance of a demonic spirit who will in turn serve the sorcerer for his entire earthly life, the understanding however is that after the magician or practitioner passes, he then will become a servant of that demon. This is why black magicians do their best to extend their lives as they know nothing awaits them after death but a life of servitude. (Hall, The Secret Teachings of All Ages The Theory of Black Magic. Page 101)

Further pacts and ceremonies are conducted between these demonic spirits and the black magician, there is a negotiation of sorts which may involve blood rituals. If the magician and the demon spirit cannot come to an agreement, other terms can be negotiated such as the spirit may say to the magician, "I will remain in your service as long as on every Friday morning you will go forth upon the public streets giving alms in the name of Lucifer, the first time you fail in this you belong to me." (Hall, The Secret Teachings of All Ages Form of Pact with the Spirit of Jupiter. Page 104)

"**What was worse, by means of the magic arts taught them by the angels Uzza and Azzael**, they set themselves as masters over the heavenly spheres, and **forced the Sun, the moon, and the stars to be subservient to themselves instead of the Lord**. This impelled the angels to ask God: " 'What is man, that Thou art mindful of him?' Why didst Thou abandon the highest of the heavens, the seat of Thy glory and Thy exalted Throne in 'Arabot, and descend to men, who pay worship to idols, putting Thee upon a level with them?" The Shekinah was induced to leave the earth and ascend to heaven, amid the blare and flourish of the trumpets of the myriads of angel hosts." (Ginzberg, Legends of the Jews Enosh. Page 55)

"What power was in them that they were able to bring them down? They would not have been able to bring them down but for Uzza, Azza and Azziel who taught them sorceries whereby they brought them down and made use of them." (Ben Elisha Chapter 5. Page 157)

Daughters of men

"When the angels saw the beautiful, attractive daughters of men, they lusted after them, and spoke: "We will choose wives for ourselves only from among the daughters of men and beget children with them." Their chief Shemhazai said, "I fear me, ye will not put this plan of yours into execution, and I alone shall have to suffer the consequences of a great sin." Then they answered him, and said: "We will all swear an oath, and we will bind ourselves, separately and together, not to abandon the plan, but to carry it through to the end." (Ginzberg, Legends of the Jews The Fall of the Angels. Page 56)

"**Shemhazai saw a maiden named Ishtar,** and he lost his heart to her. She promised to surrender herself to him, if first he taught her the Ineffable Name, by means of which he raised himself to heaven. He assented to her condition. But once she knew it, she pronounced the Name, and herself ascended to heaven, without fulfilling her promise to the angel. God said, "Because she kept herself aloof from sin, we will place her among the seven stars, that men may never forget her," and she was put in the constellation of the Pleiade."

Note: this was an astounding find, so Ishtar, the famous or infamous goddess of the Babylonian pantheon, seems to be the name of the "daughters of men" that the head Angel of Rebellion Shemhazai desired.

"Shemhazai and Azazel, however, were not deterred from entering into alliances with the daughters of men, and to the first two sons were born. Azazel began to devise the finery and the ornaments by means of which women allure men. Thereupon God sent *Metatron* to tell Shemhazai that he had resolved to destroy the world and bring on a deluge. The fallen angel began to weep and grieve over the fate of the world and the fate of his two sons. If the world went under, what would they have to eat, they who needed daily a thousand camels, a thousand horses, and a thousand steers?" (Ginzberg, Legends of the Jews The Punishment of the Fallen Angels. Page 9)

Note: Metatron is not a Biblical angel, his name is connected with the Kabala and many New Age movements.

Giant Destruction

"Giants begotten by flesh and spirits will be called *evil spirits on earth*, and on the earth will be their dwelling-place. Evil spirits proceed from their bodies, because they are created from above, and from the holy watchers is their beginning and primal origin; they will be evil spirits on earth, and evil spirits they will be named. And the spirits of heaven have their dwelling in heaven, but the spirits of the earth, which were born upon the earth, have their dwelling on the earth.

"And the spirits of the giants will devour, oppress, destroy, attack, do battle, and cause destruction on the earth, and work affliction. They will take no kind of food, nor will they thirst, and they will be invisible. And these spirits will rise up against the children of men and against the women, because they have proceeded from them. Since the days of murder and destruction and the death of the giants, when the spirits went forth from the soul of their flesh, in order to destroy without incurring judgment--thus will they destroy until the day when the great consummation of the great world be consummated. And now as to the watchers who have sent thee to intercede for them, who had been aforetime in heaven, say to them: You have been in heaven, and though the hidden things had not yet been revealed to you, you know worthless mysteries, and in the hardness of your hearts you have recounted these to the women, and through these mysteries women and men work much evil on earth. Say to them therefore: You have no peace!" (Ginzberg, Legends of the Jews The Fall of the Angels. Page 56)

"These two sons of Shemhazai, Hiwwa and Hiyya by name, dreamed dreams. The one saw a great stone which covered the earth, and the earth was marked all over with lines upon lines of writing. An angel came, and with a knife obliterated all the lines, leaving but four letters upon the stone. The other son saw a large pleasure grove planted with all sorts of trees. But angels approached bearing axes, and they felled the trees, sparing a single one with three of its branches."

"When Hiwwa and Hiyya awoke, they referred to their father, who interpreted the dreams for them, saying, "God will bring a deluge, and none will escape with his life, excepting only Noah and his sons." When they heard this, the two began to cry and scream, but their father consoled them: "Soft, soft! Do not grieve. As often as men cut or haul stones, or launch vessels, they shall invoke your names, Hiwwa! Hiyya!" This prophecy soothed them." (Ginzberg, Legends of the Jews The Punishment of the Fallen Angels. Page 9)

"Shemhazai then did penance. He suspended himself between heaven and earth, and in this position of a penitent sinner he hangs to this day. But Azazel persisted obdurately in his sin of leading mankind astray by means of sensual allurements. For this reason two he-goats were sacrificed in the Temple on the Day of Atonement, the one for God, that He pardon the sins of Israel, the other for Azazel, that he bear the sins of Israel." (Ginzberg, Legends of the Jews The Punishment of the Fallen Angels. Page 9)

Men of Renown

The further I have dug into fallen angels; the picture becomes apparent. The Bible speaks of these "men of renown," elsewhere, they are mythology gods, and in history, many are ancient rulers. These are all the same entities referred to as the "sons of God," the fallen angels and their offspring, that established false religion and worship of themselves. The sons of God taught mankind all types of knowledge, while their "sons," the giants (whether in size or status in life), ruled the planet. Anyone doing this historical research has come to similar conclusions. Here is an account from a very high New Age source, which combines the Light-bearer, sons of God, men of renown, and the gods of the earth. This legend starts with a very complex account of creation, matter, etc., slightly different but not much from the version of creation reviewed in an earlier chapter. We pick up the story from the chaotic situation on the "earthly plane."

From the cosmic view of the situation, something had to be done. And so a massive wave of *light bearers* numbering in the 10s of thousands descended upon this planet, manifesting a physical body pattern after the body idea imagined in their souls by spirit.

They moved among those whom we know now as Neanderthal, and later Cro-Magnons, to awaken the consciousness that was trapped in the animal man. **They established what we think today as religion, with symbols and rituals...** Some of the **light bearers became priests and built temples** with paintings and music, and drama to start the imagination.

Following the law of attraction, **the light bearers began gathering in groups, creating their particular form of civilization, with technology, culture, and society much more advanced and defined than we know today**. But later, many began co-habitating with primitive man, which can be interpreted from the 6th chapter of Genesis.

> "1 And it came to pass, when men began to multiply on the face of the earth, and daughters were born to unto them. 2 That the sons of God saw the daughters of men that they were fair; and took of them wives of all which they chose." [Genesis 6:1-2]

Now the fascinating aspect in this account is that the designation *sons of God* had not been mentioned in the Bible up to this point, so obviously, the reference is to another race of people. In verse four of the sixth chapter of Genesis, we read;

> "4 There were giants on the earth in those days, and also after that, when the sons of God came in unto the daughters of men, and they bare children to them, the same became mighty men which were of old, men who of renown." [Genesis 6:4]

"This inbreeding continued for thousands of years, and the consciousness of those *light bearers* dropped further into the density of materiality, with the collective mind of the planet reflecting the darkness of the descent and rapidly moving toward critical mass. Before the final catastrophe, brought on by the disintegration of spiritual values and the misuse of their powers, many fled to other parts of the world **where their superior knowledge left a lasting effect**. Evidence of their migration was seen in northern Spain, Egypt, Greece, and Central and South America, and **legends of all those ancient civilizations before to gods who taught the secrets of the heavens and the earth.** "

This account then goes on through thousands of years, war, famine, etc., eventually leading to this history of these "light bearers" and their sons' contribution to humanity.

"Traces of the former light-bearers, the giants of the earth, were lost. The reason is that the remnants of that superior civilization returned to the higher planes to join their brothers to review the lessons learned. **In time some will walk the earth again as great teachers.**" (Price Pages 35-39)

"This would mean that future rulers would be like the pharaohs, **descendants of fallen angels.**" (The Book of Secrets – Reflections and Notes on the Royal Families of the Grail Page 54-55)

"Ruling over this favoured domain, Enki introduced civilization to mankind, founded the first cities and temples, and set down the first laws." (Talbott The Age of Kronos)

"A crew, who under **names of old renown,** Osiris, Isis, [Horus] and their train, with monstruous shapes and sorceries abused fanatic AEgypt and her priests to see their wandering gods disguised in brutish forms. Rather than human, nor did Israel the infection when their borrowed gold composed the calf in Oreb and the rebel King. Doubled that sin in Bethe and in Dan liking his maker to the grazed ox." (Milton Book I)

"In Sumerian, the word An means heaven and Anu is the god of heaven... **Osiris is sometimes known as An...**" (The Book of Secrets – Reflections and Notes on the Royal Families of the Grail Page 33-34)

"In the Atlantean Antediluvian World, twelve gods originally governed Atlantis: "These deities...were twelve in number: Zeus (or Jupiter), Hera (or Juno), Poseidon (or Neptune), Demeter (or Ceres), Apollo, Artemis (or Diana), Hephæstos (or Vulcan), Pallas Athena (or Minerva), Ares (or Mars), Aphrodite (or Venus), Hermes (or Mercury), and Hestia (or Vesta)."

"Later, Atlantis was comprised of ten regions which were ruled by **ten Kings**. In *Shambala*, *Victoria LePage* states that Atlantis' "ten districts...were ruled by ten Kings." This is verified by

Donnelly who elaborates on the sacred numeral ten as the number of rulers in ancient empires." (The Book of Secrets – Reflections and Notes on the Royal Families of the Grail Page 68)

Judgment of the Fallen

"Then the eagle would reconnect the mountains of darkness, until he had spied out the spot in which the fallen angels Azza and Azzael lie chained with iron fetters —a spot which no one, not even a bird, may visit." (Ginzberg, Legends of the Jews Solomon Master of the Demons. Page 149-150)

[1] And then Michael, Uriel, Raphael, and Gabriel looked down from heaven and saw much blood being [2] shed upon the earth, and all lawlessness being wrought upon the earth. And they said one to another: "The earth made without inhabitant cries the voice of their cryingst up to the gates of heaven. [3] And now to you, the holy ones of heaven, the souls of men make their suit, saying, "Bring our cause [4] before the Most High.' And they said to the Lord of the ages: "Lord of lords, God of gods, King of Kings, and God of the ages, the throne of Thy glory (standeth) unto all the generations of the [5] ages, and Thy name holy and glorious and blessed unto all the ages! Thou hast made all things and power over all things hast Thou: and all things are naked and open in Thy sight, and Thou seest all [6] things, and nothing can hide itself from Three. Thou seest what Azazel hath done, who hath taught all unrighteousness on earth and revealed the eternal secrets which were (preserved) in heaven, which [7] men were striving to learn: And Semjaza, to who Thou hast given authority to bear rule over his associates. And they have gone to the daughters of men upon the earth, and have slept with the [9] women, and have defiled themselves, and revealed to them all kinds of sins. And the women have [10] borne giants, and the whole earth has thereby been filled with blood and unrighteousness. And now, behold, the souls of those who have died are crying and making their suit to the gates of heaven, and their lamentations have ascended: and cannot cease because of the lawless deeds which are [11] wrought on the earth. And Thou knowest all things before they come to pass, and Thou seest these things and Thou dost suffer them, and Thou dost not say to us what we are to do to them in regard to these. [Enoch 9:1-11]

"**Chiefly the fallen angels and their giant posterity caused the depravity of mankind**. The blood spilled by the giants cried unto heaven from the ground, and the four archangels accused the fallen angels and their sons before God, whereupon He gave the following orders to them: Uriel was sent to Noah to announce to him that the earth would be destroyed by a flood, and to teach him how to save his own life. Raphael was told to put the fallen angel Azazel into chains, cast him into a pit of sharp and pointed stones in the desert Dudael, and cover him with darkness, and so was he to remain until the great day of judgment, when he would be thrown into the fiery pit of hell, and the earth would be healed of the corruption he had contrived upon it. Gabriel was charged to proceed against the bastards and the reprobates, the sons of the angels begotten with the daughters of men and plunge them into deadly conflicts with one another. Shemhazai's ilk were handed over to Michael, who first caused them to witness the death of their children in their bloody combat with each other, and then he bound them and pinned them under the hills of the earth, where they will remain for seventy generations, until the day of judgment, to be carried thence to the fiery pit of hell." (Ginzberg, Legends of the Jews The Punishment of the Fallen Angels. Page 8)

[1]They said the Most High, the Holy and Great One spake, and sent Uriel to the son of Lamech [2] and said to him Go to Noah and tell him in my name "Hide thyself!" and reveal to him the end that is approaching; that the whole earth will be destroyed, and a deluge is about to come [3] upon the whole earth and will destroy all that is on it. And now instruct him that he may escape [4] and his seed may be preserved for all the generations of the world. And again the Lord said to Raphael: Bind Azael hand and foot and cast him into the darkness: and make an opening [5] in the desert, which is in Dudael, and cast him therein. And place upon him rough and jagged rocks, and cover him with darkness, and let him abide there forever, and cover his face that he May [6,7] not see light. And on the day of the great judgment he shall be cast into the fire. And heal the earth which the angels have corrupted, and proclaim the healing of the earth, that they may heal the plague, and that all the children of men may not perish through all the secret things that the [8] Watchers have disclosed and have taught their sons. And the whole earth has been corrupted [9] through the works that were taught by Azazel: to him ascribe all sin. And to Gabriel said the Lord; Proceed against the bastards and the reprobates, and against the children of fornication: and destroy [the children of fornication and] the children of the Watchers from amongst men [and cause them to go forth] send them one against the other that they may destroy each other in [10] battle: for length of days shall they not have. And no request that they (i.e. their fathers) make of thee shall be granted unto their fathers on their behalf; for they hope to live an eternal life, and [11] that each one of them will live five hundred years. And the Lord said unto Michael; Go, bind Semjaza and his associates who have united themselves with women so as to have defiled themselves [12] with them in all their uncleanness. And when their sons have slain one another, and they have seen the destruction of their beloved ones, bind them fast for seventy generations in the valleys of the earth, till the day of their judgment and of their consummation, till the judgement that is [13] forever and ever is consummated. In those days they shall be led off to the abyss of fire: and [14] to the torment and the prison in which they shall be confined forever. And whosoever shall be condemned and destroyed will from thenceforth be bound together with them to the end of all [15] generations. And destroy all the spirits of the reprobate and the children of the Watchers, because [16] they have wronged mankind. [Enoch 10:1-16]

[2]…say to the Watchers of heaven, who have sent thee to intercede for them: "you should intercede" for men, and not men [3] for you: Wherefore have ye left the high, holy, and eternal heaven, and lain with women, and defiled yourselves with the daughters of men and take to yourselves wives, and done like the children [4] of earth, and begotten giants (as your) sons? And though ye were holy, spiritual, living the eternal life, you have defiled yourselves with the blood of women, and have begotten (children) with the blood of flesh, and, as the children of men, have lusted after flesh and blood as those also do who die [5] and perish. Therefore have I given them wives also that they might impregnate them, and beget [6] children by them, that thus nothing might be wanting

to them on earth. But you were formerly [7] spiritual, living the eternal life, and immortal for all generations for the world. And therefore I have not appointed wives for you: for as for the spiritual ones of the heaven, in heaven is their dwelling. [8] And now, the giants, who are produced from the spirits and flesh, shall be called evil spirits upon [9] the earth, and on the earth shall be their dwelling. Evil spirits have proceeded from their bodies; because they are born from men and from the holy Watchers is their beginning and primal origin; [10] they shall be evil spirits on earth, and evil spirits shall they be called. [As for the spirits of heaven, in heaven shall be their dwelling, but as for the spirits of the earth which were born upon the earth, on the earth shall be their dwelling]. And the spirts of the giants afflict, oppress, destroy, attack, do battle, and work destruction on the earth, and cause trouble: they take no food, but nevertheless [12] hunger and thirst, and cause offences. And these spirits shall rise up against the children of men and against the women, because they have proceeded from them. [Enoch 15:2-12]

Punishment of Women

[1] And Uriel said to me: Here shall stand the angels who have connected themselves with women, and their spirits assuming many different forms are defiling mankind and shall lead them astray into sacrificing to demons as gods, (here shall they stand,) till the day of the great judgment in [2] which they shall be judged till they are made an end of. And the women also of the angels who [3] went astray shall become sirens. And I, Enoch, alone saw the vision, the end of all things: and no man shall see as I have seen. [Enoch 19:1-3]

Connecting the Dots

Semjaza= leader, taught enchantments, and root-cuttings, Ishtar (fell in love), two sons, bound by Michael

Mt Hermon =priory of Scion, location of fallen angels

Azazel=ascribe all sin, taught men; swords, knives, shields, breastplates, metals of the earth, bracelets, ornaments, antimony, beautifying of the eyelids, costly stones, coloring tinctures, forced the Sun, the moon, and the stars to be subservient to themselves instead of the Lord (with Uzza), bound by Gabriel

Fallen angels=Nordics, serpentine, serpents and dragons of wisdom

Semiramis =female fallen angel, Our Lady of Fatima, Virgin Mary, Tartarus

Nephilim=human woman and angels, giants, turned against men, cannibal, sinned with; birds, beasts, reptiles, fish, drink blood, those who came down, Anakim (touched the sun with their neck), Amorites, Emim (dreaded ones), Zamzummim (schemers), Moab, child sacrifice (valley of Rephaim), Gibborim, Ivvim, devour, oppress, destroy, attack, battle, destruction on the earth, work affliction. Take no food nor drink, invisible. Rise up against the children of men and against the women because they have proceeded from them

Pandemonium=capital of Satan, Seraphic lords, Cherubim, solemn council

Neutral angels= bought grail stone

Shining Ones= Neter, Osiris, Horus (last Neter), Thoth, Watchers, Nephilim, come from Sea
Baal= prince, lord of underworld, place of dead Rephaim (Nephilim), Canaan
Ashtoreh=city, gateway to underworld, Canaanite, Moloch
Canaanites=Nephilim/Anakim/Rephaim, Ham or Ham's wife progenitor of Nephilim
Ishtar=pious maiden, Semjaza fell in love with
Naamah=Tubal-cain's sister, enticed angels, Shamdon (fallen angel), Asmodeus (son), bestial
Shem=stone, chariot, vehicle/UFO, Nephilim (people of the Shem)
Armaros=taught resolving of enchantments
Baraqijal= (taught) astrology
Kokabel= the constellations
Ezeqeel= the knowledge of the clouds
Araqiel=signs of the earth
Shamsiel= signs of the Sun
Sariel= course of the moon.
Jeqon=led astray [all] the sons of God, and brought them down to the earth
Asbeel= imparted to the holy sons of God evil counsel, defiled their bodies with the daughters of men.
Gadreel=taught men all blows of death, led astray Eve, taught shield and the coat of mail, swords, taught all the weapons of death to the children of men.
Penemue=taught children of men the bitter and the sweet, the secrets of their wisdom, writing with ink and paper
Kasdeja=wicked smitings of spirits and demons, and the smitings of the embryo in the womb, that it may pass away (abortion), and the smitings of the soul, the bites of the serpent
Son of the serpent= Taba'et.
Corrupt mankind=ruin is accomplished, secrets of the angels, violence of the Satan's and their powers, sorcery, witchcraft, molten images, metal workings
Qabala=beyond Adam and Eve's time, secrets were disclosed by Enki (Samael) and Lilith (Tree of Knowledge),
Archons=masters, from primeval chaos
Female archon=Wisdom, Tiamat, Sophia, Ashtoreth-Anath, the Shekhinah who embodied them all
Black magic=the lower planes, dark evil spirits and demons, under the rulership of the fallen Angel and his twin Princess, secret processes, ceremonial rights, spirit contact, assist in requests, contractual agreements, serve sorcerer for his entire earthly life, after death will become a servant of that demon, blood rituals.
Light bearers=10s of thousands descended upon this planet, moved among Neanderthal, and later Cro-Magnons, to awaken the consciousness that was trapped in the animal man, established religion, with symbols and rituals, became priests, built temples, paintings, music, and drama, gathered in groups, created civilization, technology, culture, society, later, cohabitation with primitive man, which can be interpreted from the 6th chapter of Genesis,

inbreeding for thousands of years, consciousness of those *light bearers* dropped, legends in all nations, remnants, returned to higher planes, sons were giants

Pharaohs=descendants of fallen angels

Enki=introduced civilization

An= heaven, Anu is the god of heaven, Osiris is known as An

Atlantis 12 rulers= Zeus(or Jupiter), Hera (or Juno), Poseidon (or Neptune), Demeter (or Ceres), Apollo, Artemis (or Diana), Hephaestus (or Vulcan), Pallas Athena (or Minerva), Ares (or Mars), Aphrodite (or Venus), Hermes (or Mercury), and Hestia (or Vesta), 10 regions

Women's punishment = sirens

16

Anunnaki

Anunnaki art

In *Thy Queendom Come*, we covered the *Anunnaki* and the *Igigi* from the Babylonian cuneiform texts of ancient times. They were "revered" as a race that belonged to the earth. The Igigi belonged to heaven. Anu was the father of both groups. This group was said to serve gods such as Marduk and Ishtar; they were severe and cruel and hated mankind. However, their brilliance consumed the lands, leading me to believe they were "the shining ones," perhaps a serpent class. (Lynn Chapter 28 Babylonian Demonology. Page 316)

"**Anunnaki, i.e., the Nephilim** which descended on Mount Hermon to marry the daughters of men, per Genesis 6. The Anunnaki were the **gods who ruled over Atlantis,** and their demonized offspring were the pre-flood civilization which God judged for its wickedness. Like a good occultist, *Robert Temple* proceeds to rewrite the Biblical account of *Noah and the Great Flood* based on the ancient Babylonian legend of Gilgamesh. The quest of *Jason and the Argonauts* for the golden fleece, a symbol of immortality, is based on *Gilgamesh and the Land of the Living*."

"In Sumerian, the word an means 'heaven' and Anu is the god of heaven...**Osiris is sometimes known as An...**" (The Book of Secrets – Reflections and Notes on the Royal Families of the Grail Page 33-34)

"In pagan renditions of the Great Flood, the Anunnaki Argonauts escape the judgment of God by simply sailing through the cosmic sea in their magical ships. The celestial barques in which they are preserved are symbolic of the *Mother goddess* who gives them birth. Having fought the dragon, they sow the dragons teeth in the earth, which spring up into people. When the cosmic battle is over, the Argonauts/Anunnaki, endowed with superhuman strength and immortality, repopulate the world with a race of demi-gods." (The Book of Secrets – Reflections and Notes on the Royal Families of the Grail Page 33-34)

In the days before the flood the operative Kings of Sumer were Nephilim guardians appointed by the Anunnaki, but after the flood came a new era of the first earthly Kings…through the presidency of Anu. **The Kings were the designated guardians of the people and their duties were both military and social**. Granted to the King were a scepter of office and a tiara a headband circlet of gold which was said to envelop the great wisdom of Anu. The Queen held the formal title of Lady (nin) and she and the King lived in a high property designated the *Great house* (the E-gal). The specified duties of a King were to administer his city, while governing the overall state on behalf of the particular god in charge. The King was also the Chief Justice and head of the temple clergy whose responsibility was;

- Interpret the will of the Anunnaki to the people
- The representation of the people before the Anunnaki
- The administration of the realm

(Gardner, Genesis of the Grail Kings Chapter Nine Shepherds of the Royal Seed. page 112-113)

"Anunnaki, *divine lofty ones*, heaven came to earth. **The fiery sons of heaven or shining ones.** The assembly of the Anunnaki met at the Temple of Nippur. Primordial father, *Apus* and his consort Tiamat the Dragon Queen who is also called Mother Hubbur along with their son *Mummu*. Mummu's siblings were male and female pairs first *Lahmu* and his sister *Lahamu*, and then *Anshar* and his sister *Kishar*. Anshar and Kishar **produce a son who was to reign overall his name was Anu**. Anu's consorts were his sisters, *Antu, lady of the sky* (also called Nammu) and *Ki*, the earth mother (called Urash).

"Anu had two sons, Enlil (or Ilu), *lord of the air* (whose mother was Ki) and Enki (or Ea), *lord of the earth and waters* (mother was Antu). Enki had two wives, one goddess *Damkina*, the mother of Marduk **who became the god of the Babylonians**. Enki's other wife was his half-sister *Nin-khursag* (Mountain Queen), the *lady of life* who was also known as Nin-mah the *great lady*."

"Enki and Enlil are the sons of the ruler of Nibiru, Anu (lord of heights) and are also eternal rivals, due to the fact that Enki, even being firstborn, is not the first in line of succession to the throne *Nibiruano*. For Enki's mother (who was not the Dragon Queen) did not belong to royalty [there is a dispute regarding the "royal blood"]. Although Enki has been literally the "lord of creation of man" on earth, the "administration" of the planet stood on the command of Enlil, which, as a direct successor to Anu, of Nibiru, asserted his authority among the Anunnaki and the men. Lord Enlil determined laws, imposed order, and performed deeds that left him as "lord of humanity." This facet was decisive for Enlil to be mistaken as the Creator logos of the universe, throughout history." (Bothelho)

Enlil was also espoused to Nin-khursag and their son *Ninurta* (Ningirsu) was a mighty hunter...

Note: Is this a possible reference to Nimrod, the mighty hunter?

Cntd. by his other wife *Ninlil* (or Sud). Enlil's second son was *Nanna* (or Suen), **known as the bright one**. Nanna and his wife *Ningal* were the parents of the well-known goddess **Inanna** (also called Ishtar) who married the Shepherd-King, Dummuzi (Ezekiel 8:15 as Tammuz)."

"A further son of Enlil and Ninlil was *Nergal, King of the Netherworld*. His wife, the *Queen of the Netherworld*, was *Eresh-kigal* (the daughter of Nanna and Ningal and their **daughter was the legendary Lilith** (handmaiden to her maternal aunt, Inanna). In all there were said to be **600 Anunnaki of the Netherworld** and **300 of the Heavens**." (Gardner, Genesis of the Grail Kings Chapter Seven When Kingship was Lowered. Page 80-82)

Let us make...

Nin-khurstag
Annunaki "Mother of all living'

At this intersection, we will delve into the most prominent Anunnaki myth, which puts them as the actual creators of humankind. *A race of aliens* specifically that created humans as a slave class to serve them. Erasing our FATHER God as the creator. While we will explore direct accounts of this story from various sources, there is almost always some truth in every myth. In no way are these entities responsible for the "man" God created. However, if these are the Nephilim or fallen ones bred with human women, could their "claim" to creation be this distortion of human DNA? The fallen ones were also said to reproduce with animals and mutate vegetation. Would this be the creation they are accounting for themselves?

"From the tablet of *Ashnan and Lahar* details that "for the sake of the good things in their pure sheepfolds, man was given breath." The instruction came firstly from Dragon Queen Tiamat, the **primeval mother of the Anunnaki** who said to Enki;

- Tiamat: O my son rise from your bed...Work what is wise, fashion servants of the gods and **may they produce their doubles.**
- Enki: "O my mother, the creature whose name you uttered, it exists. Bind upon it the image of the gods.
- Tiamat: Nin-mah, Nin-khursag, will work above you, she will stand by you at your fashioning.
- Enki: O my mother, decree upon its fate, Nin-khursag will bind upon it in the mold of the gods. It is man."

"Nin-khursag was then approached by Enki and the Assembly and was formally requested to create man to bear the yoke of the Anunnaki. Nin-khursag was an anatomical specialist and there are accounts of her research, including saving Enki's semen to be applied to the cross-fertilization of certain life-forms. The documented "creation chamber' of Nin-khursag was called the *House of Shimi*, from the Sumerian sh-im-ti, meaning breath-wind-life." (Gardner, Genesis of the Grail Kings)

"Records state that Nin-khursag's experiments were soon perfected and she was ready to create her masterpiece homo sapiens-sapiens. The *Atra-hasis* epic records that Ea and Nin-igiku (Enki and Nin-khursag) **created fourteen new humans soon after the flood**, seven girls and seven boys and the process involved the **wombs of women who had survived the deluge**. The fragmented tablet describes how Nin-khursag made use of the seven and seven wombs, having prepared fourteen pinches of clay upon which Enki had delivered his repeated incantation. In one instance the opening of a navel is detailed and the wombs are called the "Creatresses of Destiny."

"The method was scientifically induced, with human ova fertilized by the Anunnaki to be placed **as cultured embryos into the wombs of surrogate mothers**. As a result they were born as babies, table fragments state;

- Nin-khursag, being uniquely great
- Makes the womb contract
- Nin-khursag, being a great mother
- Sets the birth-giving going

"Being the daughter of the great Anu, Nin-khursag was the designated *lady of life* and her emblem (which is to be found on various tablet and cylinder representations) was a symbolic **womb, shaped rather like the Greek letter omega**. She was also called the *lady of form-giving, lady fashioner* and *lady of the embryo*, while a text entitled *Enki and the World Order* calls her the *midwife of the country*. Likewise, Nin-khursag's half-brother Enki, *lord of the earth and waters*, was called *Nudimmud*, meaning image fashioner, being the archetype of original form-the master of shaping and the charmer of making."

"This new work force was created to toil the fields build cities and work the mines. This new structure was conceived with hu-mans, by **becoming their own governors destined to perform functions hitherto carried out by the Nephilim**. The table fragment continues;

- Mother Nintur (Nin-khursag) the lady of form giving,
- Working in a dark place, the womb
- To give birth to Kings, to tie on the rightful tiara
- To give birth to lords
- To place the crown on their heads
- It is in her hands."

"In about 2100 BC the future *King Gudea* of Babylon recorded that Nin-khursag was the *mother of all children.* It is clear from the Mesopotamian texts that the Sumerians that emerged from Nin-khursag's work **believed that their main purpose in life was to serve the Anunnaki by providing them with food drink and habitation.** In return *they were educated and trained in social skills and academic affairs* and the products of this training are abundantly clear form their writings."

"Later Nin-khursag produced a child from her own womb, it was fed with Anunnaki blood as a cultured embryo. Clinically fertilized by Enki. The outcome was successful and the experiment was called *Adama* (earthling). This was a superior class of leaders. So according to this record the **biblical Adam was not the first human he was the first human of Royal seed.**"

Nin-khursag is a figure in the shadows. This name was familiar to me in the Babylonian Pantheon. Still, Nin-khursag isn't in any materials I've read about mystery religions, secret societies, pagan mythology, etc., at least under this Sumerian name. Nin-khursag appears as a mad female scientist that would fit the bill as some mother goddess or creator goddess figure. Nin-khursag is another turn in the epoch of the Kingdom of darkness building on earth.

This agenda is alive and present today. From the creation of new types of mutated humans with animals etc., it's beyond a horror story. To get the full depths of this Anunnaki account, one would have to look no further than at the back of the Kodak Theater (the theater that holds the Oscar Awards). On an upper arch that shows right through to the "Hollywood" sign, a large image of Anu (or Enki) holding a bowl of "his seed," a Kabbala tree of life, and next to it an Anunnaki, which would be his son. What does the Anunnaki have to do with Hollywood?

Babylon Court in Hollywood
Anu or Enki- Tree of Life -Anunnaki

Babylon Court at night

Connecting the Dots

Anunnaki=Nephilim, gods over Atlantis, cosmic ship, escape judgement, repopulate the world with a race of demi-gods, Kings of Sumer, guardians, scepter, tiara (wisdom of Anu), 600 netherworld, 300 heavens, sons of Anu great god,(50 of them, 50 great gods

Kings = chief justice, priest, do will of the Anunnaki ,representation of the people before the Anunnaki, divine lofty ones, heaven to earth, Fiery sons, Shining ones,

Primordial parents=Apus and Tiamat (Dragon queen), offspring: Mummu, Lahumu and Lahamu, Anshar and Kishar (son Anu)

Anu=reign over all, sons; Enlil lord of air, Enki (Ea) lord of earth and waters

Enlil=wife Damkin, son Marduk, wife half-sister Nin-khursag, administration, laws order, lord of humanity

Nin-khursag=lady of life, great lady, mountain queen, create man, work for Anunnaki, cross fertilization, Enki's seed, creation chamber, homo sapiens-sapiens. 14 humans (7 boys, 7 girls) survived the deluge, surrogate mothers, lady of form-giving, lady fashioner, lady of the embryo, Midwife of the country, daughter of Anu, mother of all children, produced her own offspring Adama (Adam)

Enki- first born, not of royal blood , lord of creation of man

Nibiru=ruled by Enki and Enlil, Enlil succeed throne due to mother's lineage

Ninurta=mighty hunter, close to Ninus, Nimrod

Nanna=Enlil's second son, right one

Nanna and Ningal=Inanna (Ishtar) married Tammuz
Enlil and Ninlil=Nergal (King of netherworld)
Nergal and Eresh-kigal (Queen of netherworld) = Lilith (daughter)
Timat (Dragon Queen)= primeval mother of Anunnaki, instructs Enki to produce doubles, servants of gods, Nin-khursag works above

SECTION VI

United Nations of Lucifer

UNITED NATIONS OF LUCIFER

17

United Nations of Lucifer

Guardian of International Peace (now removed)
UN Headquarters, NY

The United Nations represents hope, peace, and world democracy. On the political and socio-economic front, little does the public realize the United Nations, first and foremost, is a world religion. A headquarters for spirituality, steeped in specific spiritual beliefs.

The problem? The head of this religion is LUCIFER!

Not, in theory, their own words, their artwork, and even their veiled beliefs. The United Nations is undoubtedly the most prominent world organization, bar none. The U.N. houses the highest level of medical (WHO), banking (IMF and World Bank), Education (UNESCO), and hundreds of other organizations under the banner of the U.N.

Since its inception, the United Nations has spiritually prepared for the Luciferian, one world, Age of Aquarius. This chapter will expose the content of the rituals, ceremonies, invocations, beliefs, and practices in the not-so-public view of the unsuspecting citizens of the world.

> "³ For when they shall say, Peace and safety; then sudden destruction cometh upon them, as travail upon a woman with child; and they shall not escape." [I Thessalonians 5:3]

Prophetess of the United Nations

Alice A. Bailey
June 16, 1880–December 15, 1949

Alice A. Bailey
June 16, 1880-December 15, 1949
Founder; Lucis Trust, Arcane Schools

Born in Manchester, England (June 16, 1880), Alice lost her parents to tuberculosis before the age of nine; she has one sibling, a younger sister. Alice describes her childhood as *miserable*. "They were for me the years of greatest physical comfort and luxury, they were years of freedom from all material anxiety, but they were at the same time, years of miserable questioning, of disillusionment of unhappy discovery of loneliness." Alice claims she was exposed to, as she describes, "the narrowest type of Christianity" from the Church of England as a youth.

An unusual encounter at the age of 15 would mold her entire life. She decided to stay home on one particular Sunday while everyone else in the household attended regular Sunday worship. The young Bailey was at home alone (except for the servants), sitting in her room, when suddenly her door opened. At the door was a stranger, a tall man dressed in fine European clothing and a turban. He walked into the room without being invited. Alice was petrified, shocked, and afraid but allowed this strange man to sit beside her on the bed.

As she recalls it, this man begins speaking with her, "He told me I had work to do in the world." This "work" would involve her gaining self-control and becoming more "pleasant." This strange man told her further that she would be helpful to him in the future, and the world's fate depended on how she handled herself. He told her the key to gaining this primary mission was gaining self-control because she had to be trusted to travel around the world doing "the master's work." The mysterious man said, "he would be in touch during intervals several years apart."

Seven years later, at 22, a brilliant light entered her room, and she heard the master speak; she didn't see him this time; she only heard him. He came to give his approval that he was pleased with the work she'd been doing and her progress. He told her, "The master is a busy executive, and his job is world direction." He also revealed, "The real founders of America were the brave Pilgrim mothers, and the **United States is a feminine civilization**."

Alice married and had three daughters, and became an occult student. She then met a man named Foster Bailey in 1919 while studying Theosophy. Alice divorced her husband and married Foster Bailey. Foster became the Nation Secretary of the Theosophical Society founded by famous occultist and mother of the New Age Movement, *Madame Helena P. Blavatsky.*

"Theosophy is, then, the archaic Wisdom-Religion, the esoteric doctrine once known in every ancient country having claims to civilization. This "Wisdom" all the old writings show us as an emanation of the divine Principle; and the clear comprehension of it is typified in such names as the Indian Buddha, the Babylonian Nebo, the Thoth of Memphis, the Hermes of Greece; in the appellations, also, of some goddesses – Metis, Neitha, Athena, the Gnostic Sophia, and finally the Vedas, from the word "to know." (What is Theosophy?)

Note: Theosophy is the revived Mystery Religion of Babylon

Theosophy logo

In November 1919, Alice first made contact with an *entity* that would come to be known as "The Tibetan." One afternoon she began to hear music from the sky, in the hills, and within herself; a voice said, "There are some books which it is desired should be written for the public. You can write them. Will you do so?" Initially, she declined. The voice went away, and she forgot about the encounter. Three weeks later, she heard the voice again; she then decided to give it a try. The first work would be, "Initiation, Human and Solar." She claims this work was not automatic writing; Alice claims automatic writing is dangerous.

"Automatic writing is gained by permitting an outside intelligence's etheric arm to control the medium's physical arm. This is impossible until the medium removes his etheric double from the arm, for two things cannot occupy the same place simultaneously. Periodically separating the life forces from the physical arm is hazardous, often resulting in paralysis. "(Lynn Chapter 18 New Age. Page 218)

The controversy she had was over the identity of the Tibetan; *Jung* said, "The Tibetan is her higher self, and Alice Bailey is the lower self." Bailey claims the Tibetan is a real presence or entity. Others say it's her subconscious. She argues that the style of writing she does for the Tibetan is "dictation" from him to her, and she would only change words to make them more coherent in English.

She worked for the Tibetan for 27 years. Eventually she could "snap into telepathic relation with him without the slightest trouble by that time."

The overarching theme of the work Alice did for the Tibetan was to, relay the message that *the Hierarchy was taking the first steps to approach closer to humanity*. "The purpose is to **restore the ancient Mysteries,** externalize the manifestation of the physical plane of the *masters* and their groups of disciples, the ashrams." Alice Bailey claimed that she was one of the ashrams working under the Tibetan.

From the Tibetan;

"I have since the year 1931 been training a group of men and women, scattered all over the world in the techniques of accepted discipleship, academically understood. Out of the many possible neophytes, I indicated to Alice A. Bailey a group of 45 people – some known to her personally and some quite unknown. The people received direct personal instructions from me which embodied the new approach to the Hierarchy." (Bailey Page 253-254)

Bailey on the United Nations;
"When I wrote the pamphlet called *The Present World Crisis* and the succeeding papers on the world situation, I stated that the Hierarchy endorsed the attitude and aims of the United Nations, fighting for the freedom of the whole of humanity and for the release of the suffering people." (Bailey Page 252)

"Blavatsky and Bailey were avid trance-channelers who claimed to receive messages from spirit entities and both recorded many predictions that were made to them regarding the inevitable appearance of "The Lord Maitreya" or "The Christ" on the earth immediately prior to earth's initiation into the utopian "New Age." Because these women engaged in the Biblical forbidden practice of spiritism and because the messages they received were deeply anti-Christian, mocking and ridiculing traditional Christianity, Bible-believing Christians have understood that the appearance of the man whom Bailey and Blavatsky predicted was not a reference to the second coming of Jesus Christ, but was in fact a prediction of the future Anti-Christ." (Atrayu)

Alice Baileys' teaching is the complete spiritual foundation of the United Nations. Bailey's formula interweave with the U.N.'s education programs under veils and layers of secrecy. Alice Bailey is the undisputed Prophetess and High Priestess of the United Nations *of Lucifer*.

Lucis Trust

Lucis Trust Logo

The Lucis Trust is located on the GROUNDS of the U.N Headquarters
866 United Nations Plaza Suite 482 in New York

"The Lucis Trust is dedicated to the establishment of a new and better way of life for everyone in the world based on the fulfillment of the divine plan for humanity. Its educational activities promote recognition and practice of the spiritual principles and values upon which a stable and interdependent world society may be based. The esoteric philosophy of its founder, Alice Bailey, informs its activities which are offered freely throughout the world in eight languages." (Lucis Trust History)

The Lucis Trust has what they term *Consultative Status* with the Economic and Social Council of the United Nations (ECOSOC) and World Goodwill is recognized by the Department of Global Communications at the United Nations as a Non-Governmental Organization (NGO)... "Since their inception Lucis Trust and World Goodwill have given their support through **meditation, educational materials and seminars**, by highlighting the importance of the UN's goals and activities as they represent the voice of the peoples and nations of the world." (Lucis Trust About US)

History

Initiation, Human and Solar, Alice A. Bailey
Lucifer Publishing

"A publishing company, initially named *Lucifer Publishing Company*, was established by Alice and Foster Bailey in the State of New Jersey, USA, in May 1922 to publish the book, *Initiation Human and Solar*. **The ancient myth of Lucifer refers to the angel who brought light to the world.** Lucifer Publishing literature which had been edited for a number of years by theosophical founder, *H.P. Blavatsky*. It soon became clear to the Bailey's that **some Christian groups have traditionally mistakenly identified Lucifer with Satan,** and for this reason, the company's name was changed in 1924 to Lucis Publishing Company."

"Lucifer" and "Lucis" come from the same Latin generative root word, Lucis, meaning light. The Baileys, like the great teacher H.P. Blavatsky, sought to elicit a **deeper understanding of the sacrifice made by Lucifer.** Alice and Foster Bailey, followers of Theosophy, a spiritual tradition which **views Lucifer as one of the Solar Angels, those advanced Beings who Theosophy says descended (thus "the fall") from Venus to our planet eons ago to bring the principle**

of mind to what was then animal-man. In the theosophical perspective, the descent of these Solar Angels was not a fall into sin or disgrace but rather an act of **great sacrifice, as is suggested in the name Lucifer which means light-bearer."** (Lucis Trust History)

Note: Do you see the connection with the "evolution" of man, as discussed earlier, through the mineral, vegetable, and animal?

Fallen Angels Sacrifice

The Lucis Trust is not DONE! In no uncertain terms, the Lucis Trust blatantly ANNOUNCE their reverence and service to Lucifer. Keep in mind this is an organization on the GROUNDS of the United Nations, not merely connected to it. The Lucis Trust conducts all of the spiritual activity at the U.N., including the management of the Meditation Room, which contains a "black stone."

"The secret of the "fallen angels" is essentially the mystery which lies behind the very **Plan of evolution, for the solar angels' willingness to "fall"**, to sacrifice themselves in order to bring the light of the principle of mind to what was then animal man, marked the coming into action of the great *Law of Duality* by which matter, form—negative and passive—could be quickened by spirit. *This act of sacrifice at the dawn of human history is a thread woven throughout the great scriptures and mythologies of the world*, including the myth of Prometheus who stole fire (mind) for man, and the biblical story of the Prodigal Son, who left the Father's home to embark upon the path of experience in the life of form and the senses—the journey to "the far country".

Note: Interestingly the role of "light-bearer" is linked with Mercury, or Hermes—the divine messenger for the Gods in Greek and Roman mythology.

"The fact that *The Secret Doctrine* equates **Venus with Gaia (Earth),** and the awakening consciousness of the Gaia theory recognizes that Earth is a living and unified organism, suggests that **humanity may now be beginning to awaken and cooperate somewhat with the reason for which the angels descended into matter:** for the salvaging of substance and the awakening of mind in form so that the *Purpose of Deity* could be registered and expressed in substance.

"THE SOLAR ANGELS "FELL" AS AN ACT OF CHOICE AND OF SUPREME SACRIFICE ON BEHALF OF HUMANITY." (McKechnie)

On the occasion of that first conference, *Mary Esther Crump,* a friend of an ABC radio correspondent reporting from San Francisco, was so inspired by the proceedings that she wrote a poem entitled *"The Song of the Seraph* of San Francisco." Herein she wrote:

"...and now, approaching our planet's night, one of the *Lord God's Seraphim*, comes, Ambassador sent from Him, to implement a cosmic Plan, on behalf of the Family of Man." (Urso)

Note: Seraph refers to the Seraphim class of angelic hosts

> ¹² For we wrestle not against flesh and blood, but against principalities, against powers, against the rulers of the darkness of this world, against spiritual wickedness in high places. [Ephesians 6:12]

Spiritual Foundation of the U.N.

The beguiling serpent strikes again! If you had no idea what the United Nations was about, by now, you are already shocked and perhaps in disbelief. The United Nations, like any Mystery Religion, veils its beliefs under organizations and various movements. In the name alone, UNITED NATIONS denotes a reversing of the Tower of Babel. God separated the nations under Nimrod's rule and confused the languages. The United Nations aims to bring the countries back together under one totalitarian system and RETURN to the One World Religion of Babylon under Lucifer's authority. The Anti-Christ will no doubt have a significant role in the United Nations.

"The succession of Secretaries-General who have presided over this organization, have understood that it exists for, and must serve the needs and hopes of all people, everywhere. As such, the United Nations is clearly, **an Aquarian organization**."

Note: This statement admits that the U.N. is a New Age, Age of Aquarius organization.

"There is an opportunity to creatively reflect on the relationship between the work of the **United Nations and the spiritual welfare of humanity**; on the needed planetary conditions that will allow humanity to realize its spiritual destiny and the ways in which the **United Nations can help create these conditions**."

"Thus, the **Spiritual Mysteries** can then once again be openly taught, and a knowing humanity will then become a willing participant in the transformation of planetary consciousness." (Urso)

Note: Here, the admission is made that in fact the United Nations will foster the Mystery System of Babylon, (see Thy Queendom Come Section III for details on the Mystery System)."

"The Plan of *Love and Light* that is the spiritual destiny of humanity, and the goals and objectives of the United Nations. " (Urso)

LOVE AND LIGHT is a highly New Age, witchcraft buzzword. It sounds excellent and lovely but dark and devoid of love. Be careful with repeating trends.

"*William Jasper,* author of "A New World Religion" describes the religion of the UN;

"A weird and diabolical convergence of New Age mysticism, pantheism, aboriginal animism atheism, communism, socialism, Luciferian occultism, apostate Christianity, Islam, Taoism, Buddhism, and Hinduism...a strange admixture of crystal worshipers, astrologers, feminists, environmentalists, Kabbalists, human potentialists, Eastern mystics, pop psychologists, and 'liberal' clergymen one would normally associate with the offbeat, sandals-and-beads counterculture of the 1960's. But, today's worshipers in this rapidly expanding movement are as likely to be scientists, diplomats, corporate presidents, heads of state, international bankers, and leaders of mainstream Christian churches." (Atrayu)

Meditation

"Within the United Nations is the germ and the seed of a great international and meditating, reflective group—a group of thinking and informed men and women in whose hands lies the destiny of humanity...Their point of meditative focus is the intuition or Buddhic plane." (Bailey, Discipleship in the New Age Page 218-219)

U Thant was the U.N. Secretary-General from 1961-1971 here is what he stated about the spiritual foundation or goals of the United Nations;

"Meditation is a process that cleanses the mind of impurities. It cultivates such qualities as concentration, awareness, intelligence and tranquility, leading finally to the attainment of the highest wisdom." U Thant, Sec. General U.N., 1961-1971.

Ladies and gentlemen, that was the SECRETARY GENERAL of the United Nations, which is the highest position. Why is meditation necessary, and how involved is the United Nations?

"The effect of human meditation at this time is to **change conditions, to invoke the higher spiritual potency**, to work with concentration—both vertically and horizontally—**within the world of spiritual energies** and within the world of human affairs. The ultimate result of effective meditation in the consciousness of the individual **is enlightenment and illumination**—leading to an increased ability to cooperate in the creative and redemptive purposes of our planetary life."

"The technique of meditation governs all expansions of consciousness, including the entire process of evolutionary development within the planet. It is the technique of spiritual contact and apprehension, the means of furthering the evolution of human intelligence, the capacity to love, and the ability to bring the personal will into alignment with the trans-personal or divine will." (Creative Meditation -A Planetary Service)

The Aquarian Age Community is another NGO associated with the United Nations Department of Global Communications, which organizes monthly meditation meetings for Lucis Trust. The name Aquarian Age indicates the New Age of Aquarius, which you can read about in detail in *Thy Queendom Come*.

Monthly Meditation meetings are scheduled under the corresponding Zodiac for that particular month.

Join in the monthly Webinar meditation meetings to help transform planetary consciousness by supporting and strengthening the spiritual work of the United Nations on the following dates in 2022 from Noon –1:00 p.m. (NY Eastern Time):

Registration for each meeting in 2022 is required.
(Please click on links below.)

Capricorn Monday January 17	Aquarius Tuesday February 15	Pisces Thursday March 17
Aries/Easter Saturday April 16	Taurus/Wesak Sunday May 16	Gemini Christ Festival Thursday June 13
Cancer Wednesday July 13	Leo Thursday August 11	Virgo Friday September 9
Libra Sunday October 9	Scorpio Monday November 7	Sagittarius Saturday December 7

Monthly Meditation Schedule (2022)
Aquarian Age Community an official U.N. Partner

"The point which I seek to emphasize, and which I hope will remain in your minds, is that this technique of meditation is the outstanding creative agent on our planet. When you, as an individual, are endeavoring **to `build the new man in Christ'** which will be an expression of your true spiritual self, meditation is, as you well know, your best agent; but the meditation process must be accompanied by creative work or else it is purely mystical, and though not futile, is nevertheless negative in creative results." (Discipleship in the New Age, Vol. II, p. 202) (Arcane School Meditation at the New Moon)

This is a quote directly from Lucis Trust, do not be deceived. This Christ is not the CHRIST you and I serve; this is one of the leading New Age deceptions.

Meditation Room

U.N Meditation Room
U.N. Headquarters

"The *Cult of the All-Seeing Eye* has existed under many names and guises for thousands of years. Through the ages, its high priests have worshiped before unhallowed altars dedicated to the adoration of a nameless deity — an *Unknown God*. This "unknown" deity is honored through an elaborate system of veiled allegories and secret symbols. Followers of this pseudo-mystical, humanistic, occult system of beliefs affirm oral traditions handed down from an ancient priesthood in Egypt. The Cult projects a minimum belief in a god which excludes God, The Divine Redeemer and rejects Jesus Christ, the Son of God. The Cult's leaders tell its initiates that their doctrine's foundation is a hidden master religion. The secret master religion is agreeable to all men due to the pre-Christian, pagan models that appear not to conflict with reputable faiths. This offspring of the ancient *idolatrous mystery cults* have existed in America for centuries. Still, its leaders have never dared to admit that they hope to replace Christianity with the Cult. However, in recent years, they have dared to establish small, public temples in the United States: namely, the **Meditation Room in the United Nations** and at Wainwright House, Rye, New York, and the **Prayer Room in the U.S. Capitol.**'

"The altar is four feet high and rests on two narrow cross pieces. It is a dark gray block of crystalline iron ore from a Swedish mine and weighs six and one-half tons. The Swedish Government presented this block of ore —the largest of its kind ever mined — to the U.N. in early 1957. The chunk rests on a concrete pillar that goes straight to bedrock. The area and passageway beneath the room are closed to the public."

"But the stone in the middle of the room has more to tell us. We may see it as an altar, empty not because there is no God, not because it is an altar to an unknown God, but because it is dedicated to the God whom man worships under many names and in many forms."

"The stone in the middle of the room reminds us also of the firm and permanent in a world of movement and change. The block of iron ore has the weight and solidity of the everlasting. It is a reminder of that cornerstone of endurance and faith on which all human endeavor must be based." (Hammarskjöld) (Spenser)

"There are 72 geometrical figures (and shadings) in the mural. The two crescent shapes and the four long triangles — white, yellow, blue and black —which are located in the two upper tiers of the mural, are each counted as one figure. The number 72 denoted from the earliest days the Divine Name of 72 words. This number is derived from a permutation of the values assigned to the four letters of the Tetragrammaton (JHVH: Jehovah), the Ineffable, Unpronounceable Name of God. This Name, in its multitude of forms, can be used to work miracles or magic, so say the Cabalists."

Note: See Thy Queendom Come for the hidden meaning of the Tetragrammaton

The mysterious mural also helps the worshipers tune into esoteric energies and helps facilitate a state of altered consciousness.

"The U.N. Meditation room at U.N. headquarters in New York is off-limits to most visitors, including Americans who pay most of the bills up there. It has been described as a pagan temple. It includes no traditional religious symbols. Secretary-General *Kofi Annan* was married to his Swedish wife in this room."

"The room is also 33 feet long and tapers inward to form a truncated pyramid. There is an abstract mural on the front wall, which is full of witchcraft symbols, and in the middle of the room, is a black stone block, which weighs exactly 6.5 tons or 13,000 pounds." (Atrayu)

Note: The Meditation Room is 33 feet long, the U.N. logo has 33 segments. 33 is the number of Satan, as well as the 33 degrees of Freemasonry.

"I was in the United Nations while on my seventh trip to New York City. I stood in the meditation room, which contains Satan's altar." (Last Trumpet Newsletter)

Moon Charts

"The time of the full moon is a period when spiritual energies are uniquely available and facilitate a closer rapport between humanity and the Spiritual Hierarchy."

MOON CHART 2022

Table of new and full moons for the twelve months of 2022:

UNITED STATES TIME

DATE	MOON	FESTIVAL **	EASTERN	CENTRAL	MOUNTAIN	PACIFIC	GMT	DAY/GMT
Jan 2	NEW	Capricorn	1:33:19pm	12:33:19pm	11:33:19am	10:33:19am	6:33:19pm	2
Jan 17	FULL	Capricorn	6:48:15pm	5:48:15pm	4:48:15pm	3:48:15pm	11:48:15pm	17
Feb 1	NEW	Aquarius	12:45:50am	11:45:50pm(-)	10:45:50pm(-)	9:45:50pm(-)	5:45:50am	1
Feb 16	FULL	Aquarius	11:56:20am	10:56:20am	9:56:20am	8:56:20am	4:56:20pm	16
Mar 2	NEW	Pisces	12:34:36pm	11:34:36am	10:34:36am	9:34:36am	5:34:36pm	2
Mar 18	FULL	Pisces	3:17:24am*	2:17:24am*	1:17:24am*	12:17:24am*	7:17:24am	18
Apr 1	NEW	Aries	2:24:14am*	1:24:14am*	12:24:14am*	11:24:14pm(-)*	6:24:14am	1
Apr 16	FULL	Aries	2:54:52pm*	1:54:52pm*	12:54:52pm*	11:54:52am*	6:54:52pm	16
Apr 30	NEW^	Taurus	4:27:55pm*	3:27:55pm*	2:27:55pm*	1:27:55pm*	8:27:55pm	30
May 16	FULL#	Taurus	12:13:58am*	11:13:58pm(-)*	10:13:58pm(-)*	9:13:58pm(-)*	4:13:58am	16
May 30	NEW	Gemini	7:30:06am*	6:30:06am*	5:30:06am*	4:30:06am*	11:30:06am	30
Jun 14	FULL	Gemini	7:51:35am*	6:51:35am*	5:51:35am*	4:51:35am*	11:51:35am	14
Jun 28	NEW	Cancer	10:52:05pm*	9:52:05pm*	8:52:05pm*	7:52:05pm*	2:52:05am	29
Jul 13	FULL	Cancer	2:37:27pm*	1:37:27pm*	12:37:27pm*	11:37:27am*	6:37:27pm	13
Jul 28	NEW	Leo	1:54:51pm*	12:54:51pm*	11:54:51am*	10:54:51am*	5:54:51pm	28
Aug 11	FULL	Leo	9:35:34pm*	8:35:34pm*	7:35:34pm*	6:35:34pm*	1:35:34am	12
Aug 27	NEW	Virgo	4:16:57am*	3:16:57am*	2:16:57am*	1:16:57am*	8:16:57am	27
Sep 10	FULL	Virgo	5:58:52am*	4:58:52am*	3:58:52am*	2:58:52am*	9:58:52am	10
Sep 25	NEW	Libra	5:54:23pm*	4:54:23pm*	3:54:23pm*	2:54:23pm*	9:54:23pm	25
Oct 9	FULL	Libra	4:54:48pm*	3:54:48pm*	2:54:48pm*	1:54:48pm*	8:54:48pm	9
Oct 25	NEW^	Scorpio	6:48:31am*	5:48:31am*	4:48:31am*	3:48:31am*	10:48:31am	25
Nov 8	FULL#	Scorpio	6:01:58am	5:01:58am	4:01:58am	3:01:58am	11:01:58 am	8
Nov 23	NEW	Sagittarius	5:57:03pm	4:57:03pm	3:57:03pm	2:57:03pm	10:57:03pm	23
Dec 7	FULL	Sagittarius	11:07:59pm	10:07:59pm	9:07:59pm	8:07:59pm	4:07:59am	8
Dec 23	New	Capricorn	5:16:42am	4:16:42am	3:16:42am	2:16:42am	10:16:42am	23

Moon Chart Schedule 2022
Lucis Trust

> In all meditation it is of value for the student to remember that, from the standpoint of permanent benefit, it is easier to meditate effectively during the period from the new moon to the full moon, than from the full moon to the new moon. The first half of the lunar cycle is one of intensification, absorption and accretion; the second half is one of assimilation and distribution. More real progress over a long period can be made by observing this cyclic law.
>
> Wisely utilizing newly acquired energies keeps inflowing and outflowing channels open and prevents emotional, mental, and psychical congestions, which may otherwise be experienced, with their accompanying physical consequences.

KEYNOTES FOR THE DISCIPLE

These keynotes for the disciple may be used in sequence as the seed thought for the meditation work done each month at the time of the full moon.

ARIES:	I come forth and from the plane of mind, I rule.
TAURUS:	I see and when the eye is opened, all is light.
GEMINI:	I recognise my other self and in the waning of that self, I grow and glow.
CANCER:	I build a lighted house and therein dwell.
LEO:	I am That and That am I.
VIRGO:	I am the Mother and the Child. I, God, I, matter am.
LIBRA:	I choose the way that leads between the two great lines of force.
SCORPIO:	Warrior I am and from the battle I emerge triumphant.
SAGITTARIUS:	I see the goal. I reach that goal and then I see another.
CAPRICORN:	Lost am I in light supernal, yet on that light I turn my back.
AQUARIUS:	Water of Life am I, poured forth for thirsty men.
PISCES:	I leave the Father's home and turning back, I save.

Moon Chart Disciple Notes
Lucis Trust

(Moon Charts 2022)

New Age at the U.N.

Let the Plan of Love and Light work out

"Love and Light" is a major New Age "catch phrase"
Lucis Trust home page

We've established the United Nations has New Age, Age of Aquarius philosophy for a spiritual basis. To understand the dangers of the New Age Movement, please review Chapter 19 in the first installment of the Mystery Babylon Series. Here we expose the inner teachings of the United Nations through the education of Alice Bailey, their undisputed Prophetess, through her many books. These books are available directly on the Lucis Trust website and disseminated throughout their organization.

"One of the English Masters is also exceptionally active, and **the Master in America is laying his plans toward an active participation in the work**. These consecrated Workers form a nucleus around the Christ and direct much of the preparatory work."

"To this fact can be traced **the interest people are now showing in occultism and in the work of the Masters;** more and more people are becoming sensitive to and conscious of Their presence, and more and more are finding their way into the groups of disciples." (Bailey, Lucis Trust, Online Books Page 502)

"*The Master Morya* is at this time acting as the **inspirer of the great national executives throughout the world**. Even those whose ideals coincide not with yours are being welded into the world plan, and much of their immediate work is **organizing the individual nations and welding them into an homogeneous whole**, preparatory to their entrance into the great international thought-form."

"The Master K.H. works also with the prelates of the great **Catholic Churches—Greek, Roman and Anglican—with the leaders of the Protestant communions**, with the foremost workers in the **field of education**, and also through, and with, the dominant demagogues and organizers of the people. His interests lie with all those who, with unselfish intent, strive after the ideal, and who live for the helping of others."

U.N. HQ of Fallen Angels

"**They are the angels who guard the sanctuaries of all the churches, cathedrals, temples and mosques of the world. They are now increasing the momentum of their vibration for the raising of the consciousness of the attendant congregations.**" (Bailey, Lucis Trust, Online Books Page 505-506)

"The aspirants and disciples of the world must realize that the hour has struck, and that the forces of the Christ are being marshaled for a supreme endeavor. These forces include **both the human and the angel evolution.**" (Bailey, Lucis Trust, Online Books Page 503-504)

"With Him works the **great Angel or Deva of the spiritual plane,** referred to in the *Treatise on Cosmic Fire* as the *Lord Agni*; He seeks to touch with the hidden spiritual fire the head centres of all intuitive statesmen." (Bailey, Lucis Trust, Online Books Page 505)

"*The Master K.H....* is attempting to transmute the thought-form of religious dogma, **to permeate the churches with the idea of the Coming and** bring to a sorrowing world the vision of the Great Helper, the Christ. He works with the *rose devas* and with the *blue devas* on astral levels, with the wise help of the great guardian Angel of that plane, called (in Hindu terminology) the *Lord Varuna.*"

"With the aid of **certain groups of angels, He works to open up the world of departed souls to the seeker,** and much that has of late convinced the materialistic world of life beyond has emanated from Him." (Bailey, Lucis Trust, Online Books Page 505-506)

"He whom you call the *Master D.K.* works much with those who heal with pure altruism; He occupies himself with those who are active in the **laboratories of the world,** with great philanthropic **world movements such as the Red Cross**, and with the rapidly developing welfare movements. His work also embraces teaching, and he does much at this time to train the various disciples of the world, taking the disciples of many of the master's and so relieving them temporarily, in this hour of crisis, from their teaching responsibilities. **Many of the healing angels, such as those referred to in the Bible, cooperate with him.**"

U.N. Anti-Christ Agenda

"*The Master Jesus* works especially with the masses of the Christian people who inhabit the occidental countries, and who gather in the churches. He is distinctively a great leader, an organizer, and a wise general executive. **A special group of devas work under his command**, and his connection with all true church leaders and executives is very close. He acts ceaselessly on the **inner esoteric council of the churches**, and with him the groups of violet angels cooperate. In church matters **he himself carries out the behests of the Christ**, saving him much and working as his intermediary... No one knows or understands so fully and wisely as he the problems of the Western culture, nor the needs of the people who carry forward the destiny of Christianity."

"One of the English Masters has in hand the **definite guidance of the Anglo-Saxon peoples** towards a joint destiny. The future for the Anglo-Saxon is great and not yet has the highest flow of the tide of its civilization been reached. History holds much glory for **England and America when they work together for world good,** not supplanting each other or interfering with each other's empire but working in the fullest unison for the preservation of the peace of the world and the right handling of world problems in the field of economics and of education."

"**The Tibetan has asked me to make clear that when he is speaking of the Christ, he is referring to his official name as Head of the Hierarch**y. The Christ works for all men, irrespective of their faith; He does not belong to the Christian world any more than to the Buddhist, the Mohammedan or any other faith. There is no need for any man to join the Christian Church in order to be affiliated with Christ. The requirements are to love your fellowmen, lead a disciplined life, recognize the divinity in all faiths and all beings, and rule your daily life with love."

New World Order

"In the New World Order of which we speak, there can be no coercion of humanity's free will. In this NWO there are two outstanding characteristics: One is that greater numbers of us will become more experienced and successful in our exploration of the one remaining unconquered frontier--**the frontier of inner space**; the depths of our humanity from which have arisen such forerunners as a Plato, or a Shakespeare, a Beethoven, or even a Moses, or a Buddha. **This inner, spiritual dimension of our lives will be studied and explored just as carefully and scientifically as we have to date explored and studied our outer environment.**"

"The NWO to which we refer must **recognize that the resources of the earth must be set free to be used justly and fairly by all of the world's people**. Ended must be the sorry spectacle of those nations and those people who suffer from overabundance and the often-corollary sense of meaninglessness, and alienation and the opposite experience of nations and people who suffer from want and destitution."(Urso, The New World Order and the Work of the United Nations)

"**Government by a recognized Spiritual Hierarchy**. This Hierarchy will be related to the masses of the people by a chain of developed men and women who will act as the intermediaries between **the ruling spiritual body and a people who are oriented to a world of right values**. This form of world control lies indefinitely ahead. When it becomes possible so to govern, the **planetary Hierarchy will have made a major approach to earth,** and there will then be thousands of men and women in touch with their organization because they will be developed enough to be sensitive to Its thoughts and ideas."

"**Government by an oligarchy of illumined minds**, recognized as such by the massed thinkers, and therefore chosen by them to rule. This they will do through the education of the thinkers of the race in group ideas and in their right application. **The system of education, then prevalent, will be utilized as the medium of reaching the masses and swinging them into line with the major ideas and this will be done not by force, but through right understanding, through analysis, discussion and experiment**. Curiously enough (from the point of view of many) the spiritual Hierarchy **will then work largely through the world scientists** who, being by that time convinced of the factual reality of the soul and wise in the uses of the forces of the soul and of nature, **will constitute a linking body of occultists**." (Bailey, The Externalisation of the Hierarchy)

Portals

Nations, for instance, have seven centres, as have all forms of existence from the human and animal upwards, and it is an interesting study to discover these centres and note the type of **energy which flows through them.**

United States of America
Chicago is the solar plexus centre
New York is the throat centre
Washington the head centre
The heart centre is Los Angeles
Germany
The heart centre of Germany is Munich
The head centre is Nuremberg
Berlin is the throat centre
British Empire
London is, of course, the heart centre for Great Britain
(and temporarily it is also the head centre, though this will not always be the case),
Ottawa is the throat centre
Sydney is the solar plexus centre
(Bailey, Lucis Trust, Online Books)

Five Exits for Energies

The physical plane areas or localities which constitute the present modern exits for energies, through which directed energies can pass to carry out the creative process, are five in number: **New York, London, Geneva, Darjeeling and Tokyo.**

These five form a five-pointed star of interlocking energies, symbolic of the major divisions of our modern civilization. I would have you bear in mind that all that I am here giving you anent energy is in relation to the **human kingdom** and to nothing else; I am not relating these energies to the other kingdoms in nature; I am here concerned with physical plane **utilization of energy through the power of directed thinking and on behalf of the evolution and well-being of mankind**.

At each one of these five centres;

- One of the master's will be found present,
- His ashram,
- A vortex of spiritual forces will there be organized to hasten and materialize the plans of the Christ for the new and coming world cycle.

The organising of these five centres will be done slowly and gradually. A senior disciple will appear and will work quietly at the foundation work, gathering around him *the needed agents, aspirants and assistan*ts. All these workers at any particular centre will be trained to think, and the effort now present in the educational and social world to force men to think for themselves is a general part of this training process.

Already the centres in *London and in New York* are showing signs of life, and disciples are active in both places and along all lines of human expression.

The centre in Geneva is also active, but not so thoroughly and inclusively; it waits for a greater calm and a firmer sense of security in Europe. The centre in Darjeeling is what is termed occultly "vibrating", but this is in response to the relative nearness and propinquity of the Himalayan Brotherhood; In Tokyo there is small activity as yet, and what there is of no great moment. The work at this centre will actually be brought into being through the work of the *Triangles* (these are groups of three that invoke the Hierarchy daily around the world).

These energies which we have been considering are released into our planetary life through the medium of certain great inlets. At this time there are five such inlets, scattered over the world. Wherever one of these inlets for spiritual force is found, there will also be present a city of spiritual importance in the same location. These five points of spiritual influx are:

- London- For the British Empire.
- New York- For the Western Hemisphere.
- Geneva- For Europe, including the U.S.S.R.
- Tokyo- For the Far East.
- Darjeeling-For India and the greater part of Asia.

Thus the expressed aims and efforts of the United Nations will be eventually brought to fruition and a new church of God, gathered out of all religions and spiritual groups, will unitedly bring to an end the great heresy of separateness. Love, unity, and the Risen Christ will be present, and He will demonstrate to us the *perfect life*.

Table of nations

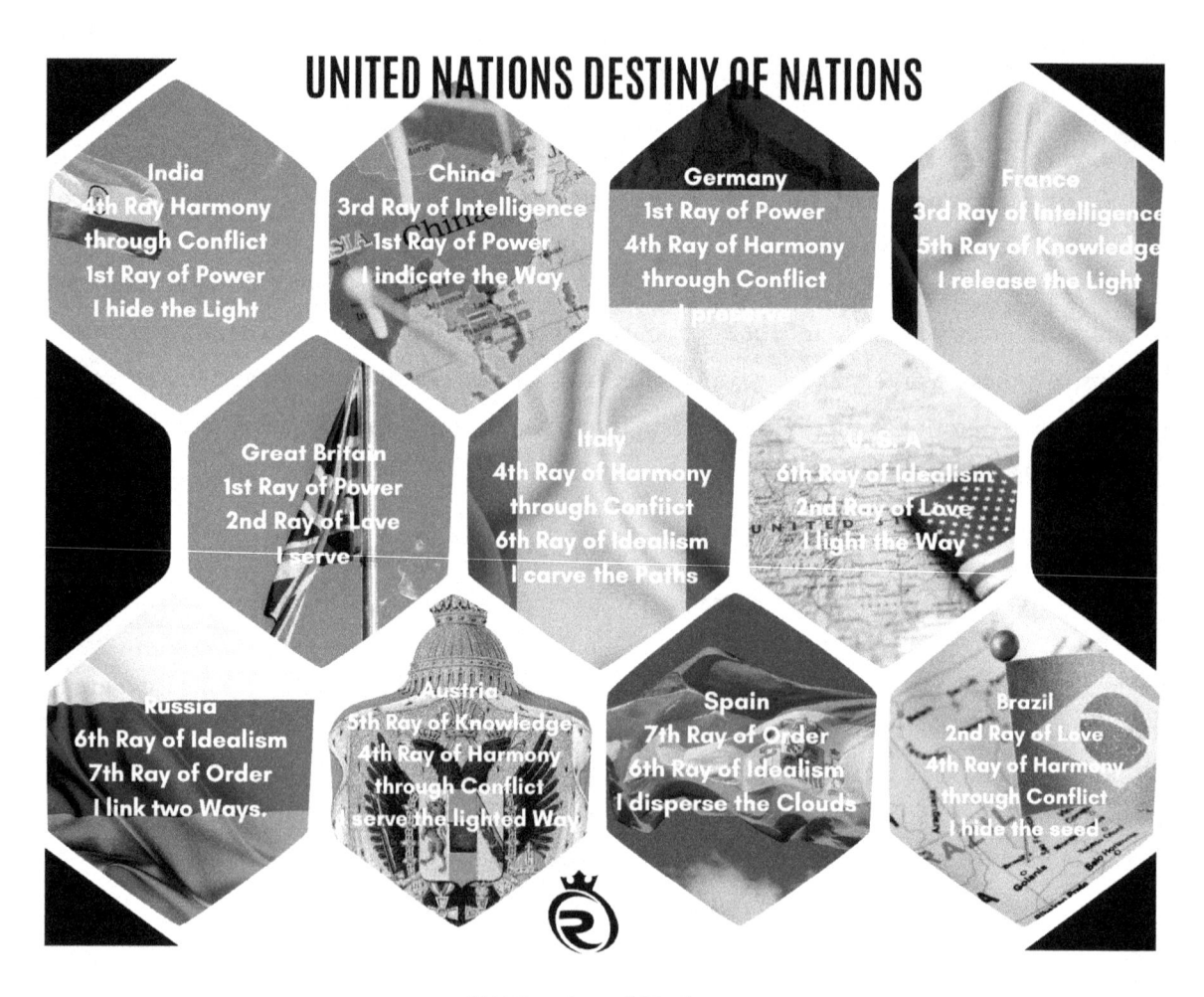

UNITED NATIONS DESTINY OF NATIONS

India
4th Ray Harmony through Conflict
1st Ray of Power
I hide the Light

China
3rd Ray of Intelligence
1st Ray of Power
I indicate the Way

Germany
1st Ray of Power
4th Ray of Harmony through Conflict

France
3rd Ray of Intelligence
5th Ray of Knowledge
I release the Light

Great Britain
1st Ray of Power
2nd Ray of Love
I serve

Italy
4th Ray of Harmony through Conflict
6th Ray of Idealism
I carve the Paths

U.S.A
6th Ray of Idealism
2nd Ray of Love
I light the Way

Russia
6th Ray of Idealism
7th Ray of Order
I link two Ways.

Austria
5th Ray of Knowledge
4th Ray of Harmony through Conflict
I serve the lighted Way

Spain
7th Ray of Order
6th Ray of Idealism
I disperse the Clouds

Brazil
2nd Ray of Love
4th Ray of Harmony through Conflict
I hide the seed

U.N Destiny of Nations
Revelations Publishing House

The Hierarchy

"That group of spiritual beings on the inner planes who are the intelligent forces of nature, and who control the evolutionary processes....Some may call it the Will of God; others, the inevitable trends of the evolutionary process; still others may believe in the spiritual forces of the planet; others may regard it as the spiritual Hierarchy of the planet, or the great White Lodge; many millions speak of the guidance of Christ and his disciples. Be that as it may, there is a universal recognition of a guiding Power, exerting pressure throughout the ages, which appears to be leading all towards an ultimate good."

Public Relations

Much has already been done in familiarizing the general public with the concept of the Hierarchy. Much of it has been done in such a manner as to bring the whole subject into disrepute, as well you know. **The groups now occupied with the dissemination of occult teaching** would be well-advised to change their methods if—beneath their pronounced ignorance and their love of the spectacular—there lies a true belief and a real humanitarian desire. Information about the Hierarchy should take the following lines:

1. **Emphasis should be laid on the evolution of humanity with peculiar attention to its goal, perfection.** This is not the idealistic perfection of the visionary mystic, but the control of the instrument, man in incarnation, by the indwelling and overshadowing soul. The constitution of man should be increasingly taught.
2. The relation of the individual soul to all souls should be taught, and with it the recognition that the **long-awaited kingdom of God is simply the appearance of soul-controlled men on earth** in everyday life and at all stages of that control.
3. From a recognition of this relationship, **the fact of the spiritual Hierarchy can then be deduced and the normality of its existence emphasized.** The fact will appear that the Kingdom has always been present but has remained unrecognized, owing to the relatively few people who express, as yet, its quality.
4. When this recognition has become general, the idea (by this time permanently present in the human consciousness everywhere) and good sense also will testify to the fact of the presence of those who have achieved the goal.

Their demonstration of divinity will be regarded as normal, as constituting a universal objective, and as the guarantee of humanity's future achievement; degrees of this divine expression can then be pointed out, ranging from that of the probationary disciple, through disciples, to Those Who have achieved mastery, and up to and inclusive of the Christ.

1. **Thus gradually the idea or concept of the existence, in bodily presence, of the**

master's will be inculcated and steadily accepted; a new attitude to the Christ will be developed which will be inclusive of all the best that the past has given to us but which will integrate men into a more sane and acceptable approach to the entire problem.

2. **The time will come when the fact of the presence on earth of the Christ as Head of the Hierarchy and the Director of the Kingdom of God will be accepted;** men will also realize the truth of the present revolutionary statement that at no time has he ever left the earth.

3. Emphasis will also increasingly be laid upon the unfolding plan, and men will be brought to its recognition through a study of the evolution of the human family, through a close consideration of historical processes, and through a comparative analysis of ancient and modern civilizations and cultures. The thread of purpose will be noted and followed through, century after century, integrating not only history into one complete story of the revelation of divine qualities through the medium of humanity, **but integrating with it and into it all world philosophies, the central theme of all creative art, the symbolism of architecture and the conclusions of science.**

Masters of Wisdom

"Senior members of Hierarchy are Masters of the Wisdom. A Master of the Wisdom is one who has undergone the fifth initiation or Spiritual Kingdom, the Kingdom of Souls. Having progressed through the four lower kingdoms:—the mineral, the vegetable, the animal and the human—the master's centre of consciousness has, through meditation and service, expanded till it now includes the plane of spirit through successive incarnations. The discipline of meditation is the only way in which this can be accomplished. Masters of the wisdom choose to stay upon our planet and limit themselves for the sake of men and women who are pressing forward on the wave of evolution. They serve the evolutionary process through meditation, or the manipulation of thought matter, and by work on the mental bodies of humanity."

Great White Lodge

"Wisdom teachings throughout the ages affirm the fact of an intelligent spiritual direction, a chain of being, underlying the evolution of consciousness. The name given to that guiding purpose varies in different traditions. Some refer to it as the spiritual Hierarchy of the planet, or the great White Lodge."

Custodians of the Plan

"The Hierarchy directs world events, as permitted by human free will, so that the evolving consciousness may express itself through adequate social, political, religious and economic forms. The Hierarchy directs world events, as far as humanity will permit (for the free will and free decision of humanity may not be ignored), so that the unfolding consciousness may express itself through developing and adequate social, political, religious and economic world forms. They give direction; They throw a light; They impress those who are in contact with them, and through the inflow of ideas and through revelation they definitely influence the tide of human affairs. The Hierarchy directs and controls, more than is realized, the unfolding cyclic cultures and their resultant civilizations. **There is a Plan for humanity and this Plan has always existed."** . The Spiritual Hierarchy (Booklet Adaptation ed.). *Profound statement!*

The lords

Thus the incoming focused energy, called forth in response to right invocation, is stepped down still nearer to humanity, and the masses can then respond to the new impulses. You have, therefore:

1. *The lords of liberation,* reached by the advanced spiritual thinkers of the world whose minds are rightly focused.
2. *The rider* on the white horse or from the secret place, reached by those whose hearts are rightly touched.
3. *The lord of civilization,* the *Master R.,* reached by all who, with the first two groups, can stand with "massed intent."

On the united work of these three, if **humanity can succeed in calling them forth,** will come the alignment and the correct relation of three great spiritual centres of the planet, a thing which has never occurred before.

Externalization of the Hierarchy

How will these Members of the Hierarchy in their various grades appear on earth? Will They come through the methods of ordinary birth, of childhood and maturity?

- Some initiates may follow this ordinary pattern, some are already passing through it today and are in the **stages of infancy and adolescence**; to them will be given a large share of the preparatory work.

Note: This was written in the 40s, so think about the people born in that era; many may have died by now. Reflect on those prominent figures born during that time.

- Some will not pass through these relatively limiting phases but will pass back and forth between the outer world and the world of hierarchical endeavor; they will be sometimes present in physical bodies and sometimes not.

- This method of activity will not be possible as long as the present rules of national and civilian identification, of passports and of drastic airport and seaport inspection are required by the authorities; such people as these "transiting initiates" would not be able to identify themselves. This form of appearance is therefore postponed for some time.

Will all the Members of the Hierarchy make their appearance at the same time? Certainly not.

- The appearing of these initiates and master's will begin with isolated members appearing and **living among men, coming forth one by one, doing the required work, returning through the portals of apparent death to the inner subjective Ashram**
- Again appearing by one or other of the methods mentioned above. This process has been going on for some time and began around the year 1860. The work of these disciples in the human consciousness is already being recognized, and already they have su**cceeded in changing the consciousness and the thinking of many millions**.

Their ideas are already permeating world thinking.

One thing only will I say:

- They will take modern life and what it means and will proceed to demonstrate how that life (the normal product of the evolutionary process) can be lived divinely.
- They will express the highest ideal of marriage (I would here remind you that many of the masters are married and have raised families) and demonstrate the principle which underlies the perpetuation of the race of men.
- They will express ordered, temperate living in all things, and will demonstrate also the possibility of the existence of people on earth who have no wrong inclinations and no bad qualities in their natures.
- They will stand forth as living examples of goodwill, of true love, of intelligent applied wisdom, of high good nature and humor, and of normalcy.
- They may indeed be so normal that recognition of **what they are may escape notice.**
- They will, finally, demonstrate to all around them the significance of right motive, the beauty of selfless service and a vivid intellectual perception.

Event of Externalization

Two things must be realized as the interested student considers this event of externalization:

The senior Members of the Hierarchy will not at first be the ones who will make the needed approach. Under their direction and their close supervision, this approach will be made—in the early stages—by initiates of and under the degree of the **third initiation,** and also by those disciples who will be chosen and designated to implement Their efforts and so will work under Their direction. It is only in the later stages, and when the time has come **for the return into recognized physical expression of the Christ,** leading to the **definite restoration of the Mysteries,** that certain of the **senior Members of the Hierarchy** will appear and take outer and recognizable physical control of world affairs. The time for this will be dependent necessarily upon the success of the steps taken by the members of the Hierarchy who are not so advanced.

Members of the Hierarchy, whether working in the early stages or later when the true externalization takes place, **will work as members of the human family and not as proclaimed members of the kingdom of God or of souls, known to us as the Hierarchy;**

They will **appear in office of some kind or another; they will be the current politicians, business men, financiers, religious teachers or churchmen; they will be scientists and philosophers, college professors and educators; they will be the mayors of cities and the custodians of all public ethical movements.**

The spiritual forcefulness of their lives, their clear, pure wisdom, the sanity and the modern acceptableness of their **proposed measures in any department in which they choose to function, will be so convincing that little impediment will be set in the way of their undertakings.**

Their immediate group work, when they are coming into power and recognition, will consist of a **sweetening and a clarification of the political situation and the presentation of those ideas which will eventually lead to a fusion of those principles which govern a democracy** and which also condition the hierarchical method—which is somewhat different; this effort will produce a *third political situation which will not be entirely dependent upon the choices of an unintelligent public or on the control which the hierarchical technique evidently involves.* The mode of this **new type of political guidance will later appear.**

THIS SECOND GROUP WILL IMPLEMENT THE NEW RELIGION;

By the time they come into control the old theological activities will have been completely broken;

- Judaism will be fast disappearing;
- Buddhism will be spreading and becoming increasingly dogmatic;
- **Christianity will be in a state of chaotic divisions and upheavals.**

When this takes place and the situation is acute enough, the Master Jesus will take certain initial steps towards reassuring control of his Church; the Buddha will send two trained disciples to reform Buddhism; other steps will also be taken in this department of religions and of education, over which the Christ rules, and he will move to restore **the ancient spiritual landmarks, to eliminate that which is nonessential, and to reorganize the entire religious field**—again in preparation for the **restoration of the Mysteries.**

THESE MYSTERIES, WHEN RESTORED, WILL UNIFY ALL FAITHS.

The stage wherein Christ and the Masters of the Wisdom can make **public appearance and begin to work publicly, openly and outwardly in the world of men.** The time of their coming will be dependent upon the success of the work undertaken by the first two groups; it is not possible for me to prophesy about this matter. So many factors are involved: the earnest work of the two groups, the readiness and the willingness of mankind to learn, the rapidity with which the forces of restoration and of resurrection can rehabilitate the world, the responsiveness of advanced humanitarians and intelligentsia to the opportunity to rebuild, to recreate and to reorganize the factors which the *new culture and the new civilization will demand. Even the Hierarchy Itself, with all Its sources of information, does not know how long this will take,* **but they are ready to move at any time.**

The Christ and the masters are occupied with the task of preparing for **the restoration of the Mysteries.** This restoration will fall into three phases and will cover and include in its symbolism all phases of human unfoldment. **The story of mankind will be pictorialized.**

These three phases correspond broadly and in a general sense to the **three degrees of the Blue Lodge in Masonry**. The analogy is not entirely accurate, owing to the unavoidable degeneracy of Masonry, but with the restoration of the Mysteries, Masonry also will come into its own. These phases are:

1. The stage of a general recognition of light in all departments of human living. This is inferred in the first stanza of the new Invocation. If the ritual of the E.A. is studied in the light of this information the significance will emerge. The poor and destitute candidate emerges into the light.

2. The stage of **complete economic reorientation**; in this, humanity is relieved of all economic anxiety and is free to receive its due wages and the right reward of all service rendered in the **building of the Temple of the Lord**; this building proceeds with rapidity.

3. The stage wherein the reward of light is received and the reward of service rendered; spiritual status is recognized through the medium of what is regarded as a major initiation, for which the first two initiatory degrees are only preparatory. **This first great initiation will be objectively staged and the general public will recognize it as the major rite and ritual of the new religious institution of the period.** This is the stage where the forces of resurrection are active, when the Lord is with his people and Christ has returned to earth.

RELIGION IS THEN RECOGNIZED AS AN ATTITUDE GOVERNING ALL PHASES OF HUMAN EXPERIENCE.

2025

(January 1946)

" Thus a great and new movement is proceeding and a tremendously increased interplay and interaction is taking place. This will go on until A.D. 2025. During the years intervening between now and then very great changes will be seen taking place, and at the great **General Assembly of the Hierarchy—held as usual every century—in 2025 the date in all probability will be set for the first stage of the externalization of the Hierarchy.** The present cycle (from now until that date) is called technically "The Stage of the Forerunner." It is preparatory in nature, testing in its methods, and intended to be revelatory in its techniques and results. You can see therefore that Chohans, Masters, initiates, world disciples, disciples and aspirants affiliated with the Hierarchy are all at this time passing through a cycle of great activity."

Destruction

Negative Groups

The Masses, The Churches and religions, The Esotericists in their turn.

Positive Groups

The Intelligentsia, The esotericists, aspirants and occultists, The Planetary Hierarchy.

The problem before the Hierarchy at the **beginning of the new or Aquarian Age** was how to fuse and blend these two distinct groups, attitudes or states of consciousness so that from their fusion a **third group could emerge** which would be exterior in its activity and yet consciously alive to the interior values; they should be able to function upon the **outer plane of appearances** and, at the same time, be equally awake and active upon the **inner plane of reality and of spiritual living.** This type of dual functioning is the easiest activity for the Members of the Hierarchy and constitutes the sine qua non prior to association with that Hierarchy.

It is interesting to note (though it is of no immediate moment) **that the work of destruction initiated by the Hierarchy** during the past one hundred and seventy-five years (therefore since the year 1775) has in it the seeds—as yet a very long way from any germination—of t**he final act of destruction which will take place when the Hierarchy will be so completely fused and blended with Humanity** that the hierarchical form will no longer be required. **The three major**

centres will then become the two, and the Hierarchy will disappear and only Shamballa and Humanity will remain, only spirit or life, and substance as an expression of intelligent love will be left. This corresponds to the experience of the individual initiate at the fourth initiation, when **the causal body, the soul body, disappears and only the monad and its expression, the personality (a fusion of soul and form) are left.** This event of final dissolution will take place only at the **close of our planetary existence,** when the door to individualization is finally closed for a pralayic period and the Way of the Higher Evolution will be more closely trodden than the Path of Initiation.

The material goal which all who love their fellowmen and serve the Hierarchy must ever have in mind and at heart is the defeat of totalitarianism. I do not say the defeat of Communism, but the defeat of that evil process which involves the imposition of ideas, and which can be the method of the **democratic nations and of the churches everywhere,** just as much as it is the method of the U.S.S.R. This we call totalitarianism. I would ask you to have this distinction clearly in your minds. Your material goal is **the defeat of all that infringes human free will and which keeps humanity in ignorance; it applies equally to any established system—Catholic or Protestant—which imposes its concepts and its will upon its adherents.** Totalitarianism is the basis of evil today; it is found in all systems of government, of education; it is **found in the home** and in the community. I refer not here to the laws which make group relations sound, possible and right; such laws are essential to community and national well-being and are not totalitarian in nature. I refer to the imposition of the will of the few upon the total mass of the people. The defeat of this undesirable tendency everywhere is your definite material goal. **Your spiritual goal is the establishing of the Kingdom of God.** One of the first steps towards this is to prepare men's minds to accept the fact that the **reappearance of the Christ is imminent.** You must tell men everywhere that the master's and their groups of disciples are actively working to **bring order out of chaos.** You must tell them that there IS a Plan, and that nothing can possibly arrest the working out of that Plan. You must tell them that **the Hierarchy stands, and that It has stood for thousands of years,** and is the expression of the accumulated wisdom of the ages. You must tell them above all else that God is love that the Hierarchy is love, and that Christ is coming because he loves humanity. This is the message which you must give at this time. And with this responsibility I leave you. Work, my brother.

The preparatory work of externalization, therefore, falls into three phases or stages, as far as relation to mankind is concerned:

First. The present stage in which a few isolated disciples and initiates, **scattered all over the world, are doing the important task of destruction,** plus the enunciation of principles. They are preparing the way for the first organized body of disciples and initiates who—coming from certain Ashrams—will proceed with the next phase of the work

Second. The stage of the first real externalization upon a large and organized scale will succeed upon the above endeavors.

These disciples and initiates will be the **real Builders of the new world,** of the new civilization; **they will assume leadership in most countries and take high office in all departments of human life**.

This they will do by the free choice of the people and by virtue of their advanced and proven merit.

By this means, gradually the Hierarchy will take over the control upon the physical plane—subjectively as well as objectively—**of the direction of human affairs**.

This direction will be in virtue of their known and approved capacity and will not involve the imposition of any hierarchical control or authority; it will simply signify the free recognition by free people of certain spiritual qualities and effective activities which they believe signify that these men are adequate to the demanded job, and whom they therefore choose as **directing agents in the new and coming world.**

Freedom of choice under the authority of a spiritual livingness which demonstrates competency will be distinctive of the attitude of the general public.

Men will be put into high office and into positions of power not because they are disciples or initiates, but because they are wise and intelligent servants of the public, with an internal awareness, **a deeply religious and inclusive consciousness, and a well-trained mind with an obedient brain.**

The direct quotes from the Alice Baily, the United Nations Prophetess and its affiliate organizations, as well as from people as high up as their Secretary General, are nearly implausible. This is not a Sci-Fi movie, an outer space comic book, or the latest high-tech game. This organization is the largest body in the entire world. Every nation with but a few exclusions is a member state of the United Nations. After reviewing this material, you will ponder, who runs the world? Is it possible spiritual entities or, as the Bible says, spiritual wickedness in high places controls the ruling powers of this planet?

The book of Daniel accounts for an entity called the *Prince of Persia*, who was not an earthly Prince. That account in the book of Daniel is eye-opening to the actual spiritual wickedness in high places.

> 20 He replied, "Do you know why I have come? Soon I must return to fight against the spirit prince of the kingdom of Persia, and after that the spirit prince of the kingdom of Greece will come. [Daniel 10:20] NLT

In *Thy Queendom Come*, we explained how the Babylonian rulers would venerate these spirits in statues and temple sacrifices.

- The kings and the people feared these spiritual powers.
- The kings and people reverenced them for the general protection, vegetation, and well-being of the land.
- Ritual child sacrifice to appease these gods.

Most scriptures of the Bible spent time rebuking the children of Israel for their idolatry. Idolatry and serving other gods were significant Biblical themes. These were not simply carvings of wood; Queen of Heaven [Jeremiah 7:18], weeping for Tammuz [Ezekiel 8:14], temples of Diana in the New Testament [Acts 19:35], sacrifices to Moloch [Acts 7:43] and Baal [Jeremiah 19:5], and the star of Remphan [Amos 5:26] were all "entities" that are still prominent in the occult today.

The United Nations and all its peacekeeping efforts are the epitome of the *calm before the storm;*

> 3 For when they shall say, Peace and safety; then sudden destruction cometh upon them, as travail upon a woman with child; and they shall not escape. [I Thessalonians 5:3]

"Two years ago on April 23, 1998, hundreds of thousands of people in over eighty countries stopped to pray peace for ten minutes. The goal was to show scientifically what the mystics and the sages have always said, that a focused 'feeling based' prayer is the most powerful force in the universe. *James Twyman*, one of the sponsors of the vigil, was at the **United Nations in New York with nearly forty ambassadors when the vigil took place**. Minutes before it began a woman stepped into the center of the circle and said these words:"

"Four years, four months, four weeks and four days ago, a group of Hopi elders **came to the UN to give their vision of the New World**. One of the things they said was, 'Four years, four months, four weeks, and four days from now, **something would happen at the UN that would change the world.' This is the day these great people prophesied.**" (Return of the Dove)

Connecting the Dots

Hierarchy= approaching closer to humanity, restore the ancient Mysteries

Lucis Trust=divine plan, interdependent world, meditation, Lucifer Publishing Company

Lucifer = angel who brought light to the world, Christians mistake Lucifer with Satan, solar angel, advanced being, descended (thus "the fall"), Venus, great sacrifice, light-bearer

Fallen Angels= Plan of evolution, solar angels, willingness to "fall" or sacrifice, light of the principle of mind, evolved animal man, Law of Duality, Prometheus, Prodigal Son, Seraph, dwell in Ursa Major, control entrance points

Mercury-Hermes = light-bearer

Venus= Gaia (Earth), home of fallen angels

United Nations= Aquarian organization, spiritual welfare of humanity, teach spiritual mysteries openly again, planetary consciousness, diabolical convergence of New Age mysticism, pantheism, aboriginal animism atheism, communism, socialism, Luciferian occultism, apostate Christianity, Islam, Taoism, Buddhism, and Hinduism...a strange admixture of crystal worshipers, astrologers, feminists, environmentalists, Kabbalah, human potentialists, Eastern mystics, pop psychologists, and 'liberal' clergymen, destiny of humanity

Meditation UN=cleanses the mind, attainment of the highest wisdom, change conditions, invoke the higher spiritual potencies, enlightenment and illumination, evolutionary development, spiritual contact, build the new man in Christ

The Master K.H.= (works with) Catholic Churches—Greek, Roman and Anglican—with the leaders of the Protestant communions, field of education, dominant demagogues and organizers of the people, open up the world of departed souls to the seeker, laboratories of the world, Red Cross

Angels=guard the sanctuaries of all the churches, Lord Agni; He seeks to touch with the hidden spiritual fire the head centres of all intuitive statesmen.

The Master Jesus (Ascended Master)=controls masses of the Christian people, group of Devas work under his command, connection with all true church leaders, inner esoteric council of the churches, carries out the behests of the Christ

English Masters=guidance of the Anglo-Saxon peoples, England and America

Christ= The Tibetan, official name as head of the Hierarchy.

NWO= resources of the earth must be set free to be used justly and fairly by all of the world's people, Government by a recognized Spiritual Hierarchy, planetary Hierarchy will have made a major Approach to earth, Government by an oligarchy of illumined minds, education, world scientists, will constitute a linking body of occultists.

Spiritual Hierarchy= group of spiritual beings, intelligent forces of nature, control the evolutionary processes, familiarizing the general public with the concept of the Hierarchy, groups now occupied with the dissemination of occult teaching, evolution of humanity with peculiar attention to its goal, perfection, Masters of Wisdom (senior members), Great White Lodge, Custodians of the plan (directs world events), the Lords (energy invoked through invocation), externalize 2025

Kingdom of God=appearance of soul-controlled men on earth

72=shapes in meditation room mural

SECTION VII

Lucifer Unveiled!

LUCIFER UNVEILED!

18

Lucifer Unveiled!

Black Virgin Unveiled

I learned long ago that nothing is what it seems when dealing with the Kingdom of darkness. Many people falsely believe the black version of the Madonna and the child is about her "race." Nothing could be further from the truth. The black virgin denotes that *she hides something in secret*. She's concealing a mystery; black, in this sense, means *secretive*. This black virgin mother and child are concealing many "layers" of secrets. Once we unveil them, you will understand why this black virgin is worshiped around the globe by her satanic cult.

Virgo

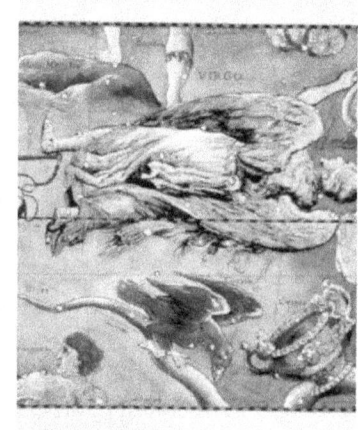

Virgo the Virgin mother goddess
Revelations Publishing House

Firstly the constellation of Virgo was thought to be the **great mother goddess** that ruled over the golden age of Lemuria, which preceded their great Atlantis.

Like many other mother goddesses, Virgo is also; Nana, Eve, Ishtar, Demeter, Herrera, Asherah, Diana, Isis, and the Virgin Mother. These are all venerations of this goddess whom they say **existed before the time of the masculine gods.**

"**Virgo will be the sign in the heavens which will precede the coming of Horus,** the pagan messiah who will avenge the Knights Templars by destroying the Roman Catholic Church."

"Should another Fatima-type apparition occur in the sign of Virgo, perhaps at Medjugorje, such an event would hardly vindicate **Roman Catholicism as the 'one true Church.'**

Eleusinian Mysteries

The Alexandrian Jews were a part of the Eleusinian mysteries, which included the abduction of Demeter's daughter Kore (Proserpine) by the god Pluto or, some say, Hades. Hades would keep her daughter for six months, and Demeter would be mourning. This story of Proserpine descending to the netherworld was a tradition preserved in a massive secret society with many rites, sacrifices, and sexual orgies, among other things. **Followers of Greek goddess worship began intertwining the Eleusinian mysteries into Christianity [Catholicism]**, which was the beginning of Gnosticism. This Mother goddess was most popular, as seen through the Egyptian goddess Isis, the highest goddess in the pantheon.

Hades abducting Proserpine

Mystery religion=initiation=mother goddess=Catholic Church

Isis

"Immaculate is our Lady Isis...the very terms applied afterwards to that personage (the Virgin Mary) who succeeded to her form, titles, symbols, rites, and ceremonies. Thus, her devotees carried into the new priesthood the former badges of their profession, the obligation to celibacy, the tonsure, and the surplice, omitting, unfortunately, the frequent ablutions prescribed by the ancient creed."

"The Black Virgins, so highly reverenced in certain French cathedrals...proved, when at last critically examined, **basalt figures of Isis!**'" (Aho)

"*Cyril*, the Bishop of Alexandria, had openly embraced the cause of **Isis, the Egyptian goddess, and had anthropomorphized her into Mary,** the mother of God." (H.P. Blavatsky)

Chartres Cathedral

After the dissolution of the Knights Templar, the Priory decision continues to **mainstream the idea of the black virgin**. The cathedrals built in the middle ages were perfect examples of this campaign. In particular, the **Notre Dame Cathedral parallels the Virgo constellation**. Many strange ceremonies were said to take place beneath these temples.

The sacred site upon which Chartres Cathedral was erected was dedicated by the Druids to the Sun.

"The Druids, like most initiatory tribal cultures, **worshiped the principle of the Eternal Feminine** as the source of all fertility."

Chartres Cathedral
Chartres, France

"The Virgin portrayed in the west facade of Chartres Cathedral is called the 'Virgini Pariturae' which means **"the virgin about to give birth."** This statue does not represent *Mary or the Biblical concept of womanhood*, but the archetypal goddesses of fertility and the *feminine principle*. Since Chartres **was dedicated to the Sun-God, the child of the sculpture is Horus, not Jesus Christ.** (Wallace-Murphy and Hopkins)

"The Black Virgin was, in reality, Virgo, the Great Mother goddess, known to the Egyptians as Isis, christened in Alexandria as Mary Magdalene."

Black Virgin=Virgo=Isis=Mary Magdalene

"According to *The Cult of the Black Virgin*, the full name of the Prieuré is the Order of the

Prieuré Notre Dame de Sion. Former Grand Master of the Prieuré, Pierre Plantard de Saint Clair, has identified **Notre Dame as Our Lady of the Light, i.e., Lucifer, the Light-Bearer.** (Begg)

Black Virgin=Virgo=Isis=Mary Magdalene=Lucifer

From 33rd Degree Freemason Christopher Knight;

"**Christianity [Catholicism] found ways to demonize Venus.** Venus formed part of the *Holy Shekhinah* and it had been the sacred hour hand of time. It represented the supreme power of the goddess, and in fact the planet still bears her name because **Venus was merely the Roman counterpart of the Egyptian Isis and the Greek Aphrodite,** who herself just another version of the great goddess. **Venus was also the symbol of the Holy Virgin,** something that would not be forgotten by Freemasons many centuries into the future, suffused as their practices would be with the beliefs of the Star families [Illuminati bloodline]."

Venus=Shekhinah=Isis=Aphrodite=Holy Virgin

"Christianity eventually shunned Venus worship altogether. True it persisted on the fringes of the Christian world, in particular in Scandinavia where **Lucifer,** *Lord of light*, became *Saint Lucie*, whose winter solstice celebrations, candles and fires became embedded in local Christian practices. But in the main, **Venus, as either a male or a female representation**, was viciously attacked. **Lucifer, who had originally been a deity or sub-deity associated with Venus was now treated as just another name for Satan.** The magical mathematical association between the movement of Venus and those of the Sun as seen from earth became the stuff of forgotten and forbidden legend as the Christian Church persecuted those who merely looked at the heavens with an intellectual curiosity."

"*The light of Lucifer* had been extinguished. Ignorance had triumphed over wisdom and superstition had replaced logic. The church spread a veil of darkness across Europe as truth became turned on its head. The dark ages were about to begin." (Knight and Butler Chapter 3 To Rescue an Empire. Page 67-68)

Venus=male or female=Lucifer

St. Lucia, born around AD 283, was a young virgin Sicilian girl devoted to Jesus. However, she had an arranged marriage to pair her with a pagan man. Lucy refused, so her fiancé turned her in to authorities after she declined to become his bride officially. Once in custody, the authorities had plans to force her into prostitution. They tortured Lucy by tying her to oxen, even burning her, but she did not die. One torture included having her eyes plucked out of her head.

For this reason, Lucy is depicted in art, holding her "eyes" on a plate or in her hands. St. Lucia eventually met her demise by being stabbed in the throat with a dagger. Lucy is considered the patron Saint of those with eyesight problems. Her relics are venerated at the Church of St Geremia. Her head was sent to Louis the 7th of France and kept at the Cathedral of the Bourges. Lucy is frequently depicted wearing a crown of seven candles. (Feast of St. Lucy)

St. Lucia
Note the cross is a Baphomet cross

Venus=male or female=St. Lucia=Lucifer

Leviathan –Baphomet Cross
Serpent intertwined at the bottom

Mother goddess and Sun god

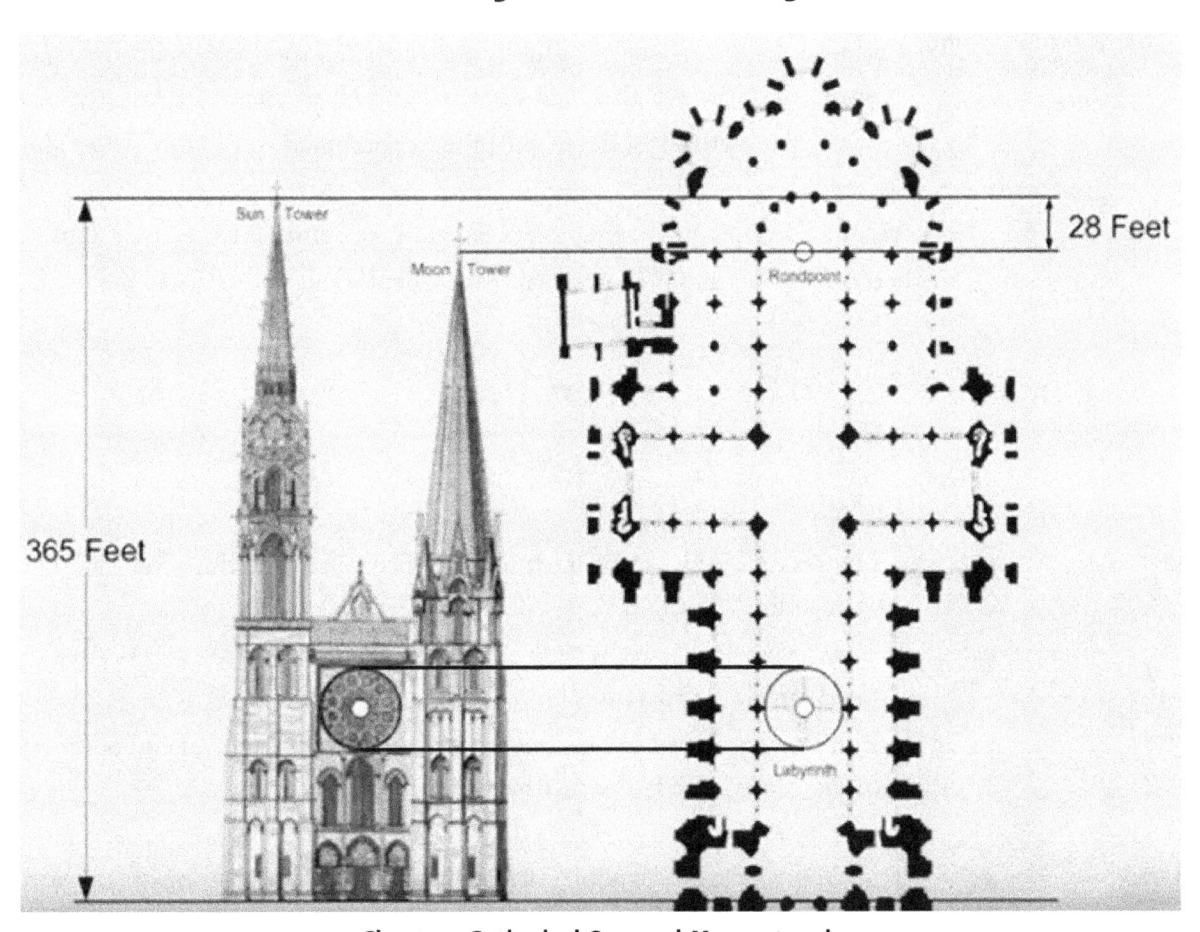

Chartres Cathedral Sun and Moon steeple

The massive and mysterious Chartres Cathedral and other Cathedrals around northern France are nearly 1,000 years old (1200-1300 A.D.). At least in concept, these structures are credited to the Knights Templar. These cathedrals are architectural wonders and are highly occultic with symbolism. Chartres has two skyscraper-size steeples representing occult dualism, sun=male, moon=female. The Statue of Liberty is 305 feet from base to torch, and the sun steeple at Chartres is 365 feet! Chartres also contains several relics, including a famous Black Madonna and Child.

As a refresher, the Knights Templar stood accused of worshiping a creature called Baphomet. This horror is a half-goat half-man, hermaphrodite beast with wings, female breasts, and other demonic elements (see *Thy Queendom Come*, Knights Templar, Chapter 23). Baphomet represents occult dualism which is the entire Luciferian belief system in a nutshell.

Author and researcher *Tracy Twyman* (now deceased) gave a provocative interview about some of the deeper secrets of the Bull, stone, Saturn, mother goddess, and Knights Templar. This is bombshell information;

Black Madonna and Child
Chartres Cathedral

- Eliphas Levi (high-level occultist that depicted the Baphomet drawing) wrote that; the Knights Templars had aimed to create "**the synthesis of all persecuted beliefs,**" meaning a combination of all heresies and pre-Christian religions.
- "Pope Pius IX accused the Templars of trying to **start a new religion,** inspired by Kabbala, Gnosticism, and heretical beliefs about *John the Baptis*t and deplorable and obscene sex rites.

Knights Templar=Kabbala=Gnosticism=One World Religion

The Great Mother Cybele

Mistress of wild nature, fertility, and protectress in times of war, her companion was a lion.
The Naassenes (Gnostic sect) secretly worshiped *Cybele*. **That means the Templars did as well.**
Romans worshiped Cybele in antiquity, and she became an embodiment of the "state." **She is the mother goddess to the Romans.**

Many worshipers adorn the great goddess as a **rock that fell from heaven.** Cybele, in legend, was a **Hermaphrodite.** In "heaven" the elders decided she was to be a woman, **so she was castrated and cast down to earth from heaven.** The rock is a portal but also an egg, signifying a portal from one plane to the next.

Great mother Cybele

Knights Templar=One World Religion=Cybele Worship=Roman= mother goddess=Hermaphrodite=rock

Note: If you follow the rabbit hole far enough, everything will start to connect; Cybele was worshiped as a rock and originally hermaphrodite. She is also divine or not fully human.

"The Church attempted to exert control over this Marian cult in its traditional manner by taking over pre-Christian forms of worship and sacred sites dedicated to various goddesses, renaming them in honour of the Holy Virgin. The symbolism, prayers and litanies associated with Demeter, **Cybele,** Ishtar and Isis **were adopted and given a Christian veneer.**"

Mary Idolatry=Cybele=Ishtar=Demeter=Isis

Mother and child

Attis Cybele's son

Cybele had a son whom she didn't want and, at his birth, left him for dead. Someone found and raised him. When he matured, the unthinkable happened. She fell in love with him, her son! Cybele began an incestuous sexual relationship with Attis when he was young. When Attis entered manhood, he fell in love with a woman and proposed. On the day of the wedding, Cybele shows up. In some versions, she filled him with madness and made him castrate himself, and he bled out and died. She felt terrible. She missed him and supposedly resurrected him.

In honor of this epoch, "The Rites of Attis" are celebrated during the last week of March, ending in April. One day commemorates the castration and the next day commemorates his resurrection.

Her priest' were castrated! The priest inductees would castrate themselves in honor of Attis, her son. The priest would have a parade where they were drunk or on drugs and then perform self-mutilation in public.

"In a Vatican poem Attis is called **the Supreme god** (hypsistos)." (Vermaseren Cybele in Rome, Italy and Sicily. Page 49-50)

"Attis, but this time winged and with burning torch, bearing the young cup-bearer Ganymede up to heaven (pi. 40). Thus the shepherd (pastor), Attis, leads another Phrygian shepherd, Ganymede, to immortality. The artist has here assigned the part of Zeus himself to Attis, who grants Ganymede eternal youth." (Vermaseren Cybele in Rome, Italy and Sicily. Page 56)

Attis=divine mother=giver of immortality=Serpent (Eve you won't surely die)=Lucifer

Phyrgian Cap Cult
Revelations Publishing House

Mithra (sun god)

Classic Mithra portrait slaying the bull

Mithra is an Iranian Sun god from the Zoroaster tradition whose worship spread literally to many parts of the world. Mithra cults appeared in Rome under the name of *Sol Invictus* (unconquered sun). Mithra is centrally important to this fundamental research; firstly, looking at Attis, he's a literal carbon copy of the images of Mithra with the Phyrigian cap. Cybele's origins are in Phrygia.

Mithra had been born from a rock instead of a woman.

To eliminate the female principle from their creation myth, the Cult of Mithra **replaced the Mother of All Living in the primal garden of paradise with the Bull named *Sole-Created*.**

- **Instead of Eve, this Bull was the partner of the first man.** (It doesn't take much imagination to figure out what happened between man and bull).

- The man engaged in bestiality by raping the Bull and then killed the Bull out of repulsion, fear, and guilt.
- The man then sought out other Bulls to do it all over again.
- Mithra, who wanted to have a son but hated the race of women, ejaculated onto a stone.
- After the appropriate time, the stone became pregnant and produced a boy called *Diorphus.* (Ps.Plutarch) *De fluviis*, XXIII. 4.

Mithra=born from a rock=virgin

This revelation about Mithra and the famous bull picture is repulsive; understand, this is not what it means. There are always interpretive meanings. The Bull, as we know, represents Taurus; the Bull is also considered the "mother" of the trinity in the zodiac.

Aries (father) = Taurus (mother) = Gemini (the fusing of the two, hermaphrodite child)

Note: the outcome of sex magick and alchemy, etc., is to create new "beings," more specifically, an androgynous, sexless race, like the angels in their heavenly state.

Earlier, we discovered the Bull as the bestow-er of light. The Bull also birthed the Golden age of Saturn. The Bull needs to birth the era, but afterward must be sacrificed to come fully into the Golden age of Saturn again. Every new era of evolution requires some pain, sacrifice or chaos.

Bull=bestower of light=Golden Age of Saturn=sacrifice

Lucifer's goal is the destruction of YAH'S creation, and it's been going on from the beginning of time. It is the most wicked of agendas, yet it's not new. Mithra's constant slaying of the Bull is his constant evolution and enlightenment. Mithra did not have a mother, and his origin was a rock. The "rock birth" could interpret his "divine" origin. Lucifer also did not have a mother. Lucifer was a created being. Mithra was divinely born, virgin birth, and he produced a son that was the same, divinely born. This is the Luciferian agenda, destroy GOD'S creation and replace it with the image of the beast (bull).

No matter what "divine feminine" energy is widespread, remember the SEED OF THE WOMAN would come to CRUSH THE HEAD OF THE SERPENT [Genesis 3:15]. Women don't have seeds, so this is the divine prophecy of the Messiah. To eliminate the woman, Lucifer, through the centuries, has given inventions to create life without a woman. This wickedness is done to corrupt creation, control procreation, and eliminate the Messiah coming through the woman forever (which failed because MESSIAH came and will return).

"The devil (is the inspirer of the heretics) whose work it is to pervert the truth, who with idolatrous mysteries endeavors to imitate the realities of the divine sacraments. Some he himself sprinkles as though in token of faith and loyalty; he promises forgiveness of sins through baptism; and if my memory does not fail me marks his own soldiers with the **sign of Mithra on their foreheads,** commemorates an offering of bread, introduces a mock resurrection, and with the sword opens the way to the crown. Moreover has he not forbidden a second marriage to the supreme priest? He maintains also his virgins and his celibates." (Geden)

Mithra=bestiality=mark in forehead

"Mithra and Cybele, though contradictory in many ways, could have been combined by the Templar magicians into one thought-form that was more **powerful than both, the Baphomet.**" (Twyman, Author, Researcher)

Mithra + Cybele = Baphomet

Here are some provocative connections with Cybele (the great mother) and earlier concepts discussed;

"Come then, and let us follow where the gods' bidding leads, let us appease the winds and seek the realm of **Gnosis**! Nor is it a long run thither; if only **Jupiter** be gracious, the third dawn shall anchor our fleet on the Cretan coast.' So he spake, and on the altars slew the sacrifices due, **a bull to Neptune, a bull to thee, fair Apollo, a black sheep to the storm-god, a white to the favoring Zephyrs.** (Vermaseren Cybele in Asia Minor and Greece. Page 25)

This poem about the Cybelene mysteries mentions Gnosis (wisdom, Sophia), Jupiter, Neptune, bull, black and white, all these are very significant.

"Since the goddess was worshipped in the shape of a meteorite **her name was connected with 'cube'** and was derived from this root (Kubaba). Her name was also translated Virgin. (Vermaseren Cybele Her Name. Page 22)

Cube = Mother goddess

"In 204 BC the king of Pergamum sent her to Rome in the shape of a meteoric stone. Thereafter she was worshipped not only as a Mountain goddess but as the **mighty Mother of the Trojans and the Romans whom legend claimed were of Trojan descent.**" (Vermaseren Introduction. Page 11)

Cybele=Mother of Trojans=Tribe of Dan=Merovingians=unholy Grail bloodline

"Mithra is brought from Persia and the hill-country of the Red Sea, a stone of varied colors that reflects the light of the sun...The Assyrians prize Eumitren the jewel of Bel their most honored deity, of a **light-green color and employed in divination.**" (Geden p.27. *History of Alexander*, book 4, chapter. 13.)

Note: The light green jewel is confirmation enough to know that Mithra is Lucifer

Mithra=green jewel=Lucifer

Babylonian Mystery Religion (one world religion)

"Thus the people, wherever the **Babylonian system** spread, were bound neck and heel to the priests. **The priests were the only depositories of religious knowledge;** they only had the true tradition, by which the writs and symbols of the public religion could be interpreted; and without blind and implicit submission to them, what was necessary for salvation could not be known. Now compare this with the early history of the Papacy, and with its spirit and modus operandi throughout, and how exact was the coincidence! In that system, **secret confession to the priest**, according to a prescribed form, was required of all who were admitted to the "Mysteries" and till such confession had been made, no complete initiation could take place." (Hislop Distinctive Character of the Two Systems. Page 5-11)

Babylon mystery system=Papacy

Six Pointed Star

Seal of Solomon
Eliphas Levi

"**The six-pointed Star** refers to the six *Forces or Powers of Nature*, the six planes, principles, etc., etc. all synthesized by the seventh, or the central point in the Star. All these, the upper and lower hierarchies included, emanate from the '**Heavenly or Celestial Virgin,' the great mother in all religions, the Androgyne,** the Sephīrāh-Adam-Kadmon." (Blavatsky) - 209:215 (Vol. I) (H. P. Blavatsky)

Cirlot's *Dictionary of Symbols* reveals that the six-pointed star **signals the birth of a god;**

"Since [Virgo] is governed by Mercury and corresponds to the number six it is symbolic of hermaphroditism, or that state which is characterized by dual - positive and negative - forces. Hence **Virgo is sometimes depicted with the symbol of the soul or the Seal of Solomon** (two triangles, representing fire and water, superimposed and intersecting to form a six-pointed star). In mythology and in religions generally, this symbol is always associated **with the birth of a god or a demi-god,** as the supreme expression of the dynamic consciousness." (Cirlot)

"**The Mark of the Beast will be a symbolic representation of the Anti-Christ's own androgynous state** (which is why he is called a 'beast') and the "transformed" condition of humanity under the perverse influence and governance of this demigod. The Anti-Christ's declaration of 'peace and safety' takes on new meaning when we understand that the "transformation of mankind" will bring God's wrath upon the world:

"The six pointed star is a Caldeo-Assyrian symbol that existed centuries before the Jewish forefathers (David et al) associated it with Judaism. Its original meaning is from the **early goddess cults** and means ritual sexual intercourse: the upright triangle represents the male (two testicles and penis) while the downright represents the female (two breasts and vagina). **The Quintile between Saturn and Venus represents the magical powers of the Goddess (Lilith, Astarte, Isis, Artemis, Venus, Eve, Mary...) having magical sex with Saturn, the Lord of Karma.** (M-Star)

Anti-Christ =goddess cults=Saturn + Venus= Androgynous child=Six Pointed Star=Mark of the Beast

Directly from the Official Website of *Priory of Sion*;

"The Merovingian Dynasty, was the first dynasty of the Frankish Kings, descended from Merovee. Our tradition teaches that Merovee, who was also a mystic and a Wizard, in addition to being a warlord, has been in **possess of a lot of ancient knowledge that today belongs to our Venerable Order.** Merovee, was not just an historical figure, but also mythical and legendary, in fact, an ancient legend depicted him as a son of a King and of a sea monster which joined his wife."

"This legend, it is actually a myth, created to pass a very essential knowledge, to make possible to unravel the ancient origins of the Merovingians, which are **going back to the ancient Babylon, as the sea monster described in the legend, is an ancient representation of Nimrod, he who built the Tower of Babel and ruled Babylon.**'

"The Priory focuses on placing one of their satanic lineage of the Merovingians on the throne. In a subtle trick bag, turn people's hearts from the FATHER and his SON to the worship and adoration of the mother goddess. The Priory, therefore, has involvement in women's rights and equal rights for women. The idea of women's rights has nothing to do with equality; instead, it usurps the authority of GOD'S order with the supremacy of women."

Directly from the obscure Priory of Sion website, the myth unravels! The "beast of the sea" who "sired" the Merovingians was referring to NIMROD, whose symbol is a FISH.

Merovee=Sea Beast=Nimrod=Origins of Merovingians=Unholy Grail bloodline=Anti-Christ

"There are in fact, different representations of Nimrod, of him with a headdress depicting the semblance of a fish; this same headdress was later adopted by the Popes of the Roman Catholic Church, up to the present day.

Lucifer put out a lie that Jesus' symbol was a fish. No where in Scripture is there a mandate or sign attached to Christ. The fish symbology was a construct of Catholicism and Gnosticism, which was perpetuating the Mystery Cult of Nimrod and Babylon and not the Savior, Jesus Christ (Y'SHUA HAMASHIACH).

Nimrod = Fish

Friday Fish Day
Catholicism "Lent" ritual

"Horus, i.e. Nimrod, who will at last unite the world under Lucifer. Recall that the myth of Horus is a distortion of the Genesis account of God's judgment on the Tower of Babel. (Gen. 10 and 11) Not happy with this arrangement, **New Agers anticipate the return of Horus as the reincarnation of Nimrod who will finally unite mankind in a glorious revolution which dethrones God.**

Horus myth=Tower of Babel=Nimrod

In preparation for the occult *New Age of the Spirit,* the high-level initiates who have infiltrated the Laodicean Church will attempt to **palm off Lucifer as the Holy Spirit**, in accordance with the Manichean tradition that the *Holy Spirit is the transformed Lucifer*. Eventually, the **Virgin-Bride (Isis) is 'married' to the Christ Child (Horus), who is the incarnation of her husband/brother, Osiris, aka Lucifer,** the Spirit with whom she united:

"Peter Dawkins wrote in The Great Vision that, in Cabalistic mysticism, the Throne (Isis) also represents the Temple in which the union of the **Virgin Soul (the initiate) to the Spirit (Lucifer) takes place**. This union, which is achieved only by the highest adepts and masters, produces the Christ Child who is the 'living embodiment of Light', which Dawkins states is the meaning of Horus. In other words, **Horus is the incarnation of the 'Spirit' Lucifer."**

Isis + Horus=Osiris=Lucifer=holy spirit

Unholy Grail

"In mockery and imitation of God's 12 tribes, *Satan blessed 12 bloodlines.* One of these bloodlines was the *Ishmaeli* bloodline from which a special elite line developed alchemy, assassination techniques, and other occult practices. One bloodline was *Egyptian/Celtic/Druidic* from which Druidism was developed. One bloodline was in the orient and developed oriental magic. One lineage was from *Canaan* and the *Canaanites*. It had the name *Astarte,* then *Astorga,* then *Ashdor,* and then *Astor. The tribe of Dan* was used as a *Judas Iscariot type seed.* **The royalty of the tribe of Dan have descended down through history as a powerful Satanic bloodline.** *The 13th or final blood line was copied after God's royal lineage of Jesus.* This was the Satanic [version of the] House of David with their blood which they believe is not only from the House of David but also from the lineage of Jesus, who they claim had a wife and children. The 13th Satanic bloodline was **instilled with the direct seed of Satan** so that they would not only carry Christ's blood--b**ut also the blood of his "brother" Lucifer**. One of the bloodlines goes back to Babylon and are d**escendant from Nimrod."** (Springmeier, Bloodlines of Illuminati. Page 2)

What a revelation! The 13 Illuminati Families supposedly all go back to the familiar Biblical enemies of the 12 Tribes of Israel. While it cannot be confirmed, the Rothschilds are said to be in the lineage of Nimrod. One possible clue into this is a young Rothschild that died at the early age of 16 (1922-1938) was named *Albert Anselm Salomon* **Nimrod** *von Rothschild.*

666

"We should, therefore, understand that the archangel Michael's battle with the dragon, in Revelation 12:7, corresponds to the conflict between the Zadokite succession and the "**beast of blasphemy**"-Imperial Rome. The "second beast" was that of the rigidly **strict regime of the Pharisees,** who thwarted the ambitions of the Hellenist Jews by segregating Jews from Gentiles. **This was the beast to which was attributed the number 666** (Revelation 13:8) the numerically evaluated polar opposite to the spiritual energy of water in the solar force." (Gardner Chapter Four The Early Mission. Page 44)

This statement alleges that the beast of Revelation is two fold;

1. Rome, Vatican, Papacy
2. Pharisees (Talmudism, Kabbala, Synagogue of Satan)

> ⁹ I know thy works, and tribulation, and poverty, (but thou art rich) and I know the blasphemy of them which say they are Jews, and are not, but are the synagogue of Satan. [Revelation 2:9]

We've reviewed earlier that genetic testing and history have eliminated most professing "Jews" as the legitimate ethnic heirs of the Semitic line. The Semitic line means the descendants of Shem (Noah's son), from which came the 12 Tribes of Israel. This lineage is the "Chosen People of God." Specifically, the lineage of Judah, which is the Royal line of King David and Christ.

All European nobility claim lineage from Judah or one of the 12 tribes, it's the reason why they have assumed rulership. These claims extend to the families such as the Rothschild and Merovingians that run areas of industry such as banking, media, entertainment, business etc.

I can't stress enough this lineage in the end times is critical. This lineage is how the Anti-Christ will "claim" the *divine right to rule* and sit on the throne at the rebuilt temple in Jerusalem.

"The Synagogue of Satan" do not follow the Torah as many falsely believe. The Torah is the basis, but the Babylonian Talmud is the Rabbinical interpretation, and the Kabbalah is a book of esoteric mysticism.

You must completely understand this very complex belief system and its history. As a point of reference, most that follow Judaism today follow the Talmud and have taken up the *doctrines of devils* Christ fought against vehemently. The Kabbalah specifically was a central theme in *Thy Queendom Come*.

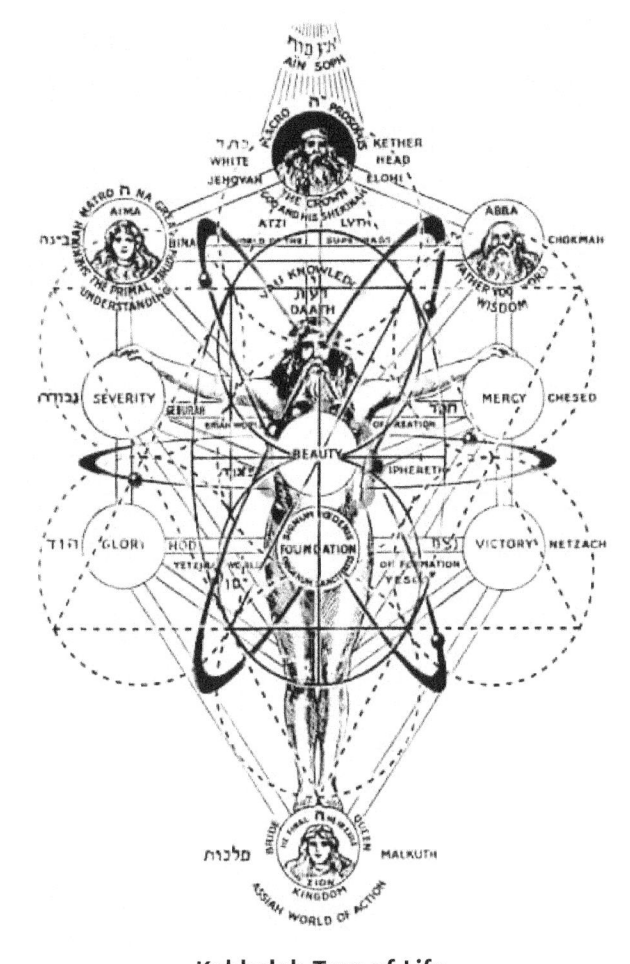

Kabbalah Tree of Life
Malkhut is on the bottom- this is also Shekhinah

I will refer to this apostate group as "The Synagogue of Satan."

"The [Synagogue of Satan], then, will be their own Messiah. The Kabbalah tells us that [Synagogue of Satan] shall rise from the depths of the abyss. First, the goddess *Malkuth*, united sexually with her phallic consort, *Hesod*, shall elevate them upwards, toward the *Crown of Life*. Along the way, the Serpent shall watch over and guide the [Synagogue of Satan]. The Serpent is their symbol, providing chaos and destruction of the world of the Gentiles. From this chaos and destruction comes, finally, order." (Marrs, Holy Serpent of the Jews: The Rabbis Secret for Satan to Crush Their Enemies and Vault the Jews to Global Dominion. Chapter 15 We shall be our own god)

Note: Order out of Chaos. Ordo Ab Chao, the motto of the 33rd Degree (Scottish Rite Freemasonry).

"According to the highest-ranking Kabbalistic rabbis, the Serpent represents not only a **specific deity, Lucifer,** but **also the whole nation,** or [The Synagogue of Satan]. The collective of all the [Synagogue of Satan] wherever they may reside on this planet, is said to be the **body of the Serpent**. The head is claimed to be the *Illuminati* initiates who, behind the scenes, are masterminding and guiding the Serpent in his path of global dominion." (Marrs, Holy Serpent of the Jews: The Rabbis Secret for Satan to Crush Their Enemies and Vault the Jews to Global Dominion)

"And do the [Synagogue of Satan] not foresee that their overshadowing Messiah, **the Holy Serpent Leviathan,** and the combined false deity of *Malkuth* and *Hesod* represent not the [Synagogue of Satan] themselves but the Beast with the prophetic number 666 (Revelation 13)?"

"The [Synagogue of Satan] actually teach in their Kabbalah Zohar that the number 666 is not an unholy number but is instead, for Judaism, an exalted and befitting gematria number for Messiah. *Rabbi Moses Hayesod,* cited in the *Vilna Goan commentary of the Zohar,* happily admits this. He states, "The **number 666 contains within it exalted and lofty messianic potential.**"

If the Pope is, as we have seen, the legitimate representative of Saturn, the number of the Pope, as head of the Mystery of Iniquity, is just 666. But still further, it turns out, as shown above, that the original name of Rome itself was Saturnia, "the city of Saturn." The Pope has a double claim to the name and number of the beast."

Serpent=fish=Nimrod=Babylon=Synagogue of Satan=Vatican=Saturn =Lucifer=666

The Vatican is also connected to the Serpent. These are pictures of Vatican Audience Hall, an obvious temple for he worship of the Serpent.

Lucifer Unveiled

United States of Lucifer

Lady Liberty

"A century ago the Frenchman, *Auguste Bartholdi*, built a statue and placed it in New York Harbor. It's construction was funded in large part by the Freemasons in France and America. The figure stands dressed in a Roman toga-and in her hand, a golden cup-like torch. Could it represent the Grail? **Does it symbolize *the Magdalene bloodline* enlightening the world?** The official name is "Liberty Enlightening the World." But, doesn't that sound a bit like blasphemy? Jesus Christ is the Light of the world- not Liberty. Could the statue really be that of **Mary, the Magdalene?**

Statue of Liberty

This age-old worship of the Magdalene appears to be the result of an esoteric mystery religion, which I believe is described in Revelation 17 as "Mystery, Babylon the Great." This undue preoccupation with "goddess worship" is also a motivating force for women's movements, women's liberation, feminism, and the New age movement. **Which are all seeking to replace Christ with a WOMAN."**

"I wonder if that is why the psalmist wrote in Psalm 87:4 "I will make mention of *Rahab* and Babylon to them that know me..." Rahab was a notorious harlot in the days of Joshua, and the verse appears to be a reference to the harlot Babylon. According to Psalm 87, the harlot will one day be revealed. At this point we can only pose the question. We can only say that her name is "Mystery."(Church Chapter Four The Myth of Mary Magdalene. Page 74-77)

"The Mery's were the high Priestesses, and so **Jesus was born from a Virgo Mary on the Horus day.** Magdala, is a Hebrew word meaning Tower. It was the name given to Miriyam, one of Yeshua's female disciples, who in all likelihood was his wife. She was called Mary of Magdala, or Mary Magdalene. We also believe she was co-Messiah with Yeshua. God-the-Father and God-the-Mother both chose to incarnate themselves upon the earth together in order to draw their created selves (all of us) back to Them. **And now they are returning....**" (Finney)

The Statue of Liberty holds a light; she bears a light in her hand. The Statue of Liberty is, therefore, a light-bearer (Lucifer).

The Congressional Medal of Honor Society issues medals for military achievements. On their website, it states directly the inspiration for the Statue of Liberty;

Lucifer Unveiled

"The Statue of Liberty is In addition to standing for Liberty, she is derived from the imagery of **Queen Semiramis of Babylon** who was famed for her beauty, strength and wisdom."

Air Force Congressional Medal of Honor "Liberty"
Congressional Medal of Honor Society

Vintage Queen Semiramis drawing

State of Liberty=Mary Magdalene=Semiramis=Queen of Babylon=Light Bearer=Lucifer

"**Viracocha is also analogous to Quetzalcoatl** of the Aztecs; to the Queshua, Aymara, and other tribes of South America, he is known as *Ameru,* which means 'serpent'. It will come as a shock to many Americans that the name 'America' is probably derived from '**Ameru', the serpent-god, and not the Italian voyager 'Amerigo' Vespucci!**" America, Land of the Plumed Serpent.

"This is why Masonic Lodges were already here. Since these ancient serpent legends include the Mesoamerican feathered serpent gods and can be looked upon as a historical testament of that *Angel thrown down by god,* "then perhaps *The Land of the Plumèd Serpent* may also be known as the **Land of Lucifer**," concludes Ken Hudnall in The Occult Connection II: The Hidden Race." (America the land of Lucifer, the real story behind the name)

United States = Land of the Plumed Serpent=Land of Lucifer

AMARUCA

Land of the Plumed Serpent

U.N. Unveiled

Security Council Chamber
UN HQ New York

It has already been proven, beyond the shadow or spec of doubt, that the United Nations is a Luciferian organization with a New Age of Aquarius One World Agenda. Although it takes some proverbial digging to find Lucis Trust (formerly Lucifer publishing), it's not impossible. Now, it's time to lift the veil of deceit fully.

The leaders of 193 countries of the U.N. have been at the Security Council Chamber at one time or another. The chamber is where world leaders meet to debate world crises, wars, and other global matters. Right in the middle of the room is an ominous mural.

The highly occultic mural in the U.N. Security Council Chamber is the highlight of this room. The entire mural has several disturbing images and themes (including a stork with its spirit underneath its feet"), which would take this whole book to decode. The focus of my interpretation will be on the "Garden of Eden" depiction.

My interpretation of this mural has its basis in my understanding of the Mystery System belief.

Close up of mural
UN HQ New York

- The young girl and boy do not represent children
- They represent the un-evolved man.
- Mankind (the girl and boy) is in the primitive state of evolution, or as we read earlier, the mineral/vegetable man.
- For man to evolve, he had to have knowledge.
- Lucifer, as the Serpent and as the TREE OF LIFE himself, offers Eve the fruit of his tree, which is knowledge.
- The girl (Eve) takes this knowledge and has begun to blossom (hence the flowers).

- The man (Adam) holding his hand out is ready to partake of the knowledge and have his eyes opened.
- His eyes right now are closed.
- Even the young Adam is hiding behind the tree staying safe as he was commanded.
- Eve was outside of the realm of protection, in their estimation "liberated."
- Eve is willing to take a chance on this wisdom hence she recevies the gift from Lucifer, as the Serpent.
- Adam is willing to receive this gift from his wife.
- The child out front, I believe, is Cain, the fruit from this union after their eyes "opened," who is the archetypal "Anti-Christ, savior, Horus" conceived knowing good and evil.
- The proof of this is the child is holding a dove;

Dove=holy spirit=Sophia=wisdom=serpent=Lucifer

- Remember their philosophy, man must walk past this "animal" stage to evolve to godhood, so all of the evil in the world is not evil. It's a painful part of the evolutionary process.

The United Nations, the largest inter-governmental body in the world, and their blatant worship of Lucifer is proof of who is running the world behind the scenes.

"I was told how **those who govern the power upon the earth are those who have FALLEN from the higher heavens and now indwell in the stars** known by earth-man as Ursa Major. From this threshold gate, they control one of the major entrance points into our local system from the higher heavens." (Hurtak)

"At one time, the Lucis Trust [Lucifer Publishing] office in New York was located at 666 United Nations Plaza and is a member of the Economic and Social Council of the United Nations under a slick program called "World Goodwill." (Atrayu)

*United Nations=One World Order=Tower of Babel
(reversed)=Nimrod=Cain=Serpent=Lucifer*

Annuit Coeptis

Vintage Back of Great Seal

The plans for the United States of America have been made plain on the entire dollar bill from front to back. In *Thy Queendom Come*, the back of the *Great Seal* was decoded and exposed by the "secret" society responsible for its symbolism. We will now delve into the origins of this wording "Annuit Coeptis" and "Novus Ordo Seclorum."

Virgil
5 October 70 BC – 21 September 19 BC

The inspiration for the wording come from two works;

1. From Virgil's *Aeneid*, Virgil is a famous Ancient Roman Poet who lived 5 October 70 – 21 September 19 BC;

Latin, *Juppiter omnipotes, audacibus annue coeptis*

"All-powerful *Jupiter* favor (my) daring undertakings"

2. To uncover another layer of meaning to, *Novus Ordo Seclorum* we look to Virgils' *Epologue IV: The Messiah*, which Virgil quotes the *Cumaean Sibyl* who was a priestess presiding over the Apollonian oracle at Cumae, a Greek colony located near Naples.

Cumaean Sibyl
Andrea del Castagno 1400s

Note: The poem excerpts are in bold. My interpretation is italicized;

- **Once more the circling centuries beg in...**
    - *An age or an era will begin a new.*
- **The Virgin reappears and Saturn reigns.**
    - *Virgo or some constellation alignment with Venus which will place Saturn back as "the greater light" i.e.*

- **From heav'n descends a novel progeny;**
    - *An angelic or divine "being" will come to earth.*
- **Now to this child in whom the iron race throughout the world shall cease and turn to gold.**
    - *When this divine child comes, the world will return to the Golden Age of Saturn, Eden, Atlantis, Paradise etc.*
- **Extend thy aid, Lucina, chaste and kind, For thy Apollo reigns.**
    - *Apollo is the "name" of this divine child (son of Jupiter).*
- **Under thy rule what trace may yet remain, With us of guilt, shall vanish from the earth Leaving it free for ever from alarm.**
    - *It seems to me this is an elimination of all that do not align with the return of this Golden age, the uninitiated.*
- **He will accept his life as of the gods, With whom the heroes mingle;**
    - *This is a return of the Watchers, Nephilim that intermingled with the daughters of men in Genesis 6.*
- **Seen by them, The whole world will he rule, now set at peace By his great father's power:**
    - *This is a One World Ruler, this is the Anti-Christ.*
- **To him shall bring Dear offspring of the Gods—the time is come, Start on thy road thou mighty fruit of Jove (Jupiter)!**
    - *This is the son of Jupiter, who will once again populate the earth with demi-gods and rule under the Golden Age where Saturn reigns.*

This poem is shocking and lays out a picture of the coming age. The Ancient Greeks believe time rotates in ages Golden-Silver-Bronze-Iron, and then it repeats. We are in Iron, where Jupiter rules, but time will transfer back to the Golden Age, where APOLLO, the son of Jupiter, will reign under Saturn. In other words, the Golden Age of Saturn will return, and Apollo will rule. Apollo comes from heaven and will rule over a race of "god-men" on earth, and this is the RETURN of Nephilim, the "gods of mythology" the "men of renown."

This *Virgin Reappearing* signifies this *great mother goddess,* who has many names, returning to her rightful place. Her "place" connected to her husband, is the great marriage. The two will become one again, the woman returning to the man, and this "being" will be androgynous. Humanity, as we know it now, will end.

US destiny=land of sacrifice=Golden Age=return of Saturn=Apollo=return of Nephilim=US Mystery Babylon

NASA Apollo logo
NASA

NASA has an entire program called the Apollo. The Kingdom of Darkness has been subtly announcing its plans to the world. The purpose of NASA alone is to explore "space," a domain where mankind cannot naturally survive. NASA is Nimrod's reversal of the *Tower of Babel*.

> [14] "I will ascend above the heights of the clouds; I will be like the most High." [Isaiah 14:14

Lucifer Telescope renamed LUCI (just like St. Lucy was renamed)
Not connected with the Vatican but is housed at the same observatory the Vatican utilizes

Lucifer's Last Stand

These series of succeeding events throughout the centuries may seem to be unrelated. Still, as you look at the entire picture, you will see that the goal of these Luciferian bloodlines is to eventually put somebody on the throne to rule as "the Christ." Well, we know this is actualy "the anti-Christ." So they came up with this scheme, this lie. The lie is that Christ never died on the cross, and "his bones" are proof of that, kept secret by these wicked secret societies. At the appointed time, they will prove to the world that Jesus never died, but he went on to have children with Mary Magdalene, and their seed is on the earth.

However, the secret of the Black Madonna and child and Mary Magdalene is a lot more sinister than you imagine.

"*The Enthroned Lady* or *Heavenly Queen* is the ancient title of Isis, the virgin mother of Horus, **as also of Mary, the virgin mother of Jesus**. The hieroglyphic symbol of Isis used by the Ancient Egyptians was that of a throne—Isis being the actual throne or seat upon which the child Horus sits as King of Light (the Sun King)."

"Just as a flame enables light to be manifested as a blazing orb or sun of radiant light, so the perfect Soul enables the Spirit to become fully manifest as the *christ child*. Just as the central orb of light sits enthroned in the midst of the flame, shining its radiance or glory all around, so the *christ child* sits as a *king of glory* upon his throne: **Horus sits upon Isis; Jesus sits upon Mary;** the christ consciousness sits upon man's soul. Then, just as the flame becomes identified with the light, swallowed up by its glory, **so the Mother becomes identified with her child, 'assumed' and 'married', as it were to her Son**."

"If God was Jesus' Father and Mary his mother, Mary must also have been the wife of God, and if Jesus himself was also God then Mary was his wife also. In this respect she closely resembles the Greek Demeter and the Egyptian Isis." (Knight and Butler Chapter 3 To Rescue an Empire. Page 66-67). *33rd Degree Freemason and historian, Christopher Knight.*

Just as in lure, Semiramis married her son (Nimrod) and then birthed his son (Tammuz, being technically her son and grandson) and the rest of the goddess tales like Cybele and Attis, this is the true wicked, dark, sinister meaning of the *Black Madonna and Child*.

Madonna and Child=mother and son=husband and wife=parents= Anti-Christ

So Magdalene is just a title or a term. In this sense, Mary's role as "wife" is Mary Magdalene.

PURE PERVERSION! This level of wickedness towers beyond any stretch of the sane imagination. I am sure most people bowing at various shrines of the *Madonna and Child* (whatever color) have no idea about the hidden veils of dark secrets these idols contain.

What can't be denied is that those same parishioners are undoubtedly aware of the Ten Commandments. The Second Commandment is very explicit concerning images and likenesses;

> [1]Ye shall make you no idols nor graven image, neither rear you up a standing image, neither

> shall ye set up any image of stone in your land, to bow down unto it: for I am the LORD your God. [Leviticus 26:1]
>
> 4 Thou shalt not make unto thee any graven image, or any likeness of any thing that is in heaven above, or that is in the earth beneath, or that is in the water under the earth. [Exodus 20:4]

It gets worse if that's possible. The Black Madonna has her tradition in Queen Isis and **her roots in the pre-patriarchal Lilith.** She thus represents the strength and equality of womanhood-a proud, forthwith tan commanding figure, as against the strictly subordinate image of the conventional White Madonna. It was said both *Isis and Lilith* knew the secret name of God." In Talmudic tradition Satan is Samael (the male part) and Lilith is his female. Samael + Lilith= Satan. This Madonna and child is literally the worship of Satan.

Lilith and Samael are one hermaphrodite "being"
Lilith is married to Samael (Satan)

As I was studying *the Shekhinah* for previous works, underneath many veils, I found *Lilith,* so under many veils of mystery and deceit the *Madonna* is found to be the demon *Queen Lilith*, the patroness of all demons. Lilith traces back to "the garden" and is the patroness of the *Dragon Grail succession of Cain* which goes through the Merovingians. Remember the Merovingians can be traced through most European-[Synagogue of Satan] bloodlines.

"*The Priory* focuses on placing **one of their satanic lineage of the Merovingians on the throne.** In a subtle trick bag, turn people's hearts from the FATHER and his SON to the worship and **adoration of the mother goddess.** The Priory, therefore, has involvement in women's rights and equal rights for women. The idea of women's rights has nothing to do with equality; instead, it usurps the authority of GOD'S order with the supremacy of women. "(Church)

Black Madonna=Lilith=Adam's first wife=Samuel's female=Dragon bloodline progenitor=Satan

We have now only to inquire what was the name by which *Nimrod* was known as the god of the Chaldean Mysteries. That name, as we have seen, was **Saturn**. Saturn and Mystery are both Chaldean words, and they are correlative terms. As Mystery signifies the Hidden system, so **Saturn signifies the Hidden god. To those who were initiated the god was revealed; to all else he was hidden**. Now, the name Saturn in Chaldee is pronounced Satur; but, as every Chaldee scholar knows, consists only of four letters, thus —Sttir. This name contains exactly the Apocalyptic number 666

S=60
T=400
U=6
R=200
=666

The "Hidden One;" that is, to Saturn, the "god of Mystery. (Hislop The Name of the Beast. Page 269-270)

Nimrod=Saturn=Satan=Anti-Christ

Bill Cooper (*Behold a Pale Horse, The Hour of the Time* broadcast) did a series on *Mystery Babylon* and the religion of the secret societies (mystery schools of antiquity). Mystery schools teach a series of symbolic myths that hold other meanings. The schools have a system of communication that surpasses language and stays out of the public view of detractors. After the *Tower of Babel*, languages were confused, and people were scattered. The mystery religion of Nimrod then spread throughout the earth. Due to climate, culture, and nationality, Nimrod, Semiramis, and Tammuz (original pagan Trinity) took on multiple names. Still, it was all the same goddess-based, "god-hood" religion centered around Nimrod, the first and only world ruler.

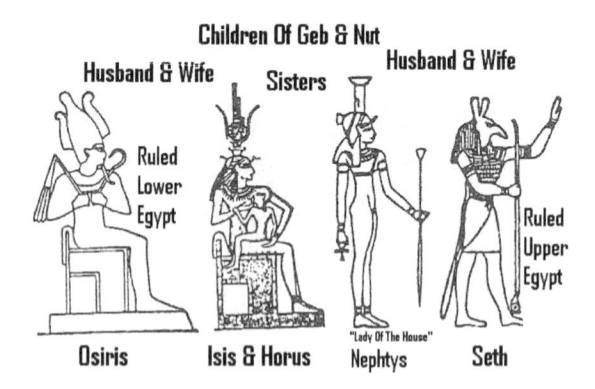

Mystery schools, like *Freemasonry*, give every degree of initiation a different focus and myth and what each means. After going through the Osiris-Isis accounts, Bill Cooper confirmed a bombshell. Osiris and Isis aren't real historical figures. They never were and were never meant to be. Osiris was Nimrod, and his murder and body being cut up into 14 pieces by his jealous brother *Set* was an allegory for "the church" and "the masses" after the *Tower of Babel*. This devil Set is intolerant and ignorant. Osiris's body "cut up" represents the remnants of the faith scattered worldwide. After Nimrod's death, Semiramis took over the mystery schools, where she became the focus, claiming to be "divine." The only thing not recovered was his "phallus"; therefore, the obelisk all over the world, including in Washington D.C., represents the phallus of Osiris. Which, one day, will be attached back to his body, and the Golden age will return.

Bill Cooper was clear to conclude that after decades of research, these were his findings. He was open to being wrong, deceived, or tricked by secret societies and their many-layered meanings and systems.

One thing is clear, to the Kingdom of Darkness, their highest deity is the Fallen Angel (Seraphim/Cherubim) Lucifer. His plan was and is to overthrow both the Kingdom of Heaven and the Earth.

"Like the goddess Isis, who found and restored all of the lost pieces of her husband, Osiris, many are restoring the unity of all life, bringing together the separate parts of humanity—different races, religions and cultures." (McLaughlin and Davidson)

Luciferian Global Network
Phallus of Osiris as their symbol

19

Conclusion

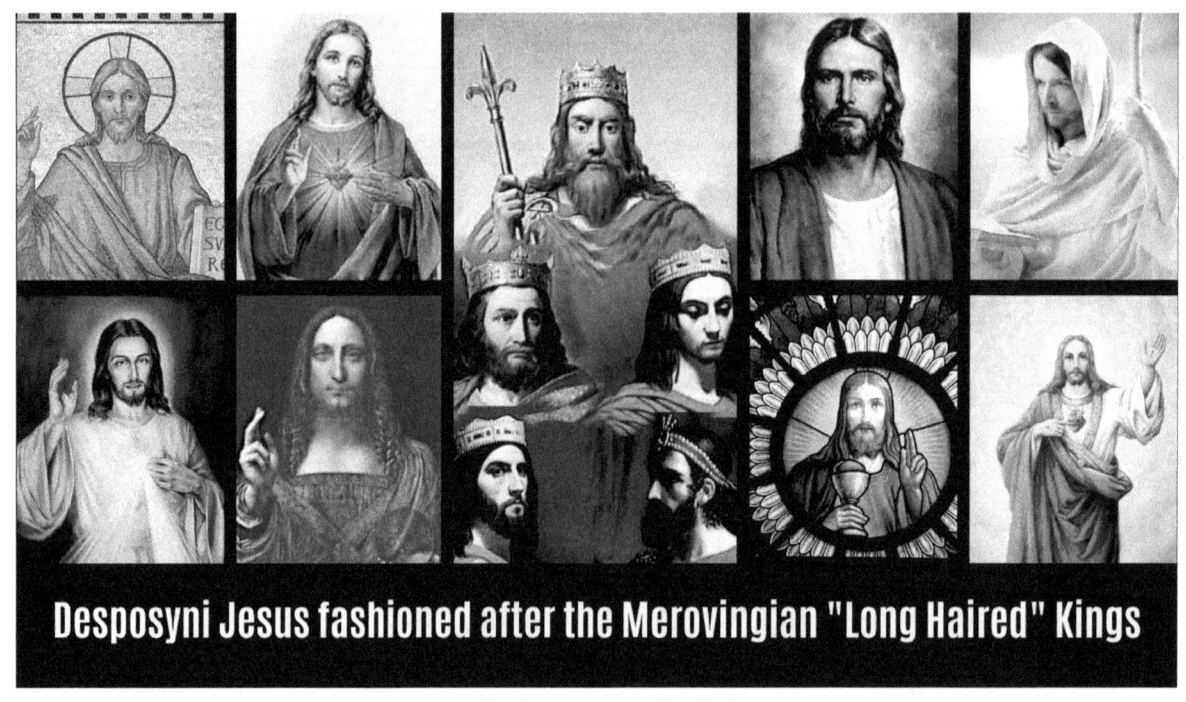

Merovingian Long Haired Kings
Crafted images of Jesus after their image– THIS IS NOT JESUS CHRIST

To the followers of the MOST HIGH. Examining the enemy's agenda from the enemy's vantage point can be confusing and exhausting. It can sometimes leave more questions than answers. We cannot combat an enemy we don't know, and the truth is, most believers do not see the cleverly laid plans of the enemy. Uncovering these plots is necessary as the WORD instructs us to expose the works of darkness;

> "And have no fellowship with the unfruitful works of darkness, but rather reprove *them*."
> [Ephesians 5:11]

"The Mystery Religions each had their secret councils which ruled them, and these councils themselves came under the guidance of a secret supreme Grand Council or Governing Body. The Mystery Religions in turn ruled the masses and the political leaders. When I first began investigating the Illuminati a clear picture developed that **the history books were doctored, and that great power was concentrated in the hands of oligarchies around the world.**"(Springmeier, Bloodlines of Illuminati. Page 3)

> " [1] And there came one of the seven angels which had the seven vials, and talked with me, saying unto me, Come hither, I will shew unto thee the judgement of the great whore that sitteth upon many waters. [2] With whom the kings of the earth have committed fornication, and the inhabitants of the earth have been made drunk with the wine of her fornication...[5] And upon her forehead was a name written, MYSTERY, BABYLON THE GREAT, THE MOTHER OF HARLOTS AND ABOMINATIONS OF THE EARTH." [Revelation 17:1-2, 5]

The Mystery Babylon net is widening. The apostate Mystery Religion predates Catholicism, Eastern Mysticism, Judaism, Christianity, and every belief in the known world. The original religion dates to the Garden, introduced to Eve by the Serpent;

- Question GOD'S authority and do what's best for you
- Obtain forbidden knowledge
- You will become immortal
- You will become "as gods."
- This religion involves duality, knowing GOOD AND EVIL (Samael + Lilith)

Alice Bailey confirmed that one of the goals for the U.N and the Hierarchy was to return to the Mysteries. This belief system has never changed, it involves various rituals, practices, and doctrines, but it all comes down to these essentials. This "doctrine of devils" is the religion of Lucifer, Satan, Samael/Lilith, and the fallen angels. This religion (historically) has passed through the bloodlines of the Nephilim and apostates of the Bible. Once driven underground from the Tower of Babel, this Mystery Religion spread worldwide. As time progressed, various mainstream, occult, Gnostic, pagan, Jewish, Christian, eastern mysticism, and New Age religions absorbed and kept these mysteries.

The Illuminati group responsible for the back of the Great Seal (see Thy Queendom Come, Chapter 31 Mystery U.S.A.) also verified the Mysteries were returning to the U.S.

In actuality, the Mystery Religions never left; but the "mysteries" have weaved their way into every area of our lives. This subversion has taken place over centuries.

Most people don't realize this *Mystery Religion* is the unofficial religion of the world; for instance, December 25 is Nimrod's birthday, and people worldwide cheerfully celebrate this! Another example of the Mystery Religion is the practice of horoscopes. The use of horoscopes is the practice of divination, which the Word of God strictly prohibits. Yet, believers haply claim "Aries, Taurus, etc." as a part of their personality. Unbeknown, people, are participating in the Mystery religion of Babylon. We read in this book the veils of secrecy behind Santa Claus, mermaids, etc. the list goes on.

Today's hermaphrodite, gender dualism, and gender erasure in the United States should prove the Mystery Religion doctrine is the New World Religion. Many religions, not just Judaism, share the six-pointed star because it belongs to the Mystery Religion. Also, the pentagram or a star interweaves with everything from the U.S. flag to the gold star given to elementary children for good behavior. These common symbols don't garner any attention. Still, they are, in fact, the highest in occult magic and practice for summoning demonic spirits.

These Mystery Religion groups run the entire world. Each branch is responsible for various factions. These families are all over the globe, scattered and working their "magic" as you would. This Mystery Religion involves the Pharaohs, The Caesars, The Royals, Entertainers, Oligarchs, Presidents, Zionist Bankers, etc.

Now the time has come when they are no longer hiding. Luciferians have poisoned society and the church to such an extent there is no need to hide. The infections, even in the church, have pulpits worldwide calling good, evil, and evil, good. Even calling on the name of the Shekhinah, this un-biblical term, invokes their goddess. Shekhinah is also Isis, Ishtar, Diana, Gaia, the Virgin Mary, Cybele, Astarte, Kali, the Queen of Heaven, and, as I learned, LILITH. Unfortunately, too many churches seem to have allowed the influence of the Kingdom of darkness into the pulpits.

The deep, twisted, new age, mystery school philosophy hidden in plain sight will deceive even the very elect in the last days. Our society is primed, like sheep in a herd, to the shrine of Lucifer.

Believers have drifted far away from the Biblical teachings of the Word of God. Without a Biblical base, Lucifer's new age, new speak, secret society, witchcraft, dark arts, and occult practices don't seem strange. These blasphemies remain hidden behind mainstream religious denominations, music, movies, video games, books, education, and our modern culture. Publicly cursing the name of CHRIST has become an everyday occurrence.

The One-World Universal Church is fastly becoming a reality. Just as the pressure people put on others to take a vaccine during the Covid-19 pandemic will be the same pressure felt to join this One World Religion (Mystery Religion). With all the religious beliefs on the planet, have you ever wondered why the entertainment industry chooses to wear upside-down crosses and crowns of thorns to mock Christ? I've never seen a mocking of the Greek or Egyptian gods. I haven't seen the many other religious symbols desecrated and disrespected. These occurrences happen more frequently without much push-back from the Body of Believers.

The tearing down of Biblical principles and the mashing together of every abomination (doctrine of devils) will be readily acceptable to many who claim the name of CHRIST. Biblical morals and standards have been so "watered down" that many will deny the only true and living God, The Only Savior, Y'SHUA HAMASHIACH (JESUS THE MESSIAH).

> " ¹³ Enter ye in at the strait gate: for wide is the gate, and broad is the way, that leadeth to destruction, and many there be which go in thereat: ¹⁴ Because strait is the gate, and narrow is the way, which leadeth unto life, and few there be that find it." [Matthew 7:13-14]

Take heed, people of GOD. We are in the most dangerous times in history, for all of the signs of the prophecies are lining up. Lucifer is not omnipresent, omniscient, or omnipotent, but on the Internet, and with advancements in science, he can be. Technology and the rise of science can now allow Lucifer's agents, the false Christs, the satanic bloodlines, to get total control over the population. AI (artificial intelligence) can look into your home, interpret your feelings, lead you and send signals.

It's high time that we wake up out of our stupor.

Should the LORD delay his coming, the next generation of young people will be the ones to feel the full force of this Luciferian agenda. They will be no match for the deception coming. This generation has grown up with normalized magic and occultism, unnatural and inordinate affections, and the breaking of every command YAH has laid down.

So we all have a mission for the Kingdom. It's not good enough that we know the truth and can warn our families of the deception. We must warn the parents, grandparents, aunts, uncles, cousins, pastors, teachers, and leaders of this present age so that they may spread the message. Unless we warn and teach the next generation about the Luciferian web that's preparing to trap them, they will be blinded sided.

> "And except those days should be shortened, there should no flesh be saved: but for the elect's sake those days shall be shortened." [Matthew 24:22]
>
> "There shall be chaos also in many places, fire shall often break out, the wild beasts shall roam beyond their haunts, and menstruous women shall bring forth monsters." [II Esdras 5:8]
>
> "And as it was in the days of Noe, so shall it be also in the days of the Son of man." [Luke 17:26]

Brothers and sisters, I wish I could tell you this was the end of the deception. We must stay vigilant, prayerful, and watchful.

> "For nothing is secret, that shall not be made manifest; neither any thing hid, that shall not be known and come abroad." [Luke 8:17]

YAH has given us a look into these dark things because the Bible does say, "everything hidden shall be revealed." Now that you are aware, what will you do with the different realities of the things you have learned? Will you run away? Will you deny them? Will you be in cognitive dissonance from the truth? Will you continue in sin so grace may abound? God forbid.

> " 37 But as the days of Noah were, so shall also the coming of the Son of man be. 38 For as in the days that were before the flood they were eating and drinking, marrying and giving in marriage, until the day that Noe entered into the ark, 39 And knew not until the flood came, and took them all away; so shall also the coming of the Son of man be. 40 Then shall two be in the field; the one shall be taken, and the other left. 41 Two women shall be grinding at the mill; the one shall be taken, and the other left. 42 Watch therefore: for ye know not what hour your Lord doth come. 43 But know this, that if the goodman of the house had known in what watch the thief would come, he would have watched, and would not have suffered his house to be broken up. 44 Therefore be ye also ready: for in such an hour as ye think not the Son of man cometh. 45 Who then is a faithful and wise servant, whom his lord hath made ruler over his household, to give them meat in due season? 46 Blessed is that servant, whom his lord when he cometh shall find so doing." [Matthew 24:37-46]

Let us spread the GOOD NEWS of JESUS CHRIST, proclaim salvation to the lost, and shed light on those in darkness because the FATHER wishes that none be lost.

"12 And, behold, I come quickly; and my reward is with me, to give every man according as his work shall be.

13 I am Alpha and Omega, the beginning and the end, the first and the last. [Revelation 22:12-13]

V. Lynn is a published author, playwright, independent journalist, researcher, and defender of the faith. V. Lynn has spent hundreds of hours of extensive on-the-ground and historical research on the Flint Water Crisis, George Floyd riots, Covid-19 pandemic, the United Nations, the World Economic Forum, Secret Societies, and the diminishing family. Ordained for Ministry in 2001, V. Lynn has organized Bible studies inside Men's Prisons, Senior Facilities, and Women's Groups. V. Lynn has served as a Sunday School administrator, and fine arts coach and has been active in combating childhood suicide and bullying. In philanthropic work, Lynn has spearheaded can good, household and infant supplies missions for communities during natural disasters. V. Lynn has dedicated her life to exposing the destructive forces of mainstream media, restoring the family, and sounding the alarm about the rapidly changing world order.

Extra Extra

Here is some supplemental information you can chew on and muddle over. A few items I could not fit into the book. Others are just my thoughts.

Melusine Cover Up

Mer has a root word meaning maritime, water, etc. It's the same root word for *Mary, Merovingians*. Recall the Melusine epoch, which connects this water fairy/serpent to European nobility. In that case, this story is, of course, a cover. Mermaids are mythical. Melusine is a cover for Mary Magdalene and the false Desposyni bloodline in all European nobility. Nimrod was the cover for the sea beast for the Merovingians. Is it a far cry that Melusine (a female sea beast) is the cover for the "alleged" progenitor of European nobility? Again, these are my thoughts.

Shining Ones

Nimrod dwelt in the plain of Shinar. After the Tower of Babel, the people spread to all parts of the world. They bought the mystery religions' traditions with them. Perhaps the "shining ones" (maybe those from SHIN - AR) have some connection to the plain of Shinar. These people set up mystery religions all over and would have unique "powers" and esoteric knowledge. Remember, they toss out these myths to distract people from the truth. You are looking for aliens instead of looking for a bloodline, a tribe, or a people. Again just my thoughts.

Annunaki

The Annunaki may be a cover for the *Elite* of the world. Remember, the whole goal of the Annunaki was creating humans for their purpose, to serve them at their will. Is it impossible to think this Annunaki epoch is about the Elite of the world creating a working class of people to do their bidding? Is that not the world we live in now? A few Elites control everyone (13 families to be exact). This Annunaki epoch may indeed be the stories of the Nephilim. Still, these Elite bloodlines claim angelic lineage, so it may be a mixing of the two tales.

Dan (the apostate tribe)

The Priory of Sion (Merovingians /Rosicrucians) had its headquarters on Mount Hermon, the fallen angels' location, the Grotto of Pan. The Grotto of Pan is the location of the Biblical "gates of hell," a portal to evil spirits. Perhaps the Tribe of Dan made a deal with the devil to bring forth children, "giants" to infect the human genome pool. Perhaps! Just a thought!

Diana was the mother goddess of the Tribe of Dan, and she was a lesbian. Is Diana an inversion of Dan himself or the tribe of Dan?

Lilith

The mystery of Lilith must be solved! Lilith is not a Biblical figure (Lilith is from the Babylonian Talmud). Still, deep down the rabbit hole, I have found that she is the goddess behind all the goddesses. This Queen of the night is veiled because open worship of Lilith would never be tolerated. Lilith is the Queen of the Night and mother of all demons. The Lilith connection is not easy to make, but when studying the Shekhinah and now the Black Virgin, Lilith was underneath several layers. Lilith is from the Talmudic tradition, but who is she?

Pan

Statue of Pan
Wisley Gardens

Pan, this hideous half goat half man is said to be ADAM! That's right. It is noted in lure and under many layers that once Adam sinned, his nature changed. He became half human, half animal, and his animal side is Pan. Again this is a very veiled symbolism. Every secret society, witchcraft, and magic tradition reveres Pan. I'm not even certain many of them are aware of Pan's origins!

"Now, Adam can be proved to be the original of Pan, who was also called Inuus (see Dymock, sub voce " Inuus"), which is just another pronunciation of Anosh without the article, which, in our translation of Gen. v. 7, is made Enos. This name, as universally admitted, is the generic name for man after the Fall, as weak and diseased. The o in Enos is what is called the vau, which sometimes is pronounced o, sometimes it, and sometimes v 01 w. A legitimate pronunciation of Enos, therefore, is just Enus or Enws, the same in sound as Inuus, the Ancient Roman name of Pan. The name Pan itself signifies " He who turned aside." As the Hebrew word for "uprightness" signifies "walking straight in the way," so every deviation from the straight line of duty was Sin; Hata, the word for sin, signifying generically " to go aside from the straight line." Pan, it is admitted, was the Head of the Satyrs—that is, " **The first of the Hidden Ones," for Satyr and Satur, " the Hidden One," are evidently just the same word ; and Adam was the first of mankind that hid himself.**" (Hislop)

Adam and Eve

I always thought it strange that Adam nor Eve (besides historical context) are ever mentioned in books of invocation, magic, or occultism. These books pervert most Biblical figures. Could it be after the fall, Adam and Eve attained "god-hood" and took on the identity of a god and goddess or evil spirits (not Biblically but from the standpoint of the occult)?

There is no mention in the Word of God that Adam and Eve turned to malevolent spirits, but is the thinking of the occult?

More Shekhinah Secrets!

Lastly, IN PLAIN SIGHT, in the actual Library of Congress, this sign is displayed;

Library of Congress

The true SHEKHINAH is man or The true GLORY OF GOD, is MAN.

LUCIFER GOT YOU AGAIN! This section was just extra information, my thoughts, and some additional information to ponder.

Please remember when we are reviewing THEIR information, it is to expose their thinking, codes, and secret plans. It's not to usurp Biblical doctrine or try to fit their thinking into Scripture, that would be heresy!

Let's stay sober and vigilant brothers and sisters!

> Be sober, be vigilant; because your adversary the devil, as a roaring lion, walketh about, seeking whom he may devour: [I Peter 5:8]

Bibliography

955.Beliar. n.d. December 2022. <https://biblehub.com/greek/955.htm>.

Agrippa, Henry Cornelius of Nettesheim. *Three Books of Occult Philosophy*. Ed. Donald Tyson. Vol. 11th. Woodbury: Llewellyn Publications, 2009, 1486-1535.

Aho, Barbara. *The Merovingian Dynasty; Satanic Bloodline of the Anti-Christ and False Prophet*. n.d. December 2022. <https://www.bibliotecapleyades.net/merovingians/merovingian_dynasty/merovingian_dynasty02.htm>.

—. *The Merovingian Dynasty; Satanic Bloodline of the Antichrist and False Prophet*. n.d. December 2022. <https://www.bibliotecapleyades.net/merovingians/merovingian_dynasty/merovingian_dynasty.htm#top>.

America the land of Lucifer, the real story behind the name. 24 April 2013. December 2022. <https://www.soulask.com/america-the-land-of-lucifer-the-real-story-behind-the-name/>.

American Zionist Movement Officially Recognized by UN: Granted Advisory Status. 3 August 2022. December 2022. <https://azm.org/american-zionist-movement-officially-recognized-by-un-granted-advisory-status>.

Anki. *The Significance of Saturn in the Jewish Faith*. 16 November 2022. November 2022. <https://religionsfacts.com/the-significance-of-saturn-in-the-jewish-faith/>.

Annuit Coeptis. n.d. December 2022. <https://www.etymonline.com/word/Annuit%20Coeptis>.

Arcane School. *Meditation the New Moon*. n.d. December 2022. <https://www.lucistrust.org/arcane_school/meditation/meditation_the_new_moon>.

Atrayu. "The Un, Lucis/Lucifer Trust, World Goodwil, Kryon, The Earth Charter and Maitreya." n.d. *Contending for Truth*. December 2022. <http://www.contendingfortruth.com/wp-content/uploads2/UN-Meditation-Room-SEAT-Maitreya-Kryon-Lucis-Trust.pdf>.

Bailey, Alice A. *Discipleship in the New Age*. Vol. II. New York: Lucis Trust, 1968;1983.

—. "Lucis Trust, Online Books." 1957. *The Externalisation of the Hierarchy*. December 2022. <https://www.lucistrust.org/online_books/the_externalisation_the_hierarchy_obook/section_four_stages_in_the_externalisation_the_hierarchy_part1 >.

—. *The Externalisation of the Hierarchy*. Lucis Trust, 1957; 1985.

—. *The Service Activities of the Arcane School*. Vol. Light on the Path Edition. Lucis Trust, 2018.

—. *The Unfinished Autobiography of Alice A. Bailey*. New York: Lucis Publishing Company, 1951, 1979.

Bakst, Joel David. *The Secret Doctrine of the Gaon of Vilna; The Josephic Messiah, Leviathan, Metatron and the Sacred Serpent.* Vol. II. City of Luz, 2013.

Baldwin, John D., A.M. *Pre-Historic Nations; or, inquiries Concerning some of the Great Peoples and Civilizations of Antiquity.* New York: Harper and Brothers, Publishers, 1874.

Bartholomew, Richard. *Mike Flynn Gets Evangelical Crowd to Recite Adapted Elizabeth Clare Prophet Prayer.* 7 October 2021. December 2022. <https://barthsnotes.com/2021/10/07/mike-flynn-gets-evangelical-crowd-to-recite-adapted-elizabeth-clare-prophet-prayer/>.

Beck, Dr. Guy L. "Celestial Lodge Above The Temple of Solomon in Jerusalem as a Religious Symbol in Freemasonry." *Nova Religion: The Journal of Alternative and Emergent Religions* 4.1 (2000): 28-51.

Begg, Ean. *The Cult of the Black Virgin.* Arcana Penguin Books, 1996.

Ben Elisha, R. Ishmael. *Hebrew Book of Enoch.* Vols. The Books of Enoch, Complete Edition. International Alliance Pro-Publishing, 2012.

Bergrun, Norman R. *Ringmakers of Saturn.* Edinburgh: The Pentland Press, 1986.

Blavatsky, H.P. *Isis Unveiled; A Master-Key to the Mysteries of Ancient and Modern Science and Theology.* Theosophical University Press, 1877, 1988.

Blavatsky, Helena P. *The Secret Doctrine. The Synthesis of Science, Religion and Philosophy.* Vol. I. New York: The Theosophical Publishing Society, 1888.

Booth, Mark. *The Secret History of the World as Laid Down by Secret Societies.* Woodstock: The Overlook Press, 2008.

Bothelho, Laura. *The Secrets of the gods.* 2011.

Brown, Dan. *The Davinci Code.* New York: First Anchor Books, 2003.

Burton, Ben. *Chukkat: The Revelation of the Holy Snake.* 6 October 2014. December 2022. <https://ladderofjacob.com/2014/10/06/holysnake/>.

Carlton, Genevieve. *The British Royal Family May Be Descended From The Mermaid On Your Starbucks Cup.* 23 September 2021. December 2022. <https://www.ranker.com/list/british-royal-family-and-melusina-starbucks-mermaid/genevieve-carlton>.

Cauley, Marty A. "Nimrod and Semiramis." 3 February 2017. Thesis.

Church, J.R. *Guardians of the Grail; and the men who plan to rule the world.* Oklahoma City: Prophecy Publications, 1989.

Cirlot, J.E. *A Dictionary of Symbols.* Barnes and Noble, 1995, 1971.

Collins, Steven M. *The "Serpent Seed" Heresy.* n.d. December 2022. <https://stevenmcollins.com/the-serpent-seed-heresy/>.

Copper, Milton William. *Behold a Pale Horse.* 1991.

Creative Meditation -A Planetary Service. n.d. Decembers 2022. <http://www.aquaac.org/un/medmtgs.html>.

Cumaean Sibyl. n.d. December 2022. <https://en.wikipedia.org/wiki/Cumaean_Sibyl>.

Bibliography

Curtis, David B. *Is Cain the Serpent's Seed.* 8 December 2019. December 2022. <https://bereanbiblechurch.org/transcripts/john-epistles/1john_03_12_cain-the-serpent-seed.htm>.

Dawkins, Peter. *The Great Vision: The Judaic-Christian Mysteries: The Vision and Birth of the New Rosicrucianism.* Banbury: Francis Bacon Research Trust, 1985.

DHWTY. *Khazars.* 29 December 2018. December 2022. <https://www.ancient-origins.net/history-famous-people/khazars-0011246>.

Doreal, ed. *The Emerald Tablets of Thoth the Atlantean.* n.d.

Dumond, Joseph F. *Shem an the Execution of Nimrod a Prophecy for our Time.* 5 February 2009. December 2022. <https://sightedmoon.com/shem-and-the-execution-of-nimrod-a-prophecy-for-our-time/>.

Eddie. *Seed of Nimrod and Semiramis.* n.d. December 2022. <https://worldtruth.tv/seed-of-nimrod-semiramis/>.

Farquhar, J.N. *A Primer of Hinduism.* Vol. 2nd Edition. London: Oxford University Press, 1912.

Farrell PhD, Joseph P and Scott D. de Hart, PhD. *Transhumanism: A Grimoire of Alchemical Agendas.* Port Townsend: Feral House, 2011.

Finkel, Avraham. *The Essence of the Holy Days; Insight from the Jewish Sages.* Lanham: J. Aronson Publishers, 1993.

Finney, Dee. *Return of the Feminine.* 14 March 2015. December 2022. <http://www.greatdreams.com/sacred/return_of_the_feminine.htm>.

Frazer, J.G., M.A. *The Golden Bough; A Study in Comparative Religions.* Vol. I. New York: Macmillan and Co., 1894. II vols.

Freedman, Benjamin. *Facts are Facts.* Carson City: Bridger House Publishers, Inc, 1954.

Freemasonry Watch. *Mark of Cain.* n.d. December 2022. <http://www.freemasonrywatch.org/markofcain.html>.

Fundamental Laws. A Report of the 68th Convocation of the Rose Cross Order. Allentown: The Philosophical Publishing Co., 1916.

Gardiner, Philip and Gary Osborn. *The Serpent Grail; The Truth Behind the Holy Grail, the Philosopher's Stone and the Elixir of Life.* London: Watkings Publishing, 2005.

Gardner, Laurence. *Bloodline of the Holy Grail.* Gloucester: Fair Winds Press, 2002.

—. *Genesis of the Grail Kings.* New York: Barnes and Noble Books, 2001.

Ginzberg, Louis. *Legends of the Jews.* Vol. 1. Philadelphia: The Jewish Publication Society of America, 1938.

—. *Legends of the Jews.* Ed. Boaz (Index) Cohen. Vol. 4. Philadelphia: The Jewish Publication Society of America, 1938.

Graber, Bishop Rudolph. "Fatima Advancing Rapidly Towards Final Fulfillment." *The Three Dimensions of Fatima* December 1977: 6.

Hall, Manly P. *The Occult Anatomy of Man.* Los Angeles: The Philosophical Research Society, Inc, 1929.

—. *The Secret Teachings of All Ages.* San Francisco: H.S. Crocker Company, 1928.

Hammarskjöld, Dag. ""A Room of Quiet" The Meditation Room, United Nations Headquarters." 1957. *United Nations.* December 2022. <https://www.un.org/depts/dhl/dag/meditationroom.htm>.

Heath, Ben. *Serpent Seed.* n.d. December 2022. <https://serpent-seed.com/>.

Heiser, Michael S. *The Unseen Realm: Recovering the Supernatural Worldview of the Bible.* Bellingham: Lexham Press, 2015.

Hill, Bryan. *The Kaaba Black Stone: A Holy Stone from Outer Space?* 3 April 2020. December 2022. <https://www.ancient-origins.net/artifacts-other-artifacts/kaaba-black-stone-holy-stone-outer-space-003661>.

Hislop, Alexander Rev. *The Two Babylons.* London: S.W. Partridge and Co., 1871.

Hoopes, Townsend and Douglas Brinkley. *FDR and the Creation of the UN.* Yale UP, 1997.

Hurtak, J.J. *The Keys of Enoch.* Vol. 7. Los Gatos: The Academy for Future Science, 2016; 1977. 7 vols.

Institute for Gnostic Studies (now defunct). *The Gnostic Handbook.* n.d.

Introduction . n.d. December 2022. <http://www.prieure-de-sion.com/4/introduction_to_the_website_796586.html>.

Irons, Lee PhD. "The Gap Theory of Genesis 1:2." *Christian Research Journal* 37.02 (2014). <https://www.equip.org/PDF/JAP372.pdf>.

James, George G.M. *Stolen Legacy: The Egyptian Origins of Western Philosophy.* Traffic Output Publication, 1954.

Jastrow, Morris Jr. and George A. Barton. *chiun.* 1906. December 2022. <https://www.jewishencyclopedia.com/articles/4345-chiun>.

Jastrow, Morris Jr., Ph.D, L.L.D. *The Civilization of Babylonia and Assyria.* Philadelphia: Philadelphia and London J.B. Lippincott Company, 1915.

John D Rockefeller Jr donated land for United Nations Headquarters. 2 May 2004. December 2022. <https://americanprofile.com/articles/john-d-rockefeller-jr-donated-land-for-united-nations-headquarters/>.

Johnson, Ken, Th.D. *Ancient Book of Jasher; A New Annotated Edition.* Bible Facts Ministries, 2008.

Josephus, Flavius. *Antiquities of the Jews.* A.D. 93.

Kennedy, D. James. *The Real Meaning of the Zodiac.* Coral Ridge Ministries, 1989.

Knight, Christopher and Alan Butler. *Solomon's Power Brokers. The Secrets of Freemasonry, The Church and the Illuminati.* London: Watkins Publishing, 2007.

Laitman, Michael. *The Serpent is the Angel of Help.* 10 February 2010. December 2022. <https://laitman.com/2010/02/the-serpent-is-the-angel-of-help/#gsc.tab=0>.

Last Trumpet Newsletter. "One World Religion on the Horizon." *Last Trumpet Newsletter* August 1999.

Love, Emily. *Black Cube: Saturn Occult Symbolism.* 9 November 2017. December 2022. <https://wearechange.org/black-cube-saturn-occult-symbolism/>.

Lucis Trust. *About Us*. n.d. December 2022. <https://www.lucistrust.org/about_us/support_un>.

—. *History*. n.d. December 2022. <https://www.lucistrust.org/about_us/history>.

—. *Lucis Trust, Arcane Schools*. n.d. December 2022. <https://www.lucistrust.org/arcane_school/talks_and_articles/the_esoteric_meaning_lucifer>.

—. "Moon Charts 2022." n.d. *Lucis Trust*. December 2022. <https://www.lucistrust.org/uploads/documents/MOON_CHART_2022-NY.pdf>.

—. *World Goodwill*. n.d. December 2022. <https://www.lucistrust.org/world_goodwill>.

Lynn, V. *Thy Queendom Come; The Devils Secret Agenda*. Vol. II. Novi: Revelations Publishing House, 2022.

Makow PhD, Henry. *Illuminati: The Cult that Hijacked the World*. Vol. I. Winnepeg: Silas Green, 2008.

Marrs, Texe. *America Shattered*. Austin: Living Truth Publishers, 1991.

—. *DNA Science and the Jewish Bloodline*. Austin: RiverCrest Publishers, 2013.

—. *Holy Serpent of the Jews: The Rabbis Secret for Satan to Crush Their Enemies and Vault the Jews to Global Dominion*. Austin: RiverCrest Publishing, 2016.

—. *Mystery Mark of the New Age: Satan's Design for World Domination*. Austin: RiverCrest Publishers, 1988.

—. *Serpent People Return to Ukraine*. n.d. December 2022. <https://www.texemarrs.com/082014/serpent_people_return.htm>.

McKechnie, Sarah. *Descent and Sacrifice*. September-October 1989. December 2022. <https://www.lucistrust.org/arcane_school/talks_and_articles/descent_and_sacrifice>.

McLaughlin, Corrine and Gordon Davidson. *Spiritual Politics: Changing the World from the Inside Out*. New York: Ballantine Books , 1994.

Metro Examiner. *Synagogue of SATAN Part 1 - From the Caucasus mountains to the Holy Land - KHAZARIAN IMPOSTERS*. November 2022. December 2022. <https://youtu.be/oXe6ycIgxXU>.

Milton, John. *Paradise Lost with Fifty Illustrations by Gustave Dore*. New York: John B. Alden, 1884.

Min. K. *Star of David or Hexagram*. 9 November 2013. December 2022. <http://www.spreadingtruthministry.com/blog/star-of-david-or-hexagram->.

Mithras: all the passages in Graeco-Roman literature. n.d. December 2022. <https://tertullian.org/rpearse/mithras/literary_sources.htm>.

"Moon Chart 2022." n.d. *Lucis Trust*. December 2022. <https://www.lucistrust.org/uploads/documents/MOON_CHART_2022-NY.pdf>.

Moore, Charles W. *The Masonic Trestle-Board Part II. Works and Lectures. Chapters, Councils, and Encampments of Knights Templars, in the United States of America*. Vol. II. Boston: The Office of the Freemasons Magazines, 1868.

—. *The New Masonic Trestle Board, Works and Lectures, The Lodges, Chapters, Councils and Encampments of Knights Templars in the United States of America.* Boston: Office of the Freemasons Magazine, 1868.

M-Star. n.d. December 2022. <https://www.gaiamind.com/m-star.html>.

NASA. *Saturn's Active North Pole*. 27 March 2007. December 2022. <https://solarsystem.nasa.gov/resources/13552/saturns-active-north-pole/>.

Nations, United. "United Nations Resolution 181." 29 November 1947. *Web Archive.* December 2022. <https://web.archive.org/web/20171010090147/https://unispal.un.org/DPA/DPR/unispal.nsf/0/7F0AF2BD897689B785256C330061D253>.

Patriot, Albion. *Christogenea Europe; Multicultural Judea.* 5 July 2015. December 2022. <https://aryanisrael.wordpress.com/2015/07/05/christogenea-europe-multicultural-judea-2/>.

Phillips, Paul A. *Saturn Occult Symbolism and "The Cube".* 4 May 2017. December 2022. <https://shiftfrequency.com/saturn-cube-symbolism/>.

Pike, Albert. *Morals and Dogma of the Ancient and Accepted Scottish Rite of Freemasonry.* 1871.

Price, John Randolph. *The Planetary Commission.* Austin: The Quartus Foundation for Spiritual Research, 1984.

Prophet, Elizabeth C. and Mark L. Prophet. *Prayers Meditations and Dynamic Decrees for Personal World Transformation.* Gardiner: The Summit Light House, 1984.

Return of the Dove. n.d. December 2022. <http://www.greatdreams.com/return_of_the_dove.htm>.

Robinson, John A.M. *Proofs of a Conspiracy against all the Religions and Governments of Europe, carried on in the Secret Meetings of Free Masons, Illuminati and Reading Societies collected from Good Authorities.* Vol. Fourth Edition. New York: George Forman. No. 64, 1798.

Ruark, Michael. *Keep the Sabbath.* 14 November 2015. November 2022. <https://michaelruark.blog/2015/11/14/keep-the-sabbath/>.

Sam. *Worship of Shivling prior to Judaism*. 8 May 2015. December 2022. <https://samofindia.blogspot.com/2015/05/worship-of-shivling-prior-to-judaism.html>.

Samuel, Maurice. *You Gentiles.* New York, 1924.

Satan and the Black Cube of Saturn. n.d. December 2022. <https://alternativepress.us/satan-and-the-black-cube-of-saturn/>.

Satanic Symbols. n.d. October 2022. <https://www.themystica.com/satanic-symbols/>.

Saturn Worship, The Black Cube. 12 December 2014. December 2022. <https://www.nicholson1968.com/nicholson1968s-post/saturn-worshipthe-black-cube>.

Schnieders, Paul C. *The Book of the Secrets of Enoch.* Ed. R.H. (translated) Charles. Vol. Enoch 2. International Alliance Pro-Publishing, 2012.

Sela, Shlomo. *Saturn and the Jews.* 10 November 2017. November 2022. <https://katz.sas.upenn.edu/resources/blog/saturn-and-jews>.

Bibliography

Sepehr, Robert. *The Serpent City Below Los Angeles*. 11 March 2022. December 2022. <https://youtu.be/y9u-jFuIClo>.

Sorenson, Richard. "Was Ham's Wife of the Nephilim?" (2020).

Spenser, Robert Keith. *The Cult of the All-Seeing Eye*. Palmdale: Omni Publications, n.d.

Springemier, Fritz. *Spiritual Warfare and Power Structures*. n.d.

Springmeier, Fritz and Cisco Wheeler. *Deeper Insights into the Illuminati Formula*. 2007.

Springmeier, Fritz. *The Top 13 Illuminati Bloodlines*. Portland: Fritz Springmeier, 1995.

Steinbuch, Yaron. *Black Lives Matter co-founder describes herself as 'trained Marxist'*. 25 June 2020. November 2022. <https://nypost.com/2020/06/25/blm-co-founder-describes-herself-as-trained-marxist/>.

Strong's Concordance. n.d. December 2022. <https://bible.knowing-jesus.com/strongs/H>.

Strongs Concordance. *H8314*. n.d. December 2022. <https://bible.knowing-jesus.com/strongs/H8314>.

Talbott, David N. *The Saturn Myth*. U.S.A.: David N. Talbot, 1980.

"The Book of Secrets – Reflections and Notes on the Royal Families of the Grail." n.d.

The Declaration of the Establishment of the State of Israel. n.d. December 2022. <https://www.jewishvirtuallibrary.org/the-declaration-of-the-establishment-of-the-state-of-israel>.

The Esoteric meaning of Lucifer. n.d. November 2022. <https://www.lucistrust.org/arcane_school/talks_and_articles/the_esoteric_meaning_lucifer>.

The Merovingians. n.d. December 2022. <http://www.prieure-de-sion.com/4/the_merovingians_850425.html>.

The Mysterious Case of Tracy Twyman. 30 March 2020. December 2022. <https://nrgiseternal.com/let-s-get-down-dirty/the-mysterious-case-of-tracy-twyman/>.

The North is Dark. 29 June 2011. December 2022. <https://www.themasonicjourney.com/the-north-is-dark/>.

"The Testament of Dan." n.d. *Internet Archive*. December 2022. <https://ia600704.us.archive.org/35/items/pdfy-7SmUFQ9bnS-7fVj9/The%20Testament%20Of%20Dan.pdf>.

The Typology of Deliverance: Rekindling the Reformation (940). Dir. Amazing Discoveries. Perf. Walter J. Professor Veith. Prod. Amazing Discoveries. 2002. Film.

Tiwari, Subhas PhD. *Yoga Renamed is still Hindu*. 2006 January. July 2022. <https://www.hinduismtoday.com/magazine/january-february-march-2006/2006-01-yoga-renamed-is-still-hindu/>.

TOI Staff. *Saudi Arabia Releases First Ever Photos of holy Kaaba stone*. 9 May 2021. December 2022. <https://www.timesofisrael.com/saudi-arabia-releases-first-ever-photos-of-holy-kaaba-stone/>.

Twyman, Tracy. "Author, Researcher." *Ancient Esoteric Cults, Elite Beliefs and Conquering the Sun*. Higherside Chats. 31 July 2017.

—. *Dead But Dreaming; The Great Old Ones of Lovecraftian Legend Reinterpreted as Sumerian/Atlantean Kings*. 2011.

U.S. Department of State. *Creation of Israel, 1948.* n.d. December 2022. <https://2001-2009.state.gov/r/pa/ho/time/cwr/97177.htm>.

Urso, Ida PhD. *In Observation of the Christ Festival/World Invocation Day 2013.* 2013. December 2022. <http://www.aquaac.org/un/relationship.html>.

—. *The New World Order and the Work of the United Nations.* 28 October 1995. World Goodwill Symposium. December 2022. <http://www.aquaac.org/un/nwo.html>.

Vera, Diane. *Theistic Satanism.* 2006, 2012. October 2022. <http://theisticsatanism.com/rituals/standard/call5gods.html>.

Vermaseren, M.J. *Cybele and Attis the Myth and the Cult.* Ed. A.M.H. (translated from Dutch) Lemmers. London, 1977.

Virgil and John (translated) Dryden. *Ecologue 4: The Messiah.* 42 BC. <https://www.poetrynook.com/poem/eclogue-4-messiah>.

Virgil and John William (translated) Mackail. 1908. December 2022. <https://en.wikisource.org/wiki/Eclogues_of_Virgil_(1908)/Eclogue_4>.

Vulgarian. *Kenneth Grant and Merovingian Mythos.* 3 September 2014. December 2022. <https://mediamonarchy.com/kenneth-grant-and-merovingian-mythos/>.

Wallace-Murphy, Tim and Marilyn Hopkins. *Rosslyn: Guardian of the Secrets of the Holy Grail.* Element , 1999.

Wasson, Donald L. *Cybele.* 4 February 2015. December 2022. <https://www.worldhistory.org/Cybele/>.

Wensinck, A.J. *The Ideas of the Western Semites Concerning The Navel of the Earth.* Amsterdam: Johannes Muller, 1916.

What do Muslims pray towards (with their backs to Temple Mount, Jerusalem)? n.d. December 2022. <https://mystery-babylon-watch.blogspot.com/2011/11/what-do-muslims-pray-their-backs-to.html>.

What is Theosophy? n.d. December 2022. <https://www.theosophy.world/resource/what-theosophy>.

Wilson, Addison. *Seven Rays Prayer to Archangel Michael by Michael Flynn.* 21 January 2022. December 2022. <https://thetruedefender.com/seven-rays-prayer-to-archangel-michael-by-michael-flynn-watch/>.

Zaidan, Henry. *25 Paintings by the Old Masters! The Legend of Semiramis.* 15 June 2015. December 2022. <https://painting-mythology.blogspot.com/2015/06/25-paintings-by-old-masters-legend-of.html>.

Zionism. n.d. December 2022. <https://overlordsofchaos.com/index.php/main-subjects/jewish-conspiracy/zionism/517-jewish-conspiracy-zionism>.

Bible Index

Introduction
    Revelation 17:5
    John 16:33

Chapter 1 Cosmic Combat
    Ephesians 6:12
    Genesis 1:1

Chapter 2 Lord of the Rings
    Genesis 1:1-1:5
    Genesis 1:16-19
    John 1:1-14
    John 14:6

Chapter 3 Black Cube of Saturn
    Amos 5:26
    Matthew 15:3

Chapter 6 The Serpent
    Genesis 3:1-5
    Genesis 3:13, 15
    Matthew 13:37-38
    I John 3:12
    Matthew 23:34-36
    Matthew 13:24-28
    Isaiah 27:1

Chapter 8 Illuminati Bloodlines
    Revelation 17:12
    Revelation 2:9
    Chapter 10
    Isaiah 14:12

Chapter 11 Symbology
    Revelation 13:1-2
    Revelation 12:9

Chapter 12 The Lost Tribe
    Genesis 49:17
    Revelation 7:4-8
    Isaiah 14:12-15

I Chronicles 2:1-2

Chapter 13 X-Man

Genesis 10:10-12
Revelation 17:8
Revelation 17:13
I Chronicles 1:10
Revelation 17:8
Genesis 25:23

Chapter 15 Fallen Angels and Nephilim

Deuteronomy 9:1-3
Genesis 6: 1-2, 4

Chapter 17 United Nations of Lucifer

I Thessalonians 5:3
Ephesians 6:12
Daniel 10: 20 NLT

Chapter 18 Lucifer Unveiled

Revelation 2:9
Isaiah 14:14
Leviticus 26:1
Exodus 20:14

Chapter 19 Conclusion

Ephesians 5:11
Matthew 7:13-14
Matthew 24:22
Luke 17:26
Luke 8:7
Matthew 24:37-46
Revelation 22:12-13

Index

Name	Page
666	118, 216, 219, 233
Abraham	32, 89, 90, 121, 122
Adam	17, 23, 27, 31, 32, 40, 57, 62, 95, 126, 142, 148, 226
Adam and Eve (garments)	126
Adama	162
Agathodaemon	63
Age of Aquarius	168, 175, 177, 194
Akkadian	73
Alchemy	35, 69, 136
Alexander the Great	68
Alien	59, 161
All Seeing Eye	12, 17, 135, 178
Allah	68
Amaru/Ameru	62, 74, 223
Amenemhet III	49
American Revolution	209
Amorites	144, 145
An	152, 159
Anakim	144, 145
Anakim	145
Androgyne	213, 229
Angels	72, 183
Anglican	182

Anglo Saxon	103,184
Anjou	65,80,82
Annuit Coeptis	227
Anshar	159
Anti-Christ	128,159,171,213,216,226,229,230
Anu	36,159,160,163
Anunnaki	50,135,158,161,163
Apep	72
Aphrodite	10,152,204
Apocalypse	67103120139
Apollo	17,26,36,68,69,71,152,211,229,230
Apophis	72,74
Apsu	73
Apus	159
Arcadia	71
Archangel Gabriel	36,153,154
Archangel Michael	9,69,153,154
Archangel Raphael	153
Archangel Uriel	153,154,155
Archons	63,148
Aries	10,152,210
Artemis	152,213
Aryan	36,37
As above so below	9,19,42
Asexual	27
Asherah	201
Ashnan and Lahar	161

Ashtaroth/reth	144,148
Asmodeus	145
Assyrian	36,37,128
Astarte	22,213,216,237
Astrology	37
Atlantis	17,18,20,72,109,136,152,158,229,230
Attis	208,209
Atum	40
Atum-Re	64,65
Automatic Writing	170
Azazael/Azzael	140,148,149,150,153,154
Aztec	62,74
Baal	143,197
Babylon	21,124,125,129,130,141,162,214,219
Babylon Gate	163
Babylonian	20,36,41,60,67,73,88,97,127,128,158,169,212
Bacchus	72
Bailey, Alice	168,170,171,173,190
Bailey, Foster	169
Baphomet	73,205,206,207,211
Bashan	144
Beast of the Sea	50
Bee (King or Queen)	111
Beehive	110
Bees	108,109,110
Beethoven	184
Beltane festival	14

Ben Ben stone	48
Benjamin (Tribe of)	103
Berlin	185
Berossus	20
Bible	35
Bistea Neptunis	92
Black cube	30,31,32
Black Madonna	98,99,100,200,202,203,204,207,231,232
Black magic	35
Black Panther (movie)	76
Black sea	88,92,122
Blavatsky, H.P.	9,37,136,169,171,173
Bloodline	84,85,86,87,90,92,97,101,102,103,104,105,113,212,216,238
Book of the Dead	67
Brazen	55
Britain	62,86,91,93,103,185
British Empire	185
British Royal family	82
Brotherhood of the Snake	102
Buddha	14,169,184
Buddhism	192
Caduceus	71
Caesars	122,237
Caesars	237
Cain	55,56,57,59,75,134,135,136,137,139,145,226,232
Canaan	120

Canaanite	22,117,143,144,145,200
Canis Mjaor	12
Cannibalism	129
Capricorn	33
Capstone	47
Cassini spacecraft	42
Castration	17,208
Catholic	35,67,86,182,195,201,204,214,236
Caucasus mountains	88,89
Celtic	216
Ceres	17,152
Chakras	27
Chaos	100,148,217
Chariot	41,113
Chartres Cathedral	202,203,206
Cherubim	58,63
Chi	27
Chicago	185
Child Sacrifice	197
China	62,64
Chiun	41
Christmas	43,45,87,236
Circumambulation	32
Clodion	92
Commonwealth Games	13
Constantinople	121
Cooper, Bill	233

Cosmos	21,27,67
Covid-19	237
Cro-Magnons	151
Cronos (Krunos)	10,18,19,20,22,23,31,37,43,64,65,73,131,
Crowley, Aleister	102
Cumean Sibyl	227
Cush	125,126,131
Custodians of the Plan	189
Cybele	99,207,208,209,211,212,237
Dagon	71,129,130
Dahomey	74
Damascus	136
Damkina	159
Dan (Tribe of)	105,116,117,118,119,122,212,216
Danites	117
Danube	21,74
Dardanus	117
Darjeeling	186,187
Dark lord	26
Dark twin	69
DaVinci Code	94
Demeter	99,152,201,202,208,200
Denmark	74
Desposyni	91,94
Deva	183
Diana	17,27,99,100,108,109,117,152,197,201
Dionysus	19,66,111

Index

Diorphus	210
Divine Feminine	20,67
DNA	59,89,130,161
Dogon People	60
Dove	41,68,113,226
Draco	12,66
Draconian Tradition	101
Dragon	9,17,27,58,62,63,64,65,67,72,75,76,79,81,101,112,134,135,159,161,232
Druids	92,202,203,216,
Ducal Luxembourg Dynast	82
Durga	75
Ea	20,73,159,161
Eagle	117,121,122,
Edom	133
Egg (cosmic)	21,65,68
Egypt	9,14,19,21,40,41,47,49,67,73,76,97,102,108,119,132,152,202,216
El Olam	36
Eleusinian Mysteries	202
Eliphas Levi	207
Elixir	82
Elizabeth Woodville	82
Embryos	161,162
Emerald	69
Emim	144,145
Emperor Augustus	68

Enki	18,20,56,135,148,152,159,160,161,162
Enlil	159,160
Enuma Elish	73
Eresh-kigal	160
Esau	132,133
Essenes	71,109,111
Ethiopia	19,70,74
Eucharist	80
European	81,86,89,90,91,93,95,100,103,105,216
Eve	27,29,55,56,58,126,134,135,148,201,209,226
Evolution	174,225,226
Externalization	190,191,194
Fairy	82
Fallen angel (knowledge)	146,147
Fallen angels	50,84,105,116,127,131,139,140,141,142,151,152, 153,174,183,226,234
Fatima	141,201
Fish	71,73,75,214
Fish Mitre	129,130
Fisher Kings	95
Five Exits for Energies	186
Flood	50,126,129,143,158,100
Fon people	74
France	93,96,100
Fraternitas Saturni	33,34
Freedman, Benjamin H.	87
Freemason (masonic)	12,27,28,35,49,50,69,93,101,102,103,105,110,179,

	193,204,221,233
French Revolution	209
Gaia	100,174,237
Gap Theory	24,25
Garden of Eden	12,17,18,27,31,56,63,126,224,229,232
Gaul	92
Geb	22
Gemini	48,210
Geneva	186,187
German	89,93,185
Giants	22,130,140,143,145,150,153,154
Gibbor	127,145
Gilgamesh	124,125,158
Giza	47,69
Gnostic	10,58,69,70,85,95,96,100,202,214
Goat	69
Goddess	67,68,69,99,102,130,144,202,213
Golden Age	12,13,14,18,24,116,210,229,233
Golden calf	72
Grail	69,71,72,82,91,92,94,95,97,104,106,109,113,135, 136,160,212,214,232
Great Seal	35,227,236
Great White Lodge	189
Greater bear	41,112
Greece	117,152
Greek	20,50,65,67,73,182,202,237
Griffins	64

Grim Reaper	31
Guardian of International Peace	167
Gucumatz	61,74
Hades	202
Hall, Manly P.	43
Halo	20
Ham	125,126,145
Hammurabi	127
Hanover-Saxe-Coburg-Gotha (House of)	95
Haphaestos	152
Hapsburgs (House of)	90,103,105,109
Harlots	21
Heaven	21
Hebrew	20,54,60,95,103
Hellenstic	37
Hera	152
Hermaphrodite	20,21,207,208,213,232,237
Hermes	10,21,63,71,105,125,126,52,169,174
Hermes Trismegistis	71
Herod	121
Herrera	201
Hesod	219
Hestia	152
Hexagram (Seal of Solomon)	35,36,39,42,104,213
Hindu	18,35,67,76
Ho Ho Ho	44
Hollywood	163

homo sapiens	161
Honey	116
Horns	33
Horus	21,70,71,72,143,152,203,215,226,231
Huang-ti	18,64
Hybrid	59
Hyperborean	20
Ichthus	72
Idaei	36
Igigi	158
Illuminati	85,93,101,236
IMF	167
Imhotep	71
Inanna	160
India	76
Indian	87
Ishmael	32,216
Ishtar	97,149,158,201,208,200
Isis	13,21,22,47,48,70,97,99,100,129,136,152,201,202, 203,204,208,215,231,000,000
Islam	35,72,84,176
Israel	37,130,150
Israel (12 Tribes)	11,59,84,89,90,117,118,120,144,216
Italy	100
Jacquetta of Luxembourg	82
Jehovah's Witness	28
jerusalem	102,105,106,144

Jesuits	35
Jesus (Christ)	25,28,57,70,94,95,109,117,134,178,203,204,214,221,231,235
Jewish	35,36,37,60,86,87,88,89,90,91,103,213,216,236
jews (Orthodox)	37
Joseph of Arimathea	91,96
Joshua	144
Judaei	36
Judah (House of)	84,91,95,107,116,117,121,216
Judaism	88,89,192,213,236,237
Judas	216
Juno	17,99,152
Jupiter	9,34,36,41,127,152,211,227,229
Kaaba	32,33,64
Kabbala	35,37,108,148,163,176,207,216,217,218
Kadru	75
Kaiun	41
Kaiwan	36
Kakadaimon	63
Kali	75,100,136,237
Kevan	40
Khalifa	32
Khazarians	87,88,90,92
Khazars	88,89,122
Ki	159
King Bulan	88
King Charles	84

King David (Israel)	35,84,91,95,105,216
King Edward IV	82
King James	86
King Meroveus	92
King Saul	95
Kings	21
Kishar	159
Knights Templar	49,80,101,104,105,106,201,206,207,208
Kodak Theater	163
Kofi Annan	179
Krishna	26
Kukulcan	61
Kundalini	68,102
Lahamu	159
Lahmu	159
Lancastrian family	82
Last Supper	104
Lebanon	119,120
Lemuria	201
Leo	48,97
Lesser bear	41,112
Levantine	37
Leviathan	59,60,72,73,206,219
Light (greater)	24
Light (lesser)	24
Light bearer	151,152,174,204
Lightning	66

Lilith	11,136,141,148,160,200,000
Lion	69,121
London	185,186,234
Lord Agni	183
Lords of Liberation	190
Los Angeles	185
Lost Tribes	103
Lucifer	9,10,14,23,25,26,27,28,29,61,63,70,86,95,102,113,119, 171,173,174,175,204,206,212,214,215,218,219,221,223, 225,226,234
Lucifer (jewel)	69
Lucifer Publishing Company	173,224
Luciferian	34,85,168,176,210,237,238
Lucis Trust	172,173,174,224
Luluwa	75
Luna	34
Lunar	37
Lusignans	90,102
Luxembourg	82
Magi	109
Magic	35,148
Mahabharat	76
Maitreya	171
Mali	60
Malkhut	135,218,219
Manabozo	18
Marduk	73,127,158,159

Mark of the Beast	213
Mars	17,41,152
Mary (mother of Christ)	70,95,100,141,203,208,237
Mary Magdalene	70,95,96,97,100,104,109,121,203,221,222,230,231
Master D.K.	183
Master Jesus	192
Master K.H.	182,183
Master Morya	182
Master R	190
Masters	182
Masters of Wisdom	189,193
Mayan	62,64
Mecca	32
Meditation	176,177
Meditation Room	174,178,179
Medjugorje	201
Mekkan	60,68,72
Melchizedek	109
Melusine	79,80,81,82,84
Mendes	73
Mercurius	40
Mercury	10,17,41,71,105,125,152,174,213
Mermaid	79
Merovee	214
Merovingian	75,91,92,93,97,104,105,108,109,110,112,113,117, 121,122,212,214,232,235,236
Mesopotamia	62,75,124

Metatron	50,149
Methuselah	142
Metis	169
Mexican	41
Mexico	47,65,67
Milky Way	48,49,50
Minerva	17,152
Mistletoe	44
Mithra	26,40,66,209,210,211,212
MK Ultra	12
Mohammad	84
Moloch	41,136,197
Montefiores	103
Montesquiou (House of)	105
Montezuma	61
Moon	11,44,177
Moon Chart	180,181
Mormon	109
Mormonism	28
Morning star	61
Moses	144,184
Mother	20,111
Mother (earth)	27
Mother (goddess)	25,70,100,117,159,201,202,206,207,229
Mothership	50
Mount Hermon	105,116,117,139,140,000
Muhammad	32

Mulsim	67
Mummu	159
Munich	185
Muslim	32
Mystery Babylon	125,182,236
Mystery school/religion	27,31,66,102,128,131,170,175,193,212,224,233,235,236,237
Naamah	145
Nachash	54,55
Nagas	75,76
Nana	201
Nanna	160
Napolen	108
NASA	422,030
Nazorites	136
Neanderthal	151
Nebo	169
Negative Groups	194
Nephilim	47,50,56,59,72,127,130,142,143,144,145,159,161,162,229
Nephtys	22
Neptune	17,50,152,211
Net of Indra	27
Neter	71,72,143
Netherworld	160
New Age	44,49,151,171,175,176,182,215,224,236,237
New World Order	184

New World Religion	176
New World Religion	192
New York	185,186,187
NGO	172,177
Nibiru	50,160
Nibiru	160
Nimrod	47,50,124,125,126,127,128,129,130,131,132,133,160, 214,215,216,226,230,232,233,236
Nin-igiku	161
Nin-khursag	136,159,160,161,162,000
Nin-mah	159,161
Ninib	36
Ninlil	160
Ninurta	20
Ninus	131
Noah	50,125,126,137,154,158
North	119
North pole (celestial pole)	23,36,39,40,42,43,112
Notre Dame	95,105,204
Novus Ordo Seclorum	227
Nudimmud	162
Nuremberg	185
Nut	22,67
Nymph	111
Oannes	20,71
Obelisk	71,234
Occult	34,35

Occultism	182,185
Odin	105
Ohrmazd	56
Oligarchs	237
Oligarchy	185
One World Order	226,229
One World Religion	207,208,212,237
Ophion	68,73
Ophis	13,70
Ophites	73
Order of the Dragon	101,102
Ordo ab chaos	28
Orion	14,46,47,49,50,128
Osiris	10,18,21,22,43,47,48,62,66,71,72,73,99,129,130,132, 143,152,159,215,233
Ottawa	185
Ouroboros	27,64
Pagan	20,33,45,70,116,126,178,
Palestine	89,116,117
Pallas Athena	152
Pan	33,142
Pandemonium	143
Papal	84
Peru	62
Phallus	64,66,68,233
Phallus	66
Philosopher's stone	69

Phoenicians	20,22,36
Phyrgian	208,209
Pike, Albert	22,102
Pillar	41,60
Plantagenet	82
Plantard (House of)	105,112,204
Plato	184
Poland	100
Polaris	20
Pope	72,219
Poseidon	152
Positive Groups	194
Presidents	237
Primordial	67,68,73,159
Prince of Persian	196
Priory of Sion	93,104,105,106,140,200,214,232
Prometheus	174
Prosepine	202
Protestant	182
Pyramid	47,49
Queen	79
Queen Elizabeth	84
Queen of Heaven	131,197,237
Quetzalcoatl	18,28,61,62,64,74,129,130,223
Rahab	221
Rainbow	64,74
Re	67

Red Cross	113,183
Remphan	36,197
Rephaim	143
Rex Mundi	26
Rhea	130
Roman	92,93,117,130,182,201,204,208,211,216
Romans	20,50,66
Rome	121
Rosicrucians	101,103,105,136
Rothschild	35,86,86,103,216,237
Rothschild, Baron Guy	86
Sagittarius	48,97,
Saint Lucie	204,205,206
Samael	58,148,232,
Samson	116,120,121
Santa Claus	39,43,44,209,236
Satan	12,23,28,34,56,57,59,65,102,108,112,116,18,119, 134,143,173,179,204,216,232
Satanists	85
Saturday	36,37,80,81
Saturn	14,16,18,19,20,21,22,23,24,26,28,30,32,33,34,36,37, 39,40,41,42,43,64,98,116,128,210,213,219,228,229, 232,233
Schnoebelen, Bill	35,141
Scorpio	47,48,97,118
Scotland (King of)	79
Sea monsters (beast)	22,84,92,128,131,214

Secret society	101,133
Security Council	224
Semiramis	124,130,131,141,221,222,231,233
Semitic	37,73,87,89,216
Semjaza	139,140,146,149,150,153,154
Seraphim	56,63,143,174,
Serpent	13,17,27,29,41,54,55,56,58,59,62,64,65,66,67,68,69, 71,72,73,74,79,92,110,117,118,120,121,130,131,175, 206,210,217,218,219,225
Serpent (brazen)	63,64
Serpent (fiery winged)	63
Serpent (plumed)	61,74,223
Serpents of Wisdom	62,70
Set	22,41,65,102,108,112
Seth	136,139,142
Sex Magick	210
Shabbat	36,37
Shakespeare	184
Shape shift	76
Sheepfold	41,113
Shekhinah	11,68,149,204,218,237
Shem	132,133
Shinar	128
Shining Ones	54,71,72,143,159
Siccuth	36
Sickle	17
Sicombrians	92

Index

Simon Magus	109
Sinclairs (House of)	90
Sirens	155
Sirius	12,13
Skull and Bones	49
Sled	40
Snake	62
Sol Invictus	209
Solar Angel	173,174
Solar orb	23
Solomon	60,61,96,109
Solstice	48,49
Sophia	10,11,13,63,70,95,100,148,169,211,226
Sorcery	35
Spain	100,152
Spanish	61
Spartans	121
Sphinx	47
Spiritual Hierarchy	180,184,188
Splash (movie)	79
St Geremia	205
Star fire	135
Star Gate	47,48
Star of David	35,37
Starbucks	79,82
Statue of Liberty	26,207,221,222
Stone	31,32,69,179

Stuart (House of)	86,90,109
Sumerian	20,23,102,125,159,161
Sun	22,23,24,27,49,62,64,102,
Sun god	26,27,40,66,69,70,203,206
Surrogate	161
Sydney	185
Synagogue of Satan	216,217,218
Table of Nations	187
Talmud	36,58,7,88,216,217
Tammuz	14,50,128,129,130,132,160,197,233
Taurus (bull)	13,14,209,210
Tefillin	37
Tehom	67,73
Tetragrammaton	179
Tezcatlipoca	61,62
The Christ	171,183,184,186,188,192,193,195
The Hierarchy	170,171,184,187,189,190,191,192,193,194,195,196. 236
The Lord of Civilazation	190
The lords	190
The Rider	190
The Shem	145
The Tibetan	170,184
Theosophy	169,173
Third Eye	37,98
Thoth	71,72,74,143,169
Throne	63

Thugees	75
Tiamat	73,127,135,148,159,161
Tibetan	21
Titans	22
Tokyo	186,187
Toltecs	61,62
Tower of Babel	124,175,214,215,226,230,233
Tree of Knowledge	148
Tree of Life	225
Trinity	233
Trinity (cosmic)	10
Trinity (Holy)	10
Trojans	117,122,211,212
Tubal-Cain	135,145
Turkisn/Mongo	90
Twyman, Tracy	207
Tyche	63
Typhon	102,112
Typhonian Tradition	101,112
Typon	72
U Thant	176
U.S. Presidents	84
Ukraine	88,90
Unesco	167
Unicorn	107
United Nations (U.N.)	167,168,171,172,174,175,176,177,178,179,196,197, 224,226,236

United States	185,230
Ursa Major	112
Utah	110
Uzza	140,148,149
Varuna	129
Vatican	84,219,234
Vatican Audience Hall	219
Vedas	27,169
Venus	9,10,17,28,41,130,135,136,152,173,174,204,206,213,228
Vespucci	74
Vesta	17,152
Vesta	152
Viracocha	62,74,130,223
Virgil	24,227
Virgin	67,201,204,
Virgo	201,202,203,213,221,238
Visogoths	92
Votan	61
Vulcan	17,135,152
Wales (House of)	91
War in heaven	9
War of the Roses	82
Washington D.C.	185,234
Watchers	72,143,150,154,155,200
Wesak festival	14
WHO	167

Index

Windsor (Royal House)	79,86
Witchcraft	35,86,179
Womb	21,107,161,162
World Bank	167
World Goodwill	172
World War II	93
Wotan	129,130
Yaldaboath	100
Yama	18,43,64
Yiddish	89
Zamzummim	144,145
Zaphon	41
Zeus	19,50,73,111,117,152,208
Zionist	35,237
Zodiac	11,13,47,67,92,130,177,181,210,236
Zohar	219
Zoroaster	40,56,65,209
Zurvan	40,65,66

CPSIA information can be obtained
at www.ICGtesting.com
Printed in the USA
BVHW021220220123
656727BV00012B/1453